THE AMA HANDBOOK OF LEADERSHIP

THE AMA HANDBOOK OF LEADERSHIP

➤ Marshall Goldsmith

➤ John Baldoni

➤ Sarah McArthur

Foreword by James M. Kouzes

HARPERCOLLINS
LEADERSHIP

AN IMPRINT OF HARPERCOLLINS

The AMA Handbook of Leadership

Published by HarperCollins Leadership, an imprint of HarperCollins Focus LLC.

Any internet addresses, phone numbers, or company or product information printed in this book are offered as a resource and are not intended in any way to be or to imply an endorsement by HarperCollins Leadership, nor does HarperCollins Leadership vouch for the existence, content, or services of these sites, phone numbers, companies, or products beyond the life of this book.

Bulk discounts available. For details visit:
www.harpercollinsleadership.com/bulkquotes
Email: customercare@harpercollins.com

ISBN 978-0-8144-1513-9 (HC)
ISBN 978-1-4002-4570-3 (paperback)

CONTENTS

FOREWORD

Imagine you're sitting in a meeting with a group of your colleagues. The door to the conference room opens, in walks a person you've never met before, and she says, "Hi, I'm your new leader."

What questions do you immediately want to ask this person?

My coauthor, Barry Posner, and I regularly present this scenario to people as part of our ongoing leadership research. People have lots and lots of questions, but by far the most frequently asked is: Who are you?

If you are the leader who walks into that room one day, it's the first question you must be prepared to answer.

People want to know about you. They want to know about your values and beliefs, what you really care about, and what keeps you awake at night. They want to know who most influenced you, what prepares you for the job you're doing, and what you're like as a person. They want to know what drives you, what makes you happy, and what ticks you off. They want to know why you want to be their leader and why they ought to be following you. They want to know if you play the piano—or something else—and they want to know something about your family. They want to know your personal story.

Wanting to know who you are isn't about prying. It's about learning to trust. We're just more likely to trust people we know, and the more we know about our leaders the more likely we are to trust them as human beings. Of course, before you can share any of this with others, you have to have clarity about it yourself. You have to know you before others can truly know you.

The second question people most frequently want to ask a prospective leader is, "Where are you going?"

People want to know about your vision of the future, your aims and aspirations, and your hopes and your dreams. They want to know where you're taking them, and what's in store down the road. They want to know why it's important to you if they move in that direction. They want to hear your story of the future.

According to the data we've collected, over 70 percent of working professionals expect a leader to be forward-looking. And being forward-looking, we have learned, is the quality that most differentiates a leader from individual contributors.

What all this means is that leadership development is self-development. The quest for leadership is first an inner quest to discover who you are. Other people can't tell you what you value. You have to discover that for yourself. Other people can't tell you what you dream for the future. You have to discover that for yourself. Other people can't tell you why they ought to be following you. You have to discover that for yourself.

Engineers have computers; painters, canvas and brushes; musicians, instruments. Leaders have only themselves. The instrument of leadership is the self, and the mastery of the art of leadership comes from mastery of the self. Self-development is not about stuffing in a whole bunch of new information or trying the latest technique. It's about leading out of what is already in your soul. It's about liberating the leader within you. It's about setting yourself free.

The intent of this handbook is to provide you with the most current knowledge and tools to more effectively forge ahead, develop people, engage people, facilitate change, and take the lead. Your challenge in moving from the page to practice is to make the lessons genuinely yours. It's essential that you do that, because making them yours is the only route to authentic leadership. Making them yours is the only route to becoming the kind of leader others will want to follow.

I wish you a safe, enjoyable, and successful journey.

James M. Kouzes

James M. Kouzes is the Dean's Executive Professor of Leadership, Leavey School of Business, Santa Clara University, and the coauthor with Barry Posner of the internationally award-winning and best-selling book *The Leadership Challenge.*

ACKNOWLEDGMENTS

We want to acknowledge the great influences on our thinking, especially Peter F. Drucker, who continues to have a great impact on leaders across the globe. We want to acknowledge the generosity of the thought leaders who contributed their time and writings and shared their ideas with us. Without them, this book could not exist. We also want to acknowledge Christina Parisi and her dedicated team at AMACOM for all of their assistance and support in creating *The AMA Handbook of Leadership*. AMACOM went above and beyond the call to make this book a success. On a personal note, we are moved by and grateful for the help and support of our families, especially Hugh, Sally, Scott, Gail, and Lyda.

ABOUT THE EDITORS

MARSHALL GOLDSMITH

Dr. Marshall Goldsmith is a world authority on helping successful leaders get even better—by achieving positive, lasting change in behavior for themselves, their people, and their teams. *What Got You Here Won't Get You There* is a *New York Times* best seller, *Wall Street Journal* #1 business book, and winner of the Harold Longman award for Best Business Book of the Year. It has been translated into 23 languages and is a top 10 best seller in seven different countries.

The American Management Association named Dr. Goldsmith as one of 50 great thinkers and leaders who have influenced the field of management over the past 80 years. Major business press acknowledgments include *BusinessWeek*—most influential practitioners in the history of leadership development; *The Times* (UK)—50 greatest living business thinkers; *Wall Street Journal*—top 10 executive educators; *Forbes*—five most respected executive coaches; *Leadership Excellence*—top five thinkers on leadership; *Economic Times* (India)—five rajgurus of America; *Economist* (UK)—most credible executive advisers in the new era of business; and *Fast Company*—America's preeminent executive coach.

Dr. Goldsmith received his PhD from UCLA. He teaches executive education at Dartmouth's Tuck School and frequently speaks at leading business schools. He is a Fellow in the National Academy of Human Resources

(America's top HR honor) and his work has been recognized by almost every professional organization in his field. In 2006, Alliant International University honored Marshall by naming their schools of business and organizational studies the Marshall Goldsmith School of Management.

Marshall is one of a select few advisers who have been asked to work with over 100 major CEOs and their management teams. He is cofounder of Marshall Goldsmith Partners, a network of top-level executive coaches. He served as a member of the board of the Peter Drucker Foundation for 10 years. He has been a volunteer teacher for U.S. Army Generals, Navy Admirals, Girl Scout executives, and International and American Red Cross leaders, where he was a National Volunteer of the Year.

Marshall's 24 books include *The Leader of the Future* (a *BusinessWeek* best seller); *Coaching for Leadership*; and his latest best seller, *Succession: Are You Ready?* Over 200 of his articles, interviews, columns, and videos are available for viewing and sharing online (for no charge) at www.MarshallGoldsmithLibrary.com. Visitors to this site have come from 188 countries and have viewed over 2.8 million resources.

JOHN BALDONI

John Baldoni is an internationally recognized leadership consultant, coach, author, and speaker. He has taught what it means to inspire at the top of a mountain in the Canadian Rockies. At sea level in Orlando, Florida, John spoke to nearly 1,000 USAF/JAG commissioned and noncommissioned officers on leadership and communication. In 2007, John was named one of the world's top leadership gurus by Leadership Gurus International.

John began his business career in a 15th-floor office with a view of a private golf course. Around the corner was a commanding view of the Pacific Ocean. In between was a recording studio where John produced and edited corporate radio spots. But John gave that all up to start his own business in the spare bedroom of a beachfront rental more than three decades ago.

In time, John established a career as a highly sought-after communications and leadership consultant and coach, where he has had the privilege of working with senior leaders in virtually every industry from pharmaceutical to real estate, packaged goods to automobiles, and finance to health care.

John speaks widely to corporate, professional, military, and university audiences. Those who attend John's keynotes and workshops find his advice to be practical and inspirational. Mixed with stories of great men and women leavened with lighthearted humor is down-to-earth practical advice that individuals can apply immediately. John's presentations blend his passion for leadership with genuine enthusiasm for helping people achieve their leadership ambitions.

John is the author of eight books, including *Lead Your Boss: The Subtle Art of Managing Up* and *Lead by Example,* which was named a "best leadership book" of 2008 as well as a Book of the Month (December 2008) selection by Entrepreneur.com. John also wrote the *Great Leaders* trilogy on communications, motivation, and results. Over the years, John's many books have been translated into multiple languages, including Mandarin, Indonesian, Japanese, and Korean.

John has created a video coaching series for AthenaOnline and a series of coaching podcasts for CXO Media. These forms of media give John the opportunity to reach a wider audience with his leadership insights designed to help managers become effective leaders.

John writes a weekly "Leadership at Work" column for *Harvard Business Publishing,* which is syndicated by Bloomberg.com. John's articles have appeared on Businessweek.com, FastCompany.com, and WallStreetJournal. com as well as in *Leader to Leader* and the *Wharton Leadership Digest.*

Readers are welcome to visit John's leadership resource Web site at www.john baldoni.com.

SARAH MᶜARTHUR

Sarah MᶜArthur is founder and president of *sdedit. With nearly 20 years' experience in the publishing field, Sarah has edited and written numerous books and articles with such influential clients and best-selling authors as Marshall Goldsmith and Anthony Robbins.

A distinguished fellow of the Global Leadership Development Center at the Marshall Goldsmith School of Management of Alliant University, Sarah's experience as the managing and developmental editor of 13 business and leadership books has made her an expert in the fields of management, leadership, executive coaching, and human resources. Her expertise has furthered the success of the best-selling management classic *Coaching for Leadership* as well as the Amazon.com, *USA Today,* and *Wall Street Journal* #1 best seller *What Got You Here Won't Get You There* and a score of other books.

Sarah is Marshall Goldsmith's editorial partner; editor of *Business Coaching Worldwide,* a forum for leadership and management experts and theorists; advertising copywriter for various clients; and a highly sought-after freelance editor of business and leadership books.

Prior to founding *sdedit, she held the positions of advertising coordinator, media manager, managing editor, and copywriter. She holds degrees in English and Environmental Studies from the University of Oregon. Sarah can be reached at sarahmc@sdedit.com and www.sdedit.com.

THE AMA HANDBOOK OF LEADERSHIP

INTRODUCTION

*"The Chinese use two brush strokes to write the word
'crisis.' One brush stroke stands for danger; the other
for opportunity. In a crisis, be aware of the danger—
but recognize the opportunity."*
    —JOHN F. KENNEDY (1917–1963), Speech in Indianapolis,
    April 12, 1959

Leading people has never been an easy task. And today, leaders have the immensely difficult job of forging a path into uncharted territories of global proportion. Amid a constantly changing business environment, sometimes confusing and often overwhelming information, and a requirement to please a variety of stakeholders, leaders are understandably often uncertain as to the right thing to do, the best avenue to take, the precise decision to make that will lead to success—and during some periods, especially of late, even survival.

As participants in and scholars of this world of incredible change, we put our heads together to see how we might contribute to—help forge, if you will—a path to a bright future. This contemplation on the crises of today, which leaders navigate on a daily basis, led us to consider where the opportunities lie. We discovered the opportunity in our great network of thought leaders. We decided to ask the world's greatest thought leaders in the fields of management and leadership to give us their ideas on the current state of the world. More specifically, we asked them: In your area of expertise, what are the trends, issues, and challenges facing leaders today and how can they lead through them successfully? Their insightful and visionary answers are encapsulated in the pages of this book.

The AMA Handbook of Leadership is a timely, timeless, informative, and important book for its readers, who must continually study and explore the world, leadership, business, and management. In it, we have brought together in one collection a global group of thought leaders who have made significant contributions to the fields of leadership and management; who run major corporations; and who advise the CEOs, managing directors, and presidents of the leading organizations and countries worldwide.

The AMA Handbook of Leadership encompasses a wide range of thoughts, practices, and theories aimed at expanding the knowledge of its target audience—primarily leaders and those in positions in which they help others lead, such as organizational development professionals, consultants, and executive coaches. Middle managers and those in different parts of the organization, such as the HR manager, the head of organizational development, and the Executive Vice President of HR, will also find this book of great interest and value.

As a reader, you will find no need to follow the chapter sequence. You may start with a favorite author, a particular issue, or even a titillating title. The place to begin is with what is most important to you!

The AMA Handbook of Leadership is divided into five parts. In Part One, "Forging Ahead: The Global Picture," our book begins with a vision of leadership for the future from Frances Hesselbein, founding president and chairman of the Leader to Leader Institute, formerly the Peter F. Drucker Foundation for Nonprofit Management. This extraordinary woman's chapter, "Diversity: The Imperative for Today's Leaders," brought tears to the eyes of one editor—what will it do for you? Long at the forefront of developing and implementing innovative concepts and strategies for maximizing organizational and individual potential through diversity management, Dr. R. Roosevelt Thomas follows Frances's train of thought in his chapter, "Leadership and Diversity Management: Unfinished Business." Maya Hu-Chan's chapter, "360 for Global Leaders: Coaching Through a World Lens," provides essential coaching practices and practical skills all global leadership should embrace. Rounding out Part One with "Asian and Western Executive Styles," D. Quinn Mills, the Albert J. Weatherhead Jr. Professor of Business Administration Emeritus at Harvard Business School, and Luke Novelli, the Chief of Intellectual Capital at Leadership Development Resources Global, describe the differences in characteristic leadership styles between Asia and the West. The authors provide implications for the development of leaders who will be able to lead effectively across global regions.

Part Two, "Developing People: The Key to the Future," begins with the insights of behavioral change expert Marshall Goldsmith. "Passing the Baton: Developing Your Successor" offers candid advice on succession from the outgoing executive's perspective. Strategic executive development expert James F. Bolt delineates 12 characteristics or success factors that can be used to develop and implement great leadership and executive talent in organizations in his chapter, "Developing Exceptional Leaders: Critical Success Factors." An internationally recognized authority on career issues and retention and engagement in the workplace, Beverly Kaye lays out step-by-step guidelines for facilitating the growth and development of new leaders, especially in a down economy, in her chapter, "The Leader's Role in Growing New Leaders." With a human resources focus on the challenges of talent management, vice president of Talent Management for Avon Products Marc Effron and PepsiCo senior manager of human resources Miriam Ort discuss the lack of status of the field of talent management and suggest ways to improve it so as to make it a more vital branch of human resources in their chapter, "Talent Pool or Talent Puddle: Where's the Talent in Talent Management?" The final chapter in Part Two is "The Cost of Investing in People Leadership Negatively Affects the Bottom Line: Fact or Fiction?" a case study by Howard J. Morgan, Manager Director of Leadership Research Institute, and Qwest executive Paula Kruger that demonstrates the benefits of "people investment."

Part Three, "Engaging People: The Force of Change," shows how a leader who engages people can create the energy to compel positive change in a forward direction. On the other hand, inertia and apathy, by-products of poor leadership, suck the life force out of any potential for positive change. If a company is fortunate, a good product or service may help maintain the organizational status quo; if not, the organization will likely fail miserably. Beginning this part is "Leadership's Silver Bullet: The Magic of Inspiration," a chapter about the value of inspiration and motivation as effective leadership behaviors by John H. (Jack) Zenger, world expert in the field of leadership development. Highly regarded management thinker Judith M. Bardwick combines cutting-edge psychological research with practical business applications to give us a clear-cut outline for change in her chapter, "Create Awareness; Create Change." With extensive expertise in the areas of survey research and change management, renowned psychometrician Joseph Folkman identifies behaviors that may cause employees to perceive a leader as uncaring. Folkman offers suggestions for becoming aware of and changing these behaviors in his chapter, "I Really Do Care!" Executive Education Professor of Strategic Leadership for the Smeal College of Business at Penn

State, Dr. Albert A. Vicere introduces us to the "DNA model" of organizations in his chapter, "The Real Legacy of Leadership: Aligning Rhetoric with Reality." Based on strategy, culture, and leadership, Dr. Vicere provides suggestions to leaders seeking to "align rhetoric to reality" by engaging employees at all levels of an organization. Finally, in this part, Dr. Paul Hersey, internationally renowned behavioral scientist and highly regarded authority on training and human resource development, discusses challenges that Generation Y workers pose to today's leaders (often from the Generation X and Baby Boomer generations) in "What Do Leaders Need to Know About Generation Y in Order to Lead Successfully?" Dr. Hersey outlines the skills, education, and expectations that Gen Yers bring to the workplace and identifies some leadership techniques for channeling these most effectively.

Part Four, "Facilitating Change: The Leader's Role," begins with a chapter by Norm Smallwood, cofounder of The RBL Group, and top business coach Dave Ulrich, ranked #1 most influential person in HR by *HR Magazine*. Their chapter, "What Is an Effective Leader? The Leadership Code and Leadership Brand," offers a clear, empirically based framework—the Leadership Code—that depicts elements that make up a good leader. Next is "Leading the Emotional Side of Change: The New 21st-Century Leadership Capability." And, who better to explore the new challenges facing 21st-century leaders and provide a fresh approach to them based on the incorporation of emotional, not just cognitive, strategies than internationally recognized psychologist Dr. Robert H. Rosen? Introducing the interesting concept "political temperature" to describe team functioning, Dr. Gary Ranker, top executive coach, and Colin Gautrey, internationally recognized thought leader in the practical use of power and influence in the workplace, give us their ideas in "Adjusting the Political Temperature of Your Team." With extensive expertise in leadership development, executive coach Patricia Wheeler helps smart executives become better leaders. Her chapter, "Making Successful Transitions: The Leader's Perspective," addresses the complicated subject of how leaders can make successful transitions from position to position and organization to organization. The final chapter in this part is by John Baldoni, internationally recognized leadership consultant, coach, speaker, and author. "A Question of Leadership: What Does the Organization Need Me to Do?" offers a fresh way of looking at leadership from the perspective of a manager's value to the organization. Baldoni emphasizes the need to engage with subordinates and the importance of values.

Part Five, "Taking the Lead: The X Factors," includes the ideas and philosophies of extraordinary thought leaders who "think outside the box" into realms that may hold the key to the future success of leadership, organizations, and possibly even humanity. Beginning this part is "Situational Intelligence," by acclaimed expert in organizational transformation Laurence S. Lyons. Lyons shares the concept of *situational intelligence*—ensuring that a business strategy is correct for the particular situation while appreciating its wider context. S. Bronfman Chair in Management at McGill University and artist in her own right, Nancy J. Adler discusses the opportunity to use the arts for creativity, inspiration, and to develop new forms of leadership in her chapter "The Arts and Leadership." The leading authority on client relationships and the skills and strategies required to earn lifelong client loyalty, Andrew Sobel introduces us to the concept of "client leadership," distinguishes it from "organizational leadership," and details its key characteristics and importance in business-to-business types of companies in his chapter, "Client Leadership: Leading in the Marketplace." And, finally, Fons Trompenaars, foremost authority on cross-cultural management, and Peter Woolliams, senior partner with Trompenaars Hampden-Turner Consulting, complete our book with "Leading for Sustainability." Outlining the "golden dilemmas" facing contemporary organizations, the authors explore the value of a cross-cultural approach to leadership both for individuals and for the "sustainability" of the organization.

We are confident that *The AMA Handbook of Leadership* will provide business leaders with the critical insights, perspectives, and frameworks to successfully navigate through today's uncharted global business arena. We hope you enjoy this book, and we hope that you will gain more understanding of leadership as it must transform to meet with our changing times.

Sarah McArthur
San Diego, CA

Forging Ahead

➤ The Global Picture

CHAPTER 1

Diversity: The Imperative for Today's Leaders

➤ Frances Hesselbein

When John Baldoni, Marshall Goldsmith, and Sarah McArthur invited me to write a chapter on "hot topics of leadership," I knew my topic instantly, and it is not only "hot," it is imperative. I have chosen for my chapter the topic "Diversity: The Imperative for Today's Leaders." Today, if we are not developing a richly diverse organization, led by a wonderfully diverse team of leaders, then we are already an organization of the past, led by leaders of the past.

As CEO of the Girl Scouts of the USA for 13 exuberant years, I never had a bad day in the nearly 5,000 days during which I led the organization. Six weeks after I left the Girl Scouts, I found myself President and CEO of the Peter F. Drucker Foundation for Nonprofit Management.

For 31 years now, I have had a philosophy, passion, and imperative for leadership that is as powerful in its impact as it is in its results, whether I was working with a Girl Scout Council in Pennsylvania or with a Drucker Foundation/Leader to Leader Institute partnership with a great corporation, university, or the military. I have encapsulated my learnings in the more than 26 books that I have written or edited.

The message is very simple:

> We manage for the mission.
> We manage for innovation.
> We manage for diversity.
> We are mission-focused, values-based,
>   demographics-driven.

These are the imperatives I have tattooed on my shoulders—in invisible ink, of course, but they are there. They are a daily reminder to me. Over the years, I have been testing these imperatives and documenting the results with leaders and organizations in all three sectors.

From July 1976 until I left on January 31, 1991, the Girl Scouts of the USA grew to a workforce of 788,000 women and men (1 percent employed staff). Coming into the position, I knew that this, the largest organization of girls and women in the world, had to take the lead in this society. We had to be an example to our own country and to the world. I believed that if we mobilized around a powerful mission; made innovation part of every deliberation, plan, and action; and developed the richly diverse, inclusive organization at every level, we could be a model to a society that in 1976 did not have "the healthy, diverse, inclusive society that cares about all of its children" as its battle cry. Building a richly diverse organization can never be seen as a challenge; it is the most remarkable opportunity for relevance, viability, and success. It is always opportunity!

The Girl Scouts board, staff, leaders, and donors were inspired with a fiery passion for change when we developed our big question: "When they look at us, can they find themselves?" That meant that when leaders, parents, and girls with richly diverse backgrounds in the major racial and ethnic groups in our country looked at our Girl Scout National Board and staff, my management team, our visuals, and the four handbooks, they could find themselves.

When I talked to the four artists who would illustrate the new handbooks, I said, "When any little girl or young woman in the United States opens her own handbook, she must be able to find herself. If I'm a little girl in a Navajo village, I open my Brownie handbook, and I can find myself. If I'm a girl in inner-city Detroit, my handbook is not filled with only New England picket fences. I can find myself in my own Girl Scout handbook." One artist asked, "Did you say 'any' little girl?" I replied, "I should have said 'every.'" The artists shared our vision and determination, and one year later, when the four Girl Scout handbooks came out, not only did they generate enormous excitement but we received prizes for "best multicultural resources for children."

We were pioneers in those days, for "diversity" wasn't everybody's favorite subject. Yet to the volunteers and staff of this great movement, "diversity-inclusion" was not only "a hot leadership topic" but also part of their vision of a bright future for our children and our country.

Along the way, a business leader took me aside and gave me some advice: "Frances, you know I really care about you and the organization, but if you don't stop this diversity stuff, you'll never raise any money." I politely thanked him. Then with John Creedon, the new president of MetLife, as our campaign chairman, we went out and raised $10 million and built a wonderful conference center near Briarcliff Manor in Westchester County, New York, on 400 deeply wooded acres that we had inherited long ago. A wonderfully diverse board and staff welcomed those Girl Scout leaders as they came to learn, to innovate, and to change lives.

In a short time, we more than tripled racial-ethnic membership at every level. We had asked ourselves, "When they look at us, can they find themselves?" The answer was a resounding "Yes!" at a time when diversity and equal access were not high on many organizations' list of imperatives. In fact, a leader from a large organization told me I was wasting my time. "Diversity will take care of itself," he said.

That was long ago. This is 2009, and it has been projected that by 2020, the majority in the United States will be the minority, and the minority will become the majority. How smoothly the change will take place will depend on how well we have built the diverse leadership organization of the future with remarkable leaders at every level who are richly representative of our country of the future. I fervently believe that if we are not "managing for diversity" today, we already are part of the past, and sadly so, for the opportunity is here now.

When we met Peter Drucker in 1981, the Father of Modern Management cheered our "mission, innovation, and diversity" focus, and he gave us some wonderful definitions as he spurred us on: "Mission is solely why we do what we do. It is our reason for being and it should fit on a T-shirt." I always say, "A mission should be short, powerful, and compelling." Which definition do you think people remember? What will fit on a T-shirt, of course.

As we worked with Peter, he gave us two or three days of his time each year. He studied us, and told the *New York Times* that we were "the best managed organization in the country. Tough, hardworking women can do anything." We took to heart Peter Drucker's philosophy, his study, and his definition of innovation: "change that creates a new dimension of performance."

As those remarkable people were transforming the largest organization for girls and women in the world, the mantra "Innovation: change that creates a new dimension of performance" made change more palatable, more reasonable. A new dimension of performance became part of the vocabulary of transformation.

I began this chapter by focusing on "diversity" as my "hot leadership topic," and then as I wrote I realized that my hot topic has three parts to it. You can't "do" just two: mission, innovation, and diversity are one powerful message. The initiative, the imperative for a bright future, is grounded by values that are palpable. With values that we live by, as mission-focused, values-based, and demographics-driven, we lead into the future. This is the organizational life we are building, the leadership life we are leading. We are the future.

Now, I can't write about my adventure in leadership with the Girl Scouts and the Drucker Foundation/Leader to Leader Institute, and meeting Peter Drucker in 1981, without adding mention of another great leader who has had an enormous impact on my life. In 1982, another man arrived at my Girl Scout office in New York. His name was Marshall Goldsmith, and he had an unusual new product he had developed that he wanted to give to the Girl Scouts—his 360-degree assessment tool. He would come to New York, begin with me, then my management team, and then move it with staff across the organization.

I was intrigued, excited, and gratified, and that began our Marshall-Frances adventure in significance that continues to this moment (1982–2009 is not a bad record for two people who think their bottom line is changing lives). We began the 360-degree assessment first with me and then my management team, which made it more acceptable to those who might be reluctant to receive feedback from their peers. Marshall's gift moved across our staff at headquarters and in the field, making an enormous difference and changing lives.

When I was taking a team to Poland for a great training opportunity, I asked, "Marshall, will you go?" Silly question! The answer was always yes. He was there when I said good-bye to the best people in the world, to the best organization in the world. And six weeks after I left the Girl Scouts, the Peter F. Drucker Foundation for Nonprofit Management was born. Marshall was the first board member to be invited, and he serves to this moment. The Drucker Foundation/Leader to Leader Institute has published 26 books, and Marshall Goldsmith and I have coedited many of them.

It is only the beginning to have a vision of "a society of healthy children, all children, strong families, good schools, decent housing, safe neighborhoods, work that dignifies, all surrounded by a healthy, diverse, cohesive community that cares about all of its people." It is quite another to find great thought leaders: leaders of quality, character, and generous hearts who share the vision, who help build the organization, who write, speak, inspire, and are always there. I think it's called "for the greater good." "Mission, innovation, diversity" began a long time ago—the imperative that is more critical than ever before measured against the darkness of our times.

When "mission-innovation-diversity" is our rallying cry, we shine a light. To serve is to live.

ABOUT THE AUTHOR

Frances Hesselbein is the Chairman of the Board of Governors of the Leader to Leader Institute (formerly the Peter F. Drucker Foundation for Nonprofit Management) and its Founding President. She was awarded the Presidential Medal of Freedom, the United States' highest civilian honor, in 1998, and serves on many nonprofit and private sector corporate boards. She was the Chairman of the National Board of Directors for Volunteers of America from 2002 to 2006 and is the recipient of 20 honorary doctoral degrees. In 2009, the University of Pittsburgh introduced The Hesselbein Global Academy for Student Leadership and Civic Engagement. Among many other awards, Frances was inducted into the Enterprising Women Hall of Fame at the 7th Annual Enterprising Women of the Year Awards Celebration and was named a Senior Leader at the U.S. Military Academy, 2008 National Conference on Ethics in America. She is Editor-in-Chief of the award-winning quarterly journal *Leader to Leader,* and a coeditor of a book of the same name. She is a coeditor of the Drucker Foundation's three-volume *Future Series* and of *The Organization of the Future 2: Visions, Strategies, and Insights on Managing in a New Era,* published in 2009. Author of *Hesselbein on Leadership and Be, Know, Do: Leadership the Army Way,* introduced by General Eric K. Shinseki, Frances is the coeditor of 26 books in 28 languages.

CHAPTER 2

Leadership and Diversity Management:
Unfinished Business

> **R. Roosevelt Thomas, Jr.**

Over the past 40 years, our society has become better at mainstreaming people previously excluded. Whether labeled as desegregation, integration, pluralism (representation), diversity, or inclusion, the reality is that we have had some notable success in identifying and accessing talent and developing leadership profiles that look like our communities.

Nowhere was this success more evident than in the election of Barack Obama as the 44th president of the United States. His election represents a giant step in creating a political leadership profile that looked like America with respect to race. Further, he appointed a cabinet that was pluralistic (representative) not only in terms of race but also of gender, ethnicity, political affiliation, ideology, experience, style, education, and other attributes. Because these people cared deeply about the United States and its challenges and opportunities, they held the potential not to be simply a pluralistic (representative) mixture but also a source of diverse behavior. President Obama expected his cabinet to generate and passionately present a multitude of diverse prescriptions for their various policy areas.

In support of his administration's priorities, the diversity management challenge for Mr. Obama became that of fostering quality decision making in the midst of these significant and critical pluralistic and behavioral differences and similarities. His leadership task has been to create an environment that minimizes distractions and divisiveness, and yet encourages the acceptance, consideration, and incorporation of multiple points of view in pursuit of effective decision making. His ultimate success, or lack of in this regard, may well determine his ability to lead in these perilous times.

Mr. Obama's diversity management challenge parallels that of a CEO whose organization has convened a demographically pluralistic (representative) workforce. As the workforce's pluralism generates diverse behavior, the diversity management task will be to ensure that a capability exists to make quality decisions in the midst of that diversity (differences and similarities). Creation of environments that facilitate effective diversity management will be a critical and urgent leadership role as our organizations and communities become more diverse and complex.

THE IMPORTANCE OF LEADERSHIP

Leadership from senior officials has always been important to the success of diversity efforts. When I first became active in the diversity arena, I regularly encountered CEOs and other senior executives exercising leadership with respect to diversity. These individuals routinely immersed themselves in details about managing workforce diversity and provided an example of involvement and exploration. They embraced the notion of pioneering a path beyond representation ("the numbers") and relationship sensitivity ("getting along").

Many of these pioneering leaders saw themselves, 25 years ago, as having made substantial progress in creating a pluralistic workforce with respect to race, gender, and ethnicity, and in fostering harmonious relationships among members of this heterogeneous workforce. Sadly, a quarter of a century later, many of these organizations and their current leaders are still celebrating pluralism (representation) and relationship gains—and still seeking guidance as to "where do we go from here."

This situation exists in many organizations perceived as diversity wise. Not long ago, a chief diversity officer said, "We're getting all kinds of awards and are on 'best practices' lists, but I don't feel as good as I should. Something is missing." Still another noted that recent analysis suggested that utilization of minorities remained an issue in his corporation. "They simply are not moving up the promotional ladder in proportion to their presence."

These comments easily could have been made 25 years ago. What has been going on in the interim? What accounts for such limited progress? In part, one contributing factor has been that, in reality, the focus has not been on diversity nor on diversity management but, rather, on creating pluralism (representation) and calling it "increasing diversity." This mislabeling has stemmed from a common conceptual confusion that results in pluralism's being equated with diversity. As a result, most organizations have not focused on diversity defined as behavioral variations, nor on diversity management capability (the ability to make quality decisions in the midst of differences and similarities). In essence, this misconception has caused many leaders to miss out on the potential benefits of diversity and diversity management.

What also has been a contributing factor is the decline of leadership in the diversity arena. Moving beyond the current limited state of progress and achieving a diversity management capability will require that today's leaders do something akin to what I saw 25 years ago at the CEO level. Those CEOs were personally involved in the managing-diversity process. Today, CEOs frequently delegate this responsibility to Chief Diversity Officers and they participate only in a limited—often ceremonial—fashion. This delegation may indeed be necessary or desirable, but it has an important caveat. CEOs must continue to display substantial leadership and involvement in the diversity management arena—even in the midst of delegation. Delegation must not be abdication in disguise.

What tasks are involved in providing the required leadership for effective diversity management? For me, leadership refers to the sum total of efforts to ensure that an enterprise has an appropriate mission, vision, strategy, and culture, and that these elements are manifested in all of the organization's activities. Leadership provides the "macro" context for "micro" managerial activity (daily efforts to achieve organizational objectives). Responsibility for creating these contextual variables and ensuring adherence to them can be a shared one throughout the organization, but it usually begins with senior executives.

One of my favorite examples of the practice of shared leadership is the story of a church janitor who, when greeting a minister scheduled to be guest preacher in the near future, first introduced himself and then launched into an hour's monologue about the church's history and traditions, its current activities, and its hopes for the future. Recollecting this experience in a discussion on leadership, the minister recognized that the janitor had acted as a leader. He wanted to make certain that the minister had an understanding of the church's mission, vision, strategy, and culture as background for preparing a suitable sermon.

In this example, obviously the senior minister had established the leadership parameters and implicitly or explicitly assigned the janitor the leadership task of reaffirming these parameters whenever possible. He had enlisted the janitor in the leadership process.

The question for this discussion is, "How can senior executives such as Mr. Obama and organizational CEOs provide this quality of leadership in energizing quests for diversity management capability?" The discussion is not academic. Many organizational leaders have not mastered the art of fostering diversity management within their organizations.

FOUR CRITICAL LEADERSHIP TASKS

Over the years as a researcher, an author, and a consultant, I have learned that the tasks detailed in this section must be dealt with if an organization is to develop a diversity management capability. Each discussion reflects my experiences in guiding leaders through their development of diversity management capability.

Task 1: Establish a conceptual milestone by which to gauge future progress. Leaders must seek specificity and agreement with respect to at least diversity and diversity management, and must strive to differentiate these concepts from the frequently pursued goal of pluralism. As senior executives talk to colleagues, practitioners, and experts in the field, they will encounter multiple definitions for diversity. It can be tempting to say, "Diversity means what we say it means." However, saying does not make it so.

Instead, executives must take the time and energy to survey meanings from what has been said, written, and done about diversity over the years. Their task is to ferret out the core essence of the definitions being used, to rationalize their differences and similarities, and to consolidate this analysis into—at the least—specific definitions of diversity and diversity management.

Here, I am calling for more than benchmarking as frequently practiced. Leaders cannot simply assume that "best practices" are best for them. Surveying, rationalizing, assessing, and integrating are all critical steps in developing conceptual milestones. Action-oriented leaders often short-change this task because it does not feel like "taking action." But indeed it is. Surveying, ferreting, rationalizing, and integrating are all "actions." Further, once leaders have agreed on definitions, they must infiltrate them throughout their organizations—another "action" step of great magnitude. Establishing conceptual milestones requires pulling together cohesive definitions and then embedding them in the enterprise. When CEOs and others give short shrift to this task, they set the stage for ongoing conceptual confusion.

What happens when there is conceptual confusion? An organization cannot even say with confidence to what it is committed. Pluralism (representation)? Behavioral diversity? Diversity management? None of the above? All of the above?

Task 2: Differentiate between capability and activity. Diversity management is not an activity or even a program but, rather, a capability. One completes or carries out an activity or a program, but uses or applies a capability. An activity has a beginning and an end, but a capability can exist indefinitely and can be used whenever, wherever, and as often as necessary. The challenge once a capability is acquired is to maintain it—to continuously improve it through practice. The old axiom applies: Use it or lose it.

Typically, we think of diversity management not as a craft to master, but more as a program, an activity, a set of tactics, or skills. However, capabilities can be approached as a craft. If individuals are asked what comes to mind when the word *craft* is mentioned, they cite items like the following: concepts, principles, skills, tactics, art, continuous learning, and the necessity of practice. Implicit in the idea of craft are the notions of practice and mastery.

Without mastery of the craft of diversity management, leaders and their colleagues lack the ability to persevere and remain focused in the midst of differences and similarities. Their ability to make quality decisions amid differences and similarities is diminished, and they go through cycles of creating pluralism (representation), floundering in representation and behavioral diversity, losing the representation and behavioral diversity, and returning to creating representation. Key to breaking this cycle is the capability to make quality decisions in spite of the tensions and complexity of diversity.

Back to Mr. Obama. Not only have he and his cabinet been charged with meeting a multiplicity of challenges characterized by different and sometimes conflicting priorities, they have had to collectively work through the mixture of their own differences, similarities, and related tensions and complexities. Going forward in the absence of a diversity management capability means their success will be less likely.

Task 3: Relate your milestone concepts to your organizational realities. Your purpose here is twofold: (1) To determine why diversity management is important for your organization, and (2) to flesh out what your diversity management aspirations should be. For more than 20 years, I have coached senior executives and diversity councils through this task by helping them to address the following questions:

➤ *How has your external environment changed in the last five years? How is it likely to change over the next five years? What, if any, implications do you see with respect to diversity?* Typically, participants cite various environmental forces and how these influences have shifted or are likely to change. They also note how the changes are likely to affect their diversity agenda. For example, one food manufacturer's expectations described how changing consciousness about health and preventive medicine would necessitate changes in the nature of the products the company offered. They predicted that this shift would generate product diversity issues for the company.

➤ *How has your mission changed over the last five years? How is your mission likely to change over the next five years? What, if any, implications do you see with respect to diversity?* Here, participants cite their corporation's purpose or provide descriptions of what the company does and why it exists. Anticipated change may range from how the company goes about its purpose to fundamental modifications around its mission.

An example of the former would be a regulated company that finds itself in a deregulated environment with different requirements for success. On the other hand, a corporation might find that a series of acquisitions has intentionally or unintentionally changed the nature of its mission. With respect to diversity, a deregulated company with different requirements for success might find itself struggling with functional diversity and integration issues as the different functions seek to adapt to the new environment. The company growing by acquisition likely would see integration issues in its future for some time.

➤ *How has your organization's vision changed over the last five years? How is your organization's vision likely to change over the next five years? What, if any, are the implications with respect to diversity?* By vision, I mean the executives' view of how things would look if they were successful in achieving their organization's mission. A frequently reported shift in visions has been with respect to geography. One company's leaders traced shifts from a regional focus to a national and, finally, to a global focus. In this instance, the implications for diversity often centered on customer variations. One CEO noted, "We not only do not know how to deal with people outside of the United States; we also do not know how to deal with people in the United States outside of the region where we are located."

➤ *How has your company's strategy changed over the last five years? How is it likely to change over the next five years? What, if any, are the implications with respect to diversity?* By strategy, I mean what the company is going to do to achieve competitive advantage. Executives often don't know what their sources of competitive advantages are. One set of company representatives reported 20 sources; however, upon closer examination, none survived scrutiny. Though all were critical necessities for business success, none was a source of competitive advantage. Diversity issues noted here often concern management of workforce diversity, global diversity, and acquisition diversity. Participants usually begin this task focused on workforce diversity and complete it with an awareness of multiple forms of diversity with strategic implications for their corporation.

➤ *How has your organizational culture changed over the last five years? How is it likely to change over the next five years? What, if any, are likely to be the implications for diversity management?* To fully address this question will require some formal research. Such research is often called a *cultural audit*. Another option is structured discussion designed to ferret out the basic cultural assumptions that drive an organization. The purpose of assessing organizational culture is to determine whether there are deeply rooted barriers to diversity management. In several organizations, we have found that the basic assumption "We are family" worked against diversity management; this assumption favored "members of the family." Outsiders (individuals without some significant connection to the family) were not welcomed. New employment and promotional opportunities went to members or friends of the family. This analysis suggests where gaining diversity management capability might require cultural change.

Task 4: Develop a formal diversity management mission and vision. This vision and mission will constitute the heart of diversity management aspirations and should be directly linked to the organization's overall mission, vision, and strategy. Indeed, the stronger this link and the more it is articulated, the more compelling will be your rationale for moving forward with diversity management.

The diversity management mission should describe what the leaders hope to achieve with diversity management and their purpose for building a diversity management capability. The diversity management vision should describe the conditions that will be generated by accomplishing the diversity management mission. The clearer leaders can be about this mission and vision, the clearer they can be about their diversity management aspirations and supporting rationales.

BARRIERS TO LEADERSHIP

The tasks described in the previous section constitute the leadership work required to facilitate the building of a diversity management capability. Where CEOs and other leaders have given serious attention to these tasks, their diversity management efforts have had greater vitality and success. Yet, many organizations routinely fail to garner the necessary enthusiasm and support for these tasks.

First, a critical source of resistance has been the perception that diversity and diversity management fundamentally are civil rights and corporate social responsibility issues. As such, they are common sense, "no big deal," and/or a "done deal." In any event, the reasoning here is that they don't require what I have called the leadership tasks.

Second, the perception that diversity and diversity management should not really be the focus has been another source of resistance. Individuals with this view accurately see the difference between pluralism (representation) and behavioral diversity, and they believe that the center of attention should be on creating a pluralistic workforce with respect to race and gender. While this pluralism *may* lead to behavioral diversity and the need for diversity management, until that happens advocates of this perspective argue that to shift focus would result in a distraction from the critical issue of fostering pluralism. Proponents of this view do not recognize or appreciate the reality that diversity management can contribute to sustained desired pluralism.

A third source of resistance is the perception that the leadership tasks represent a delay in "taking action" on diversity. This becomes especially critical when individual contributors do not trust senior management's commitment. They fear that company leaders may decide not to go beyond the leadership tasks, and indeed, this does happen. So, they argue that "we must strike with vigorous, concrete action before the window of opportunity closes."

Finally, leaders may bypass the leadership tasks simply because of the time requirements. A common explanation is, "My senior executives believe deeply in diversity and want to move forward, but they cannot devote this kind of time to establishing 'macro' parameters. There is just too much on their plate." These leaders often do support major diversity efforts, but without the grounding provided by performing the leadership tasks. A common consequence of bypassing the leadership work is gross conceptual confusion with respect to pluralism (representation), diversity, and diversity management.

A MATTER OF URGENCY: GETTING TRACTION

Key to getting traction with diversity and diversity management is addressing what I have called the leadership tasks. If these tasks are not carried out in a quality fashion, leaders and their organizations risk being ineffective in their decision making in the midst of differences and similarities. This would be at a time when our society and its organizations are becoming increasingly diverse and complex. Accordingly, there is some urgency to getting leadership in the diversity arena back on track.

ABOUT THE AUTHOR

Over the past 25 years, **R. Roosevelt Thomas, Jr.,** has been at the forefront in developing and implementing innovative concepts and strategies for maximizing organizational and individual potential through diversity management. Founder of the American Institute for Managing Diversity (AIMD), a nonprofit research and education enterprise, and Roosevelt Thomas Consulting & Training, Dr. Thomas is the author of six published books and numerous articles.

In 1998, the National Academy of Human Resources elected R. Roosevelt Thomas as a Fellow. He has also been recognized in the *Wall Street Journal* as a top business consultant, cited by *Human Resource Executive* as one of HR's Most Influential People, and awarded the Distinguished Contribution to Human Resource Development Award by the American Society for Training and Development. Dr. Thomas has served as a consultant to numerous Fortune 500 companies, corporations, professional firms, government entities, nonprofit organizations, and academic institutions. Dr. Thomas can be contacted at RThomas@rthomasconsulting.com and www.rthomascon sulting.com.

CHAPTER 3

360 for Global Leaders: Coaching Through a World Lens

> Maya Hu-Chan

Anyone who has purchased a new flat-screen TV or called a customer-service line for a major U.S. company only to be forwarded to a representative in India already knows how the global economy has immersed itself in our daily lives. The question now is no longer how a global economy will affect a leader but how a leader can best manage in the global economy.

THE LEADER OF TOMORROW

One simple analogy for the challenges leaders face in a global economy is to imagine that the owner of a roadside diner comes in to announce to the short-order cook that, along with meat loaf, pot roast, and hamburgers, he will immediately start serving Cambodian fish curry, Tunisian *brik à l'oeuf,* Botswanan *chotlho,* and 50 other exotic cuisines. The cook will likely greet him with a blank stare and many of the "regulars" at the diner will subsequently raise their eyebrows. *Bon appétit!*

As many a good chef can attest, having a specific recipe on hand is far less important than understanding the origins, preferences, and expectations of a beloved dish. Before learning the basic steps for cooking it, a chef needs to be open to understanding what makes it special. For example, as a connoisseur of won ton, I know that any noodle house worth its salt will have noodles that aren't too soft and that even "bite back" a little with each flavorful nibble. Once the chef learns the right texture and the staff learns the menu, the regulars go global. Welcome to the Global Leadership Café.

In this chapter, with the broth of survey results from actual global leaders in business, the spice of anecdotal information received through 14 extensive interviews with leaders throughout the world, and some noodles of insight from my coauthored book, *Global Leadership: The Next Generation*,[1] I will offer ingredients or perceptions that leaders have of themselves and their strengths and weaknesses in various fields. Based on our findings, I will recommend some essential coaching practices and practical skills all global leaders should embrace. These skills, if used correctly, will enable leaders to successfully manage teams from abroad, communicate effectively, and make appropriate decisions based on the uniqueness of a particular workforce. The workplace, like the café, embraces the new flavors of the clientele, and business gets bubbling.

THE DATA AND THE DESIGN FOR GLOBAL LEADERSHIP

Let's pull out the first pot and begin the boil. The survey, as implemented by Assessment Plus,[2] was designed to rate 187 leaders from 45 different companies around the world on their leadership abilities. In order to get a comprehensive understanding of the strengths and weaknesses of these leaders, the survey questioned 2,535 direct reports, peers, direct managers, and customers in 15 management categories as related to the performance of the 187 leaders. All questions were answered on a scale of 1 to 5, with 1 representing a rating of "extremely dissatisfied" and 5 being "highly satisfied."

By and large, the 187 leaders scored well in setting good examples for others but needed improvement in how they managed others. The managers had an average score of 4.45 in terms of their ability to "demonstrate honest, ethical behavior in all interactions" and a score of 4.27 that they "ensure that the highest standards for ethical behavior are practiced throughout the organization."[3] However, in terms of creating constructive dialogue with those around them, the leaders scored significantly lower (3.86) on whether they "ask people what he/she can do to improve."[4]

Thus, there is success in laying forth the recipe of integrity, but the soup needs salt. The successful global leader must add self-awareness, solicit feedback, and work to ensure ongoing communication. To be self-aware, the leader must know himself or herself. In our survey, scores were low (3.79) on the degree to which the leader "understands her/his own strengths and weaknesses."[5] They don't know, and they don't ask. This is a recipe for trouble.

An example from a recent Asian coaching client showed that neither he nor his supervisor was in tune with what it would take for the two of them to engage in constructive dialogue. The client himself was known to be highly introverted. Though he was supremely competent in his analytical abilities, among his colleagues he was perceived as lacking confidence. When speaking with him in a coaching setting, however, it became clear that he was actually a person of high ability with great self-confidence. The supervisor, equally unaware of how his own blunt communication might undermine his message, assumed that his supervisee was meek and simply told him, "You need to think out loud." To better boost performance, this global manager might have perceived the cultural factors involved and, rather than demanded instant extroversion, worked with his supervisee to share information in a way that suited them both.

Continuing in this vein, many of the survey results show that leaders excel in terms of their own attitudes and practices but do less well in how they encourage the best from those around them. They scored a high rating of 4.30 in their ability to "consistently treat people with respect and dignity"[6] and 4.3 in "embracing the value of diversity in people (including culture, race, sex or age),"[7] but scored a lower rating of 3.82 in their ability to "provide developmental feedback in a timely manner."[8] They did not "provide effective coaching to their direct and indirect reports and colleagues" (3.82)[9] nor "take risks in letting others make decisions" (3.85).[10] This ties back to not getting feedback from direct reports on what could be improved in the leader's style, and round we go.

Disconnects occur at multiple levels. For example, the leaders showed a strong ability (4.22) to "recognize the impact of globalization on their business,"[11] but did not fare as well (3.93) in "helping others understand the impact of globalization."[12] Also, the leaders scored high (4.28) on "communicating a positive, can-do sense of urgency toward getting the job done,"[13] but in the category of "creating a shared vision" failed to "develop strategy to achieve the vision" (3.82) or "inspire others to achieve the vision" (3.84).[14] These results are consistent with the findings that show leaders' inclination to perform somewhat more within themselves (without awareness of their own strengths and weaknesses, and without feedback) versus projecting a message outward that will help team members and subordinates define a clear objective for a team or company.

What these results further suggest is that the leaders of today have developed a strength of "self" and develop their skills as they navigate through their day. They have the skills and judgment needed to tackle any obstacle that lands on their desks and they can do it in an ethical, respectful manner. The question that remains is an obvious one: Can a leader truly be a leader if the only person she or he has managed to develop and inspire is herself or himself?

If this "development" includes no feedback from direct reports, colleagues, and supervisors, is it headed in the right direction? The answer is no, of course, and any inability on the part of a leader to be able to successfully interact and motivate those around him is only magnified when working in a global economy. Successfully interacting with those around one is hard enough; developing a strong, meaningful working relationship with colleagues across oceans is that much harder when the challenges of distance, time zones, languages, and cultures are thrown into the mix. For North Americans, this may create a particular challenge. My recent interviews[15] have shown that for executives from countries as varied as Germany and India a relationship must be as deep as it is wide, and what might be a "friendship" in one culture might be considered nothing more than an acquaintanceship in another.

Returning to our culinary metaphor, as the diner becomes a global café, new menu items are required. New recipes must be savored. Not only will the burger of the past take some Dijon mustard today, but in the future the chef will have to develop the confidence to serve burgers and wonton at the same table!

In the research for our book *Global Leadership: The Next Generation,* we asked the 200 leaders to rank the most important success factors for global leadership in the past, present, and future. For leaders of the past and present, "demonstrating self-confidence as a leader" was ranked as most important. For leaders of the future, however, the top-ranking success factors were "consistently treating people with respect," followed by "understanding the impact of globalization on his/her business" and "creating and communicating a clear vision for her/his organization."[16] In other words, the global leaders of the future need to move beyond themselves and focus on those around them. Fundamental as this may seem, it signals a significant shift in awareness toward a realization that in a global environment the human element (e.g., respect for others) becomes even more important.

RECOMMENDATIONS FOR THE FUTURE

As leaders move beyond themselves and widen the lens through which they see others, the true recipe for global leadership begins to develop. Successful leaders make decisions by navigating through the global village and removing any preconceptions of how others are supposed to behave. As human beings, it is natural that everybody judges others; the important point is to be aware of whether our judgment is determined by informed observation or preexisting, culturally based assumptions.

With the global context and its challenges in mind, I've developed a list of five recommendations designed to elicit some of the inherent skills leaders already possess, honing them to enable team members and subordinates to benefit from a shared vision and sense of purpose. Within each recommendation, multiple elements are included. Not every ingredient applies in every situation, of course; the idea is to select that which is most applicable to your situation.

1. Create a vision and share it with others.[17]

    ➤ With confidence and enthusiasm, inspire stakeholders with your new recipe (vision), giving as much foundational information as possible.

    ➤ After analyzing key factors in the relevant context, schedule meetings to review and update the vision.

    ➤ In setting goals, be specific and include the whole group, not just individual performers.

    ➤ Move from vision to mission and strategies, all the while remaining true to the overarching vision of the company and inspiring staff to refine strategies at the local level.

As you begin to know yourself and your lens, look for the lens of your global counterparts. Find the point of intersection. Carefully observe others and do your best to understand what makes them tick. What motivates them? Where can you find a point of common understanding? Be adaptable.

2. Give developmental feedback in a timely manner.[18]

➤ Design a development plan in conjunction with your direct report, and follow up with feedback on performance. Become a coach.

➤ When you give feedback, refer back to clearly established performance standards.

➤ After completion of each project, ask what went well and what could be done differently next time.

➤ Have stakeholders develop awareness of their own strengths and development needs.

Understand that your success, as well as the success of the company, depends on how you can improve the performance of those around you. By simply showing an interest in those around you, not only do you increase their chances for success but they will see that they truly are part of a team, regardless of time zones or language barriers.

3. Let people make decisions.[19]

➤ Determine where power might be shared, evaluating the pluses and minuses in each area.

➤ Ask the teams themselves for ideas about how they might create goals and do their jobs.

➤ Follow up with meetings to review progress, adjusting where necessary.

➤ Continue to empower stakeholders to solve their problems and make decisions independently.

Shared leadership is one of five emerging competencies from the *Global Leadership: The Next Generation* research. Creating a shared vision and empowering stakeholders with feedback and other forms of effective communication will set in motion the momentum necessary to work in a virtual environment. By encouraging others to take responsibility for a specific task or project, they also assume an ownership role and have a stake in the success of their work.

4. Empower others to take risks.[20]

➤ Help your staff to assess the risks and benefits of a decision.

➤ Work with them as you clarify, affirm, and respect their talents to make moves that require a stretch.

➤ Develop the boundaries or action areas for new ideas where staff can try them out without violating any nonnegotiable requirements.

➤ Identify assignments that could be used for development.

Your willingness to let staff take risks ties directly into the degree to which you respect them for who they are. Set aside all assumptions and ask questions until you have a clear understanding of their ideas, questions, and concerns; then you can delve deeper to try to understand the basis of these, what motivates them, and how it influences them. Keep at it and oftentimes you will be pleasantly surprised by the results.

    5. Recognize the importance of globalization and reinforce its impact on business.[21]

➤ Analyze the supply chain of your company or the global network of your organization to gain an understanding of its reach.

➤ Share your learning and inspire staff curiosity about globalization and its potential benefits.

➤ Make meaningful forecasts based on profit within a global financial context.

➤ Explore opportunities for innovation and business among your staff and stakeholders.

➤ Place yourself and your company into the future, asking "What can we do that we couldn't before?" Then come back to the present, seeing that the future is now; the globe is at your doorstep.

Congratulations! Now you're a chef at the Global Leadership Café. By creating a vision to bring others on board, giving feedback along the way, sharing leadership, helping your staff take risks, and bringing home the message of globalization, you are setting in motion a formula that will equip your team for the challenges of the 21st century. In this chapter, we have set forth the premise that a global leader is like a good cook: one flexible enough to incorporate new recipes and adjust them to ensure the quality of the mix and a successful dish.

Here's the final secret, though: today's menu is not the same as yesterday's or tomorrow's. Just as a chef adjusts recipes to taste, so the global leader of the future must adapt to changing scenarios in a volatile world. As our Global Leader of the Future Aggregate's 2,535 stakeholders have told us in our survey data, one of the key principles for moving forward is to move outside of one's own realm, changing from a reactive mindset to one of ongoing and dynamic action and communication. Then, just as the world itself goes around, so must the cycle of dialogue among leaders, colleagues, and direct reports. With a 360-degree view and curiosity in a changing global environment, you are ready to cook!

ABOUT THE AUTHOR

Rated one of the Top 100 Thought Leaders by *Leadership Excellence* magazine and Top Leadership Guru from Asia by Leadership Guru International, **Maya Hu-Chan** is an international management consultant, an executive coach, an author, and a sought-after speaker. She specializes in global leadership, executive coaching, and cross-cultural business skills.

Harvard Business School has chosen her book *Global Leadership: The Next Generation* to be one of its Working Knowledge recommended books. She is also a contributing author to six books, including *Coaching for Leadership,* edited by Marshall Goldsmith, Laurence S. Lyons, and Alyssa Freas. Maya has trained and coached thousands of leaders in Global Fortune 500 companies. She has worked with major corporations throughout North America, Asia, Europe, South America, and Australia.

Born and raised in Taiwan, Maya received her BA from National Chengchi University in Taiwan, and master's degree from Annenberg School of Communications, University of Pennsylvania. Contact Maya at mayahuchan@earthlink.net or visit her Web site at www.mayahuchan.com.

NOTES

1. Marshall Goldsmith, Cathy L. Greenberg, Alastair Robertson, and Maya Hu-Chan, *Global Leadership: The Next Generation* (Upper Saddle River, N.J.: Financial Times Prentice-Hall, 2003).

2. Assessment Plus Professional Effectiveness Assessment 360 Feedback Results, Global Leader of the Future Aggregate, December 2008.

3. Ibid., 9.

4. Ibid., 10.

5. Ibid., 19.

6. Ibid., 12.

7. Ibid., 16.

8. Ibid., 12.

9. Ibid.

10. Ibid., 14.

11. Ibid., 15.

12. Ibid., 16.

13. Ibid., 18.

14. Ibid., 11.

15. Maya Hu-Chan, 14 Interviews on Perceptions of Americans.

16. Goldsmith et al., *Global Leadership.*

17. Ibid., Resource Section, "Creating a Shared Vision," Item 24, 121–22.

18. Ibid., "Developing People," Item 33, 151–52.

19. Ibid., "Sharing Leadership," Item 20, 103–4.

20. Ibid., "Empowering People," Item 20, 168.

21. Ibid., "Thinking Globally," Item 1, 17–18.

CHAPTER 4

Asian and Western Executive Styles

> ### D. Quinn Mills and Luke Novelli, Jr.

Similar executive styles can be found in Asia and the West, but there are differences that reflect major variations in cultures and economic systems. The Western-style entrepreneur is alive and well in Asia today and is making a strong contribution, especially in China. Yet the Western-style professional manager is largely lacking, except in Japan. Western executives have yet to emulate Asian executives, except for a select few expatriates.[1]

The first question that comes up with this chapter's title is, "What is 'Asian' and what is 'Western?'" The West is a big place, including all of Europe and all of the Americas. Asia includes widely diverse countries (e.g., China, India, and the Philippines). The varieties of cultures within these two aggregations are vast, and in many ways, making comparisons at this high level of abstraction is almost more harmful than helpful. However, keeping this in mind, we do believe it can be useful to explore leadership styles associated with the two regions as a way to broaden and deepen our understanding of executive effectiveness and to begin to move these understandings in *both* directions.

We will start by distinguishing three executive roles, and then discuss some historical and contingency factors that have affected how these roles play out in various regions. We will then describe some elements of executive style and how they vary in different countries. Finally, we will discuss implications for executive effectiveness and for executive development.

LEADERSHIP, MANAGEMENT, AND ADMINISTRATION

In comparing executive styles internationally, it is useful to distinguish among three roles: leadership, management, and administration (generally, the distinction made in the West is between leadership and management, with administration confused among the other two). The three are in fact very different; yet each is valuable in running an organization effectively. The *leadership role* is about a vision of the future and the ability to energize others to pursue it. The *management role* is about getting results and doing so efficiently so that a profit or service is created. The *administration role* is about execution through rules, policies, and procedures.

These distinctions are important for communicating about how organizations are run; when the distinctions are not made, conversation becomes very confused, as happens often, even in formal academic discussion. It is common to confuse the three.

The administrative point of view is typical among the top executives of state-owned or controlled enterprises. All over the world, executives who focus on the administrator role have worked their way to the top of corporations by careful adherence to rules and policies or adroit political maneuvering within a bureaucracy. The managerial focus is on results (usually measured by financial accounts) and efficiency (i.e., cost-cutting to generate profits). MBA programs and formal training have shaped the managerial point of view among a large number of executives, especially in the United States. The leadership role involves the ability of an executive to create a vision of the organization's future and energize others to pursue the vision successfully. Jack Welch once commented to a group of younger managers in General Electric when he was CEO, "You may be a great manager, but unless you can energize other people, you are of no value to General Electric as a leader." An effective leadership role is critical, but also the most rare of the three roles.[2]

Generally speaking, administration is delegated to lower levels in Western companies than in Asian ones. Many middle-level Asian managers are primarily administrators and they lack the management skills so important to the results-driven operations of Western companies. Western managers are better at management but often falter in the administrative focus of execution.

HOW MIGHT THE THREE ROLES PLAY OUT DIFFERENTLY AROUND THE WORLD?

Taking a contingency perspective, we see that executive styles in different regions of the globe are partly a result of the history and institutional arrangements from which they emerged. For example, the Chinese possess the longest continuous civilization in the world. Human relationships there have a subtlety and depth of definition that are unknown elsewhere. The personal style of Chinese executives (whether they are in mainland China or among the overseas Chinese) reflects these cultural characteristics. It is common to find in China a highly directive leader, and in Japan a more participative leader. The empowering leader and the charismatic leader (in the American mode) are far less common.

Executive styles and executive qualities are expressed differently in different regions of the world. The role models available for business executives in different regions have a significant impact on up-and-coming executives. In America, with its longstanding experience with professional business leadership, the most readily available role model for the head of a company is the corporate CEO. In China and Chinese-related businesses, it is the head of the family. In France, it remains the military general. In Japan, it is the consensus builder. In Germany, it is the coalition builder.

Western leaders in some countries exhibit specific traits to a greater degree than in others. For example, emotionalism is more common in American leaders than elsewhere. Germans typically see American emotionalism as a sort of business demagogy and are very suspicious of it.

There are a number of components of executive style that can be identified. We have selected a few (depicted in Table 4.1) to illustrate the point that style can vary on a number of dimensions around the globe.

Table 4.1 General Asian–Western Executive Style Differences*

Style Dimension	Asian	Western
Decisiveness	low	high
Integrity	—	—
Adaptability	low	high
Emotional toughness	high	low
Emotional resonance	low	high
Humility	high	low
Self-knowledge	low	high

* "Low" and "high" refer to the relative presence of the characteristic across the two regions. There is probably no difference in levels of integrity across the two regions, but it is likely that it would be expressed quite differently.

Decisiveness is common to effective executives in all countries; however, Europeans and Japanese are the most consensus-oriented, requiring more time and exhibiting greater openness to the ideas of others, whereas Chinese and American top executives are more likely to make decisions quickly and personally.

Integrity is a complex characteristic very much determined by national culture. What behavior is perceived as honest in one society is sometimes not in another, and vice versa. The widespread public perception of corruption in business, especially in America and China, suggests that integrity is deeply challenged in much of business today.

Adaptability is a pronounced characteristic of American leadership generally, which is highly pragmatic. This is also true of the Chinese, but less true of leadership behavior in many other Asian countries where ideological, religious, and other social mores make for greater rigidity in executive behavior.

American executives have emotional toughness, but spend much time trying not to show it, for it is not generally admired. The current ideal type in American society displays emotional sensitivity, not toughness. On the other hand, toughness is a much admired quality of Asian leadership.

Emotional resonance—the ability to grasp what motivates others and appeal effectively to it—is most important in the United States and Europe, but does not currently appear as a significant element of Asian executive style, where the aspiration of masses of people for a higher living standard provides strong work-oriented motivation as a general matter of course. But as living standards in Asia improve and knowledge workers become more important, the ability of executives to motivate employees will become more important and so will understanding them (emotional resonance).

Humility is a very uncommon trait in the American CEO. It is sometimes found in Asia, where it is generally admired. It is often a trait of the most effective leaders, even in the United States, as it was in the most well-respected of all American political leaders, Abraham Lincoln. Once, when the Civil War was not going well for the Union side, a high-ranking general suggested that the nation needed to get rid of Lincoln and have a dictatorship instead. The comment came to Lincoln's ears. Lincoln nevertheless promoted the general to the top command in the army and told him, "I am appointing you to command despite, not because of, what you said. Bring us victories, and I'll risk the dictatorship."

Self-knowledge is important in avoiding the sort of overreach so common in America; it is an uncommon virtue here, however, while it is a strength of many Asian executives.

THE IMPACT OF CORPORATE FORMS ON EXECUTIVE STYLES

Executive style depends to a significant degree on the role focus of the executive in the firm, and this depends partly on the form that business takes. Thus, the executive role reflects the actual responsibilities given to the executive in a business, and this reflects the form, economic environment, and political context of the business.

The West has a dominant form of business organization: the joint stock enterprise. The recent upsurge of government equity ownership in many businesses (as a result of the financial crisis) is not likely to convert these businesses into Asian-style state-owned enterprises. Asia has four significant forms— the state-owned enterprise, government-linked business, family-controlled business, and Western-style joint stock company.

While the role of top executives is everywhere superficially the same— responsibility for the overall direction and performance of the enterprise— there is actually a great difference in what top executives do in Western versus Asian businesses. This reflects the substantial differences between the Western economic system and that of Asian countries. To understand this, we have to take a look at the origins of today's American business system.

Modern business arose in Europe in the form of the joint stock company, and the heart of the modern Western business system is the interaction of these companies with the capital market. American business arrangements quickly assumed marked characteristics of their own, different from those in Europe. In America, both government and family relationships were much weaker than in Europe—business was done primarily as arms-length transactions among people without family connections, and government was forced into a primarily regulatory role in the economy. A quasi-professional management developed and the investor achieved a prominence in the governance of business unequaled in Europe.

Today, American business exhibits four characteristics strikingly different from European business:

1. Less government involvement and direction

2. Proportionally far more professionally trained managers and executives

3. Shareholder primacy in corporate governance rather than a stakeholder model of governance

4. A single dominant chief executive (and therefore single-point accountability to the investor) rather than a committee or partnership style of management

Most large Western companies are dependent on capital markets and so pay much more attention to Wall Street than is yet common in Asia. Wall Street has strong expectations about the behavior and performance of business executives. There is less freedom of action for executives and boards in America than in Asia. Consequently, American executives are responsive to their boards and to Wall Street.

Most U.S. companies are run by professional managers who are succeeded by other professional managers, as a consequence of either retirement or replacement by the company's board of directors. The better companies have sophisticated programs for developing executives within the company, and ordinarily choose a new chief executive officer from among them. The result is the continual combination and recombination of business assets in different corporate forms. This process of asset recombination in theory generates more efficient uses of productive resources (physical, human, and intellectual) and is a major generator of wealth creation.

There is extreme flexibility in the U.S. economy with respect to (1) asset recombination and (2) entrepreneurial enterprise. These two factors give the American economy its strength and influence in the global economy. It is not just that American executives are better trained in the managerial role than those of most other nations, but that they are trained and have learned to work in an extremely flexible institutional setting that permits them to exercise imagination and initiative.

As a result, American large-company executives are good at two things: recombining productive assets and cutting costs of production. However, they are weak at two other things: attaining real efficiencies of operations and achieving organic growth for their companies (i.e., growing the core businesses of a corporation).

One might say that Asian executives are the opposite—they are good at attaining real efficiencies of operation (increasing productivity) and achieving organic growth, while less effective at recombining productive assets and cutting production costs.

What is the difference between cost-cutting and improving efficiency, it might be asked, since both reduce costs/unit of output (products or services)? The answer is that the American executive isn't usually effective at improving productivity, but is effective at reducing costs directly, by strategies such as decreasing wages, reducing staff (thus forcing cuts in unit cost of production rather than increasing output per hour at the same cost), and cutting benefit costs (including pensions, health insurance, etc.). This reflects the role focus we discussed earlier: American executives focus on management, whereas Asian executives are more likely to focus on administration.

This distinction was highlighted recently in Singapore when DBS bank, using the logic of cost-cutting as seen from the managerial role, unexpectedly announced a large layoff in response to the worsening situation in the banking sector. A senior government official (among others) chastised the bank for not seeking all means possible to reduce costs before resorting to layoffs (e.g., reduced pay, reduced work hours). The official indicated that there would be new "guidelines" about the proper procedures that employers should follow prior to announcing and implementing layoffs.[3] The government's response demonstrates the logic of the administrative rather than the managerial role. This logic was further in evidence in an article by the CEO of a prominent real estate company. He indicated that he would implement pay cuts within his organization rather than layoffs, with the largest percentage of cuts coming from the most senior levels. This "downtime" brought on by the global recession was viewed as an opportunity to upgrade the skills of employees. He considered avoiding layoffs a way of maintaining and building capability and future loyalty that would pay off in increased competitiveness.[4]

The broader American economy makes up for the weakness of its large companies in accomplishing organic growth through having the world's strongest entrepreneurial sector, one that develops new products, services, and processes and transfers these to the established business sector in a variety of ways.

This process of recombination of assets that is central to the Western economic model (whether the assets are longstanding or newly created by entrepreneurship) also permits massive speculation and recombination for other purposes than efficiency—the "ideal" process (in theory) degenerates in practice. Vast sums of capital are wasted in recombination of assets that serve no economic purpose, though they often serve the personal financial gain of those involved in the mergers and acquisitions.

In Europe, even where there is formal liquidity of assets by virtue of the joint stock company structure, both government and social partners (labor unions, communities, etc.) constrain the recombination of assets to a much greater degree than in America.

Asia is only now entering the complex institutional arrangements that form the global economy. Much of the vaunted economic advance of East Asia, for example, is actually the provision of labor to Western companies that bring both technology and capital to Asian sites. The great game of asset recombination is not played by Asian business leaders, but that is beginning to change. Can they do it successfully in an environment in which both state-owned and family-owned companies compete with joint stock companies?

Many Asian family-controlled companies are in fact mini-conglomerates with real estate, construction, hotel, residential development, manufacturing, retail, theme park, and other branches. Corporate strategy theory tells us that these companies diversify their assets and revenue sources in order to compensate for economic market failures. For example, because capital markets are weak, managers in conglomerates are given responsibility for allocating capital among different businesses. Because labor markets are inefficient and business training is weak, conglomerates train their few corporate executives and move them around different business lines. This is also the reason that family-owned conglomerates are the dominant organizational structure in Asian economies.

As a consequence of legal and institutional contingencies, the executive role focus has evolved differently in different regions. Figure 4.1 is meant to be illustrative only and represents what might be the case given our discussion.

The graphs in Figure 4.1 suggest that the administrative role focus dominates in Asia, is moderate in Europe, and is less prominent in America, whereas the managerial focus dominates in America, is prominent in Europe, and much less visible in Asia. We believe that it is likely that the leadership role focus is relatively the same across all three regions and does not dominate how executives function in any of them.

Figure 4.1 Geographic Distribution of Executive Roles

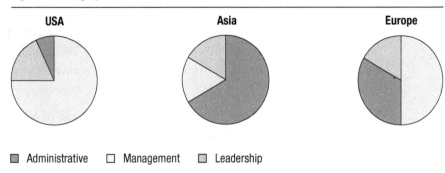

USA   Asia   Europe

☒ Administrative   ☐ Management   ☐ Leadership

WHAT ARE THE IMPLICATIONS FOR EXECUTIVE EFFECTIVENESS?

With changes in the global business environment, the key question is, "Will the styles of executive-role focus in Asia and the West become more alike or not?" One could speculate that as Asian economies grow their executive styles will come to resemble more closely those in the West. In particular, the family-controlled company and the state-owned enterprise will decline or disappear. Another view is that the rise of consumerism in Asia will not effect deeper differences between Asian and Western cultures, and that both the family-controlled corporation and the state-owned enterprise will persist to a greater degree than expected.

We would like to speculate that there are pluses and minuses to the executive styles associated with the different cultures. A key for executives who increasingly find themselves operating in the global arena will be to *adopt styles that are effective regardless of their cultural source*. This will require accentuating the positives and minimizing the negatives associated with their familiar executive role pattern. In short, there is a great deal to be learned from both Asia and the West regarding executive effectiveness. We are beginning to see this with the Tata group, for example, one of India's largest conglomerates and an extremely successful company since its founding in 1868. The chairmanship has been in family hands for nearly its entire history and is currently headed by Ratan Tata, a family member. Recently, there have been several acquisitions and/or stakes in foreign companies. For example, Tata Motors acquired Jaguar and Land Rover from Ford. Tata Steel purchased the Corus group, the Anglo-Dutch steelmaker. Tata Tea took a 30 percent share of U.S. Energy Corp. and sold it less than a year later to Coca-Cola. Tata Power bought a stake in Indonesian PT Bumi Resources, and Tata

Chemicals purchased U.S. soda-ash producer General Chemical Industrial Products, Inc. So it is clear that the giant Indian conglomerate is pursuing an aggressive acquisition strategy.[5] As described in the section about corporate forms and executive styles, this will require senior Tata executives to operate effectively in a context of asset recombination, something more familiar to executives in the West.

The Microsoft entry into China provides an illustration of Western executives having to readjust their styles to operate in Asia. After an initial period during which Microsoft stubbed its toe badly, Bill Gates and other senior Microsoft executives invested the time and energy to build relationships and operate within the context of Chinese business etiquette and the dictates of the Chinese Communist Party. Once Microsoft recognized that access to the Chinese talent base was probably a more valuable asset than access to the Chinese market, a different form and tone of relations emerged. It required much closer attention to the administrative component of the executive role than would have been the case in the West.[6]

These two examples are not meant to be definitive but, rather, illustrative of the fact that the most likely global business future will require effective executives to adopt the best of regional practices and minimize the downsides of their own region's executive role negatives.

IMPLICATIONS FOR DEVELOPMENT

In an increasingly globalized context, the question becomes, "What and how will executives need to develop to be effective across regions?" We will start with the second part of the question—how will executives develop? The research is quite clear,[7] and supports our experience working with executives around the globe in suggesting that there is good news: there does not appear to be a major difference across regions in what it takes for executives to develop.

There is a stream of research showing that, fundamentally, executive development is a learning-based process.[8] In essence, people are exposed to a variety of events. These events provoke experiences that, if reflected upon, have the potential to teach lessons about executive effectiveness. To the degree that these lessons are internalized, executives alter and reshape their attitudes, perspectives, and assessments of the skills they need. To the degree that they are able to apply, through feedback-rich practice, the insights they have gained, they can improve their executive functioning currently and in the future. So the key to executive development is placing executives into situations that have the potential to teach valuable lessons about effectiveness, and supporting them in extracting the lessons from those experiences. This also requires supporting executives in learning how to learn more effectively and in becoming more skilled at recognizing and taking opportunities to practice.

Now to the first part of the initial question: the "what" executives will need to learn is embedded in the executive roles that they need to perform. They will simultaneously need to pay attention to the role focus they are familiar with—often unlearning what they are familiar with if it will not work in a new situation. In addition, they will need to learn the unfamiliar—that is, how to be effective with people raised in different cultures. The leadership-management-administration framework can help point executives toward what they need to develop.

In summary, historical and cultural factors significantly shape the accepted practices that executives are expected to engage in. There are different configurations of executive role, with more or less relative emphasis on leadership, management, or administration, that vary between Asia and the West. This relative emphasis has served executives well in the regions they were brought up in. However, as the world becomes more globalized, it is imperative that global executives be able to distinguish the positives of other role configurations and minimize the negatives of those with which they are most familiar. The path to accomplishing this is through effective learning (i.e., development) and application of the lessons learned through practice and performance. Increasingly, senior executives will be required to be facile with both Asian and Western executive styles.

ABOUT THE AUTHORS

D. Quinn Mills is the Albert J. Weatherhead Jr. Professor of Business Administration, Emeritus, at Harvard Business School, where he has taught business and government leadership. Professor Mills consults with major corporations and is a director of several start-ups. A significant author, Mills's recent books include *The Financial Crisis of 2008–9* (2009); *Rising Nations* (2009); *Master of Illusions: Presidential Leadership in America*

(2006); *Leadership: How to Lead, How to Live* (2006); *Principles of Management* (2005); and *Principles of Human Resource Management* (2006). He is also author of three other books on financial problems: *Wheel, Deal and Steal: Deceptive Accounting, Deceitful CEOs and Ineffective Reforms*; *Buy, Lie and Sell High: How Investors Lost Out on Enron and the Internet Bubble*; and *Having It All, Making It Work*. Professor Mills's current research focuses on leadership, strategy, finance, and human resource management.

Luke Novelli, Jr., is Chief of Intellectual Capital at Leadership Development Resources Global and formerly a Senior Fellow at the Center for Creative Leadership (CCL). While at CCL, he was a faculty member in a variety of programs and held a number of leadership positions. He has been based in Singapore for six years, working with regional and global organizations to implement leadership-development initiatives. Currently, his focus is "efficient" leadership-development approaches (80 percent of the value using 20 percent of the resources). His research focuses on how to create climates for development that leverage an organization's investments in individual leadership development. Contact Luke at Novelli@ldr-g.com and www.leadership-development-resources.com.

NOTES

1. For a general introduction, see "Asian and American Leadership Styles: How Are They Unique?" *Working Knowledge,* Harvard Business School, June 27, 2005. A longer version of the same title was published by D. Quinn Mills (with the assistance of Ajmal Ahmady) in the *Peking Business Review,* August 2007, in Chinese.

2. Heard by D. Quinn Mills.

3. Debbie Yong, "New Guidelines for Layoffs," *Straits Times,* May 5, 2008.

4. Susan Long, "When Times Are Bad Prepare for Good Times," *Straits Times,* December 3, 2008.

5. "Major Overseas Acquisitions by India's Tata Group," *Economic Times,* March 26, 2008, http://economictimes.indiatimes.com/articleshow/2900293.cms.

6. Robert Buderi and Gregory T. Huang, *Guanxi (The Art of Relationships): Microsoft, China, and Bill Gates's Plan to Win the Road Ahead* (New York: Simon & Schuster, 2006).

7. Morgan W. McCall, Jr., *High Flyers: Developing the Next Generation of Leaders* (Boston: Harvard Business School Press, 1998).

8. Robert J. Thomas, *Crucibles of Leadership: How to Learn from Experience to Become a Great Leader* (Boston: Harvard Business School Press, 2008); and Cynthia D. McCauley and Ellen Van Velsor, eds., *The Center for Creative Leadership Handbook of Leadership Development,* 2nd ed. (San Francisco: Jossey-Bass, 2003).

PART TWO

Developing People

➤ The Key to the Future

CHAPTER 5

Passing the Baton: Developing Your Successor

> **Marshall Goldsmith**

At the end of a long and successful career, preparing your successor and yourself for the passing of the baton can be a leader's greatest challenge. Every leader faces this challenge eventually. Some leaders handle it well; many do not. However, if you handle it the right way while you are still at the organization, it can mean that your successor enters to applause while you exit gracefully.

Developing successors is often a task that busy leaders put off to "take care of later"—that is, until it is actually their point of departure and there is no more time to prepare! Rather than be surprised when it is time to leave, how can leaders prepare for transition? What are the personal and behavioral elements of transition—in other words, what is the human side of transition? And how can they leave their positions with class and dignity?

PREPARING FOR THE INEVITABLE

The handoff is imminent. Sooner or later, you will have to pass the baton of leadership to another leader who will take your place. It is up to you, the leader, how successful the handoff will be. As in a relay race, there are two important steps. The first is that you will have to slow down so that you and your successor do not drop the baton during the pass; the second is that you will have to coach your successor up to speed so as to carry the baton to the finish line.

During the handoff, you can't just concentrate on the pass. You have to keep a close eye on your competitors and your organization's short-term quarterly results, as well as its long-term goals, to ensure that everything runs smoothly and successfully even during the transition. You have an audience of stakeholders watching your every move—stockholders who expect to receive a return on their investments, analysts who expect you to keep your commitments, customers who want value, employees who expect your actions to match your words, and competitors who hope you'll fail or become so exhausted you can't do your part.

Then, after a successful handoff, you will disappear quietly into the sunset. There will be no great fanfare because, if you have done your job of developing your successor well, your organization will be even more successful after you leave! Your legacy will be that of a leader who ensured that the values of the organization lived on even after your departure.

SUCCESSION IS PERSONAL

The process of readying yourself for succession is personal, and it is often influenced as much by emotion as it is by logic. Experiencing a gamut of hopes and fears and probably even a sense of loss is likely as you prepare to move on. For many leaders, their job has become something like their best friend, as was the case with a coaching client of mine. Sharing how it felt to leave her job, this gracious CEO said, "It seemed like I was getting promoted every few years. I loved the company, my coworkers, and our customers. Going to work was always a joy for me. . . . The time just flew by—and then one day it was time to leave. It hurt."

She had fallen in love with being a leader. And when this happens, it can be difficult, sometimes almost impossible, to let go. The transition process will be different for each person. Nevertheless, it will be personal to you and your other executives, and the board.

MAKING A GRACEFUL EXIT

Getting through the transition process in the most positive way possible is the goal of a successful transition. Your objectives are to enjoy your final year (or so) as leader, to slow down and ready yourself for the changes ahead, to coach your successor to a position where there is a good opportunity for success, and to make room for him or her to speed up and take on the challenges of your position. Now that you know what you need to do, for the process to begin, you'll have to choose your successor.

Developing your successor is one of the greatest accomplishments you or any CEO can achieve. At the beginning of this process, one of the first issues that will come up is whether to put your energies into an internal or an external successor.

External Succession: Why Not?

There are many reasons *not* to choose your successor from outside the company. For one, the board will want a leader with a proven success record—these leaders are few and far between and can be costly to the organization to bring in. And, if they do not work out, they will likely expect a large exit package. Far beyond the monetary, the damage of external CEO failure can cost the company severely in terms of reputation, as negative stories are released in the business press, employees are let go, and resources are slashed. And, company veterans take a dim view when they are forced to take less so the failed externally hired CEO can leave with more.

Another reason not to hire from the outside is that it can be indicative of a failure of leadership development within the company. At least that's the opinion of one very famous CEO with whom I teach in a corporate leadership development program. Having been hired from outside the company himself, he has made it his personal mission to develop talent from within, to develop his own successor. So, ask yourself: if you left tomorrow, who could take your place? If no one comes to mind, then you haven't been doing your job! You have not been developing your successor, you have not been participating in developing the next generation of leaders, and you have not been participating in what you require of your line managers.

One final reason for looking on the inside rather than on the outside when choosing a successor is that external CEOs often bring their own people with them. They will likely bring in their own trusted, high-level executives, which will mean that internal executives at your organization will be passed over and promotional opportunities negated. These valued employees may leave the corporation because they don't see future promotional opportunities and may even fear that they will be fired. All of these reasons are not to say that companies should *never* hire externally.

Though your goal may be to develop an internal successor, there are sometimes forces in the business environment that eliminate this possibility. For instance, in one famous case, a high-level executive committed an ethics violation. While the CEO was not involved in the violation, he was held responsible for the damage. Feeling it important to send a message about the severity of the problems and the need for the company to change, the board decided to hire an external successor. In another example, an internal candidate, though seen as a *potentially* excellent CEO, was not chosen because an external CEO was seen as a better *immediate* choice.

When deciding when not to develop your successor from within the company, do a cost-benefit analysis. Ask yourself: What will it cost to bring in an outsider? What are the potential benefits? What will it cost to promote each candidate? What are the benefits? Are there any outsiders who cannot be matched by anyone in the company? Depending on your answers to these questions, you will know whether it will be more beneficial to hire an external canidate or to promote from the inside.

In summary, there are many cases where external hires are successful (think IBM), but hiring external CEOs does come with high risk. If it is possible to develop an internal successor, that is often the best route.

Effective Internal Succession

If hiring a CEO from the outside can bring great risk and send people the wrong message about the company's leadership development, the opposite can be said of effective internal succession. Choosing a successor internally can produce many positive outcomes.

Internal hiring shows that you are developing talent from the inside—just as you are asking your line managers to do. It will mean that another top-level position will open for the promotion of another internal executive. As CEO, your vision for the company will more likely be carried on after you leave by an internal successor who has lived it with you over years than by an external successor who will probably have no attachment to your vision whatsoever.

CHOOSING THE BEST PERSON

Whether it is to be an internal or external successor, the following talents will likely be required of your successor:

1. Bright, intelligent

2. History of success and achievement

3. Dedicated and committed to the organization's success

4. Cares about company and people

5. Integrity (candidates who commit integrity violations should not be considered for this or any other position!)

Now that you are clear on what to look for and whether to hire an external or internal candidate, there are also a few things that you should *avoid* when choosing a successor. Choosing a successor is often presented as a practical process, during which executives evaluate the abstract concepts of strategic fit, core competencies, and long-term shareholder value. Rarely acknowledged is that the process of evaluating potential successors can be influenced by emotions as much as it can be by logic! From a behavioral perspective, it is important to be aware of three very human mistakes that many leaders make when evaluating potential successors. All three diminish our objectivity and our ability to choose a great successor.

1. *Why doesn't he or she act like me?* As successful human beings, we tend to overvalue our strengths and undervalue our weaknesses when evaluating others. The more successful we are, the more likely we are to fall into the "superstition trap," which simply stated is "I behave this way. I am a successful leader. Therefore, I must be a successful leader because I behave this way." Of course, though, we are all successful *because of* many positive traits and *in spite of* some negative traits that we could diminish.

   Years ago I worked with a CEO who was a great communicator. He had the best verbal communication skills of anyone I have known. When it came time to pass the baton, he could not accept the fact that his successor, whose strengths were strategy and marketing, was not as great a communicator. He was so dogged about this point that the board had to intervene and the CEO was forced to leave. This could have been a positive succession, but it turned out to be an unfortunate event for the previous CEO. You don't want this to happen to you.

Take a look at your own strengths and challenges. Make a list of them. Know that you will have a tendency to forgive large errors that resemble your weaknesses and punish small flaws in others that occur in your strong areas. List your potential successor's strengths and weaknesses. Think like an objective outsider, as hard as this may be. Recognize that while you may feel very strongly that the candidate should exhibit a certain behavior because it has led to your success, it may not be critical to the success of the organization.

2. *Why doesn't he or she think like me?* Of course, as a successful leader, you probably believe that your strategic thinking is the right strategic thinking. However, as you proceed in the succession process you will have to let go. Your successor will make different decisions, and this may be tough for you to watch—especially since you are still the leader and have the power to reverse those decisions. As hard as it is, step back. Your successor will manage your organization in the future—not you. Let him or her slowly make a bigger and bigger difference in developing strategy.

   Ensuring that the organization is headed in a positive direction in a general sense and achieving results, recognize that your successor's alternate route may even turn out to be a better route than the one you would have taken.

3. *Why doesn't he or she respect and appreciate my friends?* If you respect and admire someone, you may overvalue his or her input, and the converse is true as well. It can be hard to face that your successor may respect and admire someone you don't. His or her personal preferences will be different from yours. Respect this and let the individual choose his or her own trusted advisers.

   You may notice after the transition that the status and power of some of your good friends is actually lessened. They may not be "in the circle" at the top. As a result of this loss, they may leave the company. Both you and they may find this tough. If you know your friends will not support the new leader, especially for personal reasons, take them aside. Try to convince them that this is the best leader for the future of the company. Explain that the leader needs support and a clean slate. Set your successor up to win. Respect your successor enough to let him or her choose those key advisers.

Developing your successor is extremely personal. Follow these steps and you'll find that this may well be the greatest accomplishment of your career!

COACHING YOUR SUCCESSOR

Your job as the exiting leader is to help your successor become the best leader he or she can be for the company. Preparing your successor to take on your position is a great challenge. If you do this right while you are still at the organization, your successor will enter to applause while you bow out gracefully—in a seamless transition that is good for all concerned.

What do you need to know about coaching so you can ensure a smooth transition? What due diligence must you do with regard to coaching your successor?

1. Decide whether and to what extent you will coach your successor.

2. Hire an executive coach for those areas in which you are not an expert.

3. Involve key stakeholders to determine your successor's strengths and weaknesses.

4. Review all of the feedback—keep in mind to look for trends, consider the organizational environment, and highlight key patterns.

5. Initiate and analyze organizational surveys so you can understand how you as a leader have influenced your organization.

In addition, gather ideas for leadership success by asking each preselected stakeholder the following questions:

➤ What are the person's strengths that will help him or her be a great leader?

➤ What are the developmental challenges that he or she may need to overcome in order to be a great leader?

➤ If you were this person's coach, what specific suggestions would you give him or her—strategic or tactical—that would help him become a great leader?

SET UP YOUR SUCCESSOR FOR SUCCESS

As you prepare to exit the company, coach your successor behind the scenes. Transfer power before it is necessary. Support your successor in whatever way you can, and build his or her confidence by involving the person in important decisions and ensuring as best you can that he or she agrees with your long-term strategies before they are announced. After all, this is the person who is going to have to live with these strategies for the next few years and is going to have to make them work.

Make tough, unpopular decisions that you know will be good for the company. Don't get caught up in "finishing on a great note" or making sure that you look good. Focus on putting your successor in a spot where he or she will succeed. Make decisions for the long-term success of the organization, rather than the short-term performance of the company.

This type of class and self-sacrifice is rare, but in the long run it is best for the company, for investors, for the successor, and even for you, the outgoing leader. This is your last chance to do the right thing for the long-term benefit of the company. Don't waste it!

PREPARE YOURSELF FOR THE NEXT PHASE OF YOUR LIFE

On a personal note, slowing down can have its advantages. You will go home a little earlier, spend more time with your family, go to your grandkids' ball games more often, and get to know your spouse again. You'll have time to explore the next team (or teams) you will lead. You'll be ready to pick up the leadership baton in a new race.

When all is said and done, this is how you might want your transition to look: In the beginning, you are running at full speed, leading the company. Your focus is not yet turned toward developing your successor and creating a great rest of your life. This is normal. Near the middle of the transition you are slowing down. You are leading the company, but you are very involved in developing and coaching your successor. You are beginning to focus on creating a great rest of your life. At the end of the process, you will stop leading the company. You will be available only when your successor asks you to help. Your focus has now turned toward creating a great rest of your life.

This is what you want to happen; however, it isn't often what actually happens. Quite frequently the leader is so focused on leading the company until the very end that little time is spent developing the successor and nearly no energy is spent creating a great rest of life. As a result, the transition is bumpy, the baton may be dropped, and there is likelihood of a rough and unpleasant start into the next stage of life.

If you would rather have a great transition for you and your successor, look more like the leader in the first example and less like the leader in the second example. Pass the baton with grace and exit with class and dignity into a great rest of your life.

ABOUT THE AUTHOR

Marshall Goldsmith is a *New York Times* best-selling author and editor of 25 books. *What Got You Here Won't Get You There* is a *Wall Street Journal* #1 business best seller and Harold Longman Award winner for Best Business Book of the Year. *Succession: Are You Ready?* is part of the Harvard Business "Memo to the CEO" series and is a *Wall Street Journal* best seller. Dr. Goldsmith is one of the few executive advisers who has been asked to work with over 100 major CEOs and their management teams. He has been recognized as one of the world's top executive educators and coaches by the American Management Association, *BusinessWeek, Fast Company, Forbes, Economist,* and the *Wall Street Journal.* His material is available online (for no charge) at www.MarshallGoldsmithLibrary.com, where visitors from 188 countries have viewed, downloaded, or shared over 2.5 million resources. Contact Marshall at Marshall@marshallgoldsmith.com.

CHAPTER 6

Developing Exceptional Leaders: Critical Success Factors

> James F. Bolt

What does it take to develop really exceptional leaders? There are 12 key characteristics of great executive/leadership development processes and programs. This chapter describes each of the characteristics, or success factors, and ends with a checklist that should prove useful for assessing and improving your own practices.

The characteristics of these programs are:

1. Linked to strategy

2. Thorough front-end analysis

3. Custom designed

4. Custom leadership profile, feedback, and development planning

5. Action-oriented learning methods

6. A strategy and system

7. Top-down implementation

8. High-potential identification and development

9. Succession management

10. Integrated talent-management system

11. Measurement

12. Driven by top management

How do we know that these factors are critical? In the last 25 years, I've had the privilege of consulting on executive and leadership development with half of the Fortune 100 companies and many Global 500 organizations. In addition, I've conducted surveys on trends in executive/leadership development approximately every two years since 1983, and have led in-depth research projects on topics such as talent management, executive coaching, and identifying/developing high-potential talent. For many years I was fortunate to lead peer-to-peer networks made up of the heads of executive development, leadership development, talent management, organizational development, human resources, and so on from leading companies all over the world. This provided a great way to keep abreast of best and innovative practices.

Before we review each of these success factors, note that the words *executive/leader* are used broadly throughout to refer to the following:

> ➤ *Members of boards of directors.* The chairman of the board, the CEO, and those who report directly to the CEO. Anyone in a C-suite position. All elected officers.

> ➤ *Corporate vice presidents (including functional heads).* Heads of/presidents of groups, divisions, business units, or profit centers and their direct reports. All people included in the executive compensation program.

> ➤ *High-potential managers.* Managers who have been formally identified as having the potential to fill any of the executive-level positions noted above.

Executive development refers to any formal activity that is aimed at broadening or building mindsets, knowledge, skills, and experience and at enhancing capabilities. *Executive development* will often be used as shorthand to include the organization's executive/leadership development and talent management strategies, systems, processes, and programs.

Of the 12 critical success factors, several are directly related to executive/ leadership development programs and others are applicable to the broader talent management system.

THE 12 CHARACTERISTICS OF SUCCESSFUL EXECUTIVE DEVELOPMENT PROCESSES AND PROGRAMS

1. Linked to Strategy. *Our executive development efforts are directly linked to our organization's strategy. It is clear how these efforts help address our business challenges and achieve our strategic objectives.*

   While trying to choose which of the 12 factors are most important might be a fool's game, in my mind, this one and the last (top-management driven) are clearly the most critical because without them it's highly unlikely that any investment in executive development will have a significant impact on either leader effectiveness or business performance. Of course, they are closely related. The best way to ensure that executive development is linked to the strategy is to work with the CEO and her or his team to ensure that whatever is done is driven by them, and specifically aimed at achieving their strategic agenda.

2. Thorough Front-End Analysis. *No significant executive development effort is begun without a thorough front-end needs assessment.*

   Two or three times in my consulting career, I've agreed to design a new executive development strategy and program without conducting a needs analysis. Big mistake! These were all failures because they ended up addressing needs that were not on target. The typical situation included a client who believed that the organization had been "surveyed to death" and that executives would not tolerate any kind of needs analysis. As a result, we essentially had to guess what the development needs were and/or use the opinions of a small number of senior executives who were not close enough to the marketplace realities and real needs of the target audience. In effect, we developed programs that were not dealing with mission-critical topics and didn't achieve the intent of the first characteristic—that is, we were not *linked to the strategy!*

   Effective needs assessment is typically done via a combination of survey and interviews of the target audience and key executives and other critical stakeholders. Regardless of the method, the assessment must identify the capabilities (mindset, knowledge, and skills) needed to achieve the vision, live the values, address the critical business challenges, and successfully execute the business strategy.

3. Custom Designed. *We custom design our programs so that they address our unique, company-specific challenges and opportunities and help create and/or drive our vision, values, and strategies.*

   The best executive development programs focus on the unique needs of the organization. They build the specific capabilities needed to address the organization's marketplace and business challenges, and as stated in item no. 2, those required to achieve the vision, live the values, and execute the strategy. Therefore, a custom-designed solution is required to meet those precise requirements; off-the-shelf solutions are typically not appropriate.

4. Custom Leadership Profile, Feedback, and Development Planning. *We use a custom-designed (linked to our vision, values, and strategies), multirater leadership instrument/inventory to provide confidential development feedback to our executives. Our executives have individual development plans based on that feedback that they actively manage.*

   It wasn't too long ago that it was unusual for individuals at the executive level to receive feedback on their leadership effectiveness. Now it's commonplace at best-practice companies. Whether the organization uses the language of "competencies" or not, the goal is to get senior management to agree on the values and leadership practices that are critical to success (preferably both today and in the foreseeable future), then to develop a 360-degree feedback instrument based on those practices that is updated at appropriate intervals. It's critical that the final practices are ironed out and consensus is built among the top management team and other key senior executives. If they do not believe these are the most critical practices, then the practices are useless.

   Now the hard part: the members of the top management team must be the role models for the process by personally leading the way. Typically that means being the first to receive feedback, creating development plans, working with a coach, actively and visibly managing their action plans, and monitoring and supporting the action plans of the people who report to them. Having a core leadership profile that top management owns and models, and that is used throughout the organization, can also be a key part of building and sustaining the desired organizational culture and identity. It is a mistake to let the members of each part of the organization use their own leadership profiles because they think they are unique. However, it's probably okay if they add items to the core profile to account for their uniqueness.

5. Action-Oriented Learning Methods. *Our executive learning experiences use active rather than passive learning methods to ensure learning by doing. Whenever feasible, we use some form of "action learning" whereby participants apply what they are learning to real, current business problems and opportunities.*

Many years ago when I attended the Harvard Advanced Management Program (the highest-level open-enrollment university executive education program), the only learning process used was the case study method, and that was considered pretty advanced. In most executive education programs, it wasn't unusual for people to spend the majority of their time sitting on their hands listening to wise experts lecture on a variety of fascinating topics. Thankfully, those days are mostly gone. The fact is that executives (and most adults) learn best when the learning process engages them actively and viscerally and the more ways the better. For executives in particular, it helps a great deal if they see the immediate relevance of what they are learning to their work and how it can be applied to improve performance. And absolute nirvana is having a chance to actually apply the learning to real work challenges immediately. Also, 360-degree feedback, business games, adventure learning, business simulations, and the like have all become extremely popular and are examples of more action-oriented versus passive learning methods.

The most popular of all of these in the last 10 years or so has been "action learning" (even though it is not new; it was developed in the United Kingdom in 1945 or so). My short definition of action learning is "working in teams on real business challenges for development purposes." There are many forms of action learning and I won't attempt to describe them here. The essence of most action learning programs is a combination of a real business challenge (typically selected and sponsored by a senior executive), an educational component that provides the knowledge/skills needed to address the challenge, and a team that has been selected to work on the challenge as a development experience.

6. A Strategy and System. *We have a strategy and long-term plan for executive development. Our programs and practices are part of a continuous system and process rather than stand-alone, ad hoc events.*

    Too many programs are created and conducted as one-off, ad hoc events that are not connected to any overall plan, strategy, or system for executive development. Typically they are the pet project of an individual senior executive or HR executive. Unfortunately, experience indicates that they usually do not have much impact. These disjointed efforts often feel like the "program of the month," with the result that participants often don't see them as part of a clear overall strategy and integrated system that is directly aimed at building the capabilities they and the organization need to achieve success. Also, a system and strategy provide much greater leverage and impact than solo events.

7. Top-Down Implementation. *Whenever our executive development efforts are aimed at organization change, our top management attends the programs first as participants. Then the programs are cascaded down through the organization.*

    The essential goal of many of the executive development programs we've been asked to create is to transform the organization in some significant way. These programs are frequently the key component of a major change effort. The content often includes the case for change, the new vision and strategy, the change strategy, and the capabilities needed for success in the "new" organization. For programs of this nature, we always insist that the top management team be the first to participate. Even though the team members have likely been involved in reviewing and approving the design of the program, it's critical that they personally experience it, for a number of reasons.

    First, they serve as the pilot group in that if there is anything that needs to be changed before the program is rolled out through the rest of the executive ranks (and likely in some form throughout the organization), they are the ones who need to decide what to change. Those decisions need to be based on firsthand experience, not on a presentation about the program. Second, they need to actually experience what it is that everyone else will be learning so that they can reinforce and support that with their direct reports. Third, any transformation or change effort will fail if it's seen that top management espouses the change desired but does not live it.

Therefore, managers need to be able to learn individually, and as a team too, so that they can role-model the new way of being and leading in the organization.

8. High-Potential Identification and Development. *Our organization has an effective process for identifying "high-potential" talent and accelerating its development.*

   No organization can achieve long-term success if it doesn't focus on the future talent pool for leaders. Some organizations have sophisticated methods for identifying who should be designated a high potential and others are content with more informal ones. Frankly, I don't think it matters as long as it is legally defensible, makes sense to those it affects, and is perceived to actually work—that is, those who are identified are seen as performing well when put into positions of significant responsibility.

   Even at the executive level (as we've defined it here), there are typically two groups that organizations pay close attention to. One is the relatively small number of people whom they think are next in line to fill vacancies in the top management team. The development tends to be tailored to each individual and often includes extensive assessments, an executive coach, and external development experiences such as a board membership at another organization and high-end executive education experiences such as the Harvard Advanced Management Program or the Center for Creative Leadership's "Leadership at the Peak" program.

   Next is a larger group a level down being groomed as a talent pool to be prepared for executive-level positions. While the group members also typically get assessments and coaching, it is common practice that they attend custom-designed internal programs as a cohort aimed at accelerating their development/preparation. Action learning is a very popular learning method for this type of program. Significant potential benefits of these programs are developing this group as a learning community beyond the formal program, and building strong working relationships that will serve the group members well when they are promoted into key executive roles.

9. Succession Management. *We have an effective succession-management system that ensures that we have the right executive in the right job at the right time. Seldom are we forced to hire from outside the organization to fill a key executive-level job opening as a result of not having a qualified internal candidate prepared.*

High-potential identification and development is critical. However, best-practice organizations also have a sound system for planning succession to the executive ranks. The foundation of that system is a deep understanding and agreement among members of top management about these types of things: What kind of executives and executive capabilities will they need, when, and where? Who (by name or from a pool of talent) will be ready to replace any key job or person when they expect them to be needed or in an emergency? What balance of external talent versus homegrown is right for them in order to ensure they are primarily providing growth potential for their own people and yet have the capability to hire for unique capabilities not available? Or to interject new perspectives and thinking when needed? Succession planning or management is something that most well-established organizations are quite good at, although the further into the future they try to predict their needs, the more difficult the task, even for the best.

10. Integrated Talent-Management System. *We have a well-integrated talent-management system (recruiting, succession management, external and internal executive education, leadership development, on-the-job development, coaching/mentoring, performance management, retention, etc.) rather than independent, stand-alone processes.*

    Nirvana! For several years it's been clear that the goal is to have a truly integrated system, but frankly, few organizations have achieved this. Apparently it's easier said than done. Despite the fairly rapid rise in the number of people with titles that include the words "talent management," in many organizations the individual processes still operate in silo fashion, often with different managers responsible for them. For instance, even in fairly advanced organizations, it's not unusual for there to be both a head of talent management and a chief learning officer who may not even report to the same person.

11. Measurement. *We set clear, measurable objectives when we create new executive development strategies, systems, processes, and programs. Then we measure the effectiveness and business impact using metrics that matter to senior management and communicate the results effectively.*

Surprisingly, there is still considerable controversy over how important metrics are in this field. Some feel that either members of top management believe in the value of executive development (and therefore metrics are a waste of time) or they don't (and no metrics will change their minds). The fact is that whether they want them or not, solid metrics are needed to manage the operations of executive development effectively, so it's a silly argument. Although sophisticated evaluation methods are typically extremely costly, there are many simple yet effective ways to measure the effectiveness of our work as long as we set measurable objectives when we first establish any new strategy, system process, or program. In the last executive/leadership trends survey conducted by Executive Development Associates, it was clear that this was a top priority for professionals. More than half said it would be a top priority for them, but only 20 percent said they were good at it. As one summed it up, "Measurement will be our biggest challenge in the next few years."

12. Driven by Top Management. *Our CEO and top executives champion our executive development efforts. We have a senior executive advisory board. Our top executives attend the programs as participants so that they can role-model and reinforce what is being taught, and they also teach when appropriate.*

    No executive development effort can be truly successful without the deep commitment and support of top management, starting with the CEO. Some just seem to "get it," to somehow be genetically predisposed to understanding the impact of executive development and have a gut-level belief in its importance and value. Lucky you if you work in an organization with such a CEO; you can skip the rest of this section! I've found a couple of approaches that help when that's not the case.

    One approach is peer pressure/example. It is very effective to brief members of the top team on examples of what other companies they admire are doing and the results they are achieving, including, of course, the key role that the CEO and top management plays. Another is that there is nothing that compares to a mind-changing experience. For many senior executives, their mental picture of executive development is neutral to negative based on their personal experience. Typically, that experience is limited to attending a university open-enrollment executive-education program where they may have enjoyed them-selves, made some great contacts, and even been intellectually stimulated. But for most, they did not make an application or connection to improved business performance.

Therefore, if you can get them to sponsor, teach in, and, best of all, attend the first session of your top-level executive development program, and *it's as good as it should be* (see the previous 11 characteristics), it is highly likely to change their mindset about the power of executive development. Best-practice companies often have an advisory board for executive development made up of top high-potential leaders from all key parts of the organization. The board is usually selected by members of top management and reports to them, and they ensure that the board is trained on what constitutes exceptional executive development. This helps provide broad line-ownership and direction for executive development.

SUMMARY

Knowledge of these success factors isn't of much use if it isn't applied. Early on I promised to provide a checklist for assessing your own practices in order to help identify areas of strength and things that could be improved. That checklist follows. After you complete it, it might be useful to consider how to leverage the areas of strength and decide what to do about the areas of weakness. For instance, if you think an area of weakness is mission critical, what can be done to improve it? If not, perhaps it can be left alone.

If you are in an HR/executive development position, this assessment might be beneficial to do as a team to see what level of agreement there is. More important is to have a candid discussion about the current state and what actions should be taken, and then to create an action plan. I also recommend thinking about using some version of this checklist for customer input. Simply determine who your key stakeholders/customers are and if they could provide feedback that would be valuable. Then administer the check-list as a survey to get their input.

Good luck!

STRATEGIC EXECUTIVE DEVELOPMENT CHECKLIST

Directions: Rate how effective you think your organization is on each item by circling 1–5, with 1 being "poor" and 5 "exceptional":

1. *Linked to Strategy:* Our executive development efforts are directly linked to our organization's strategy. It is clear how these efforts help address our business challenges and achieve our strategic objectives.

   1   2   3   4   5

2. *Thorough Front-End Analysis:* No significant executive development effort is begun without a thorough front-end needs assessment.

   1   2   3   4   5

3. *Custom Designed:* We custom design our programs so that they address our unique, company-specific challenges and opportunities and help create and/or drive our vision, values, and strategies.

   1   2   3   4   5

4. *Leadership Profile, Feedback, and Individual Development Plans:* We use a custom-designed (linked to our vision, values, and strategies), multirater leadership instrument/inventory to provide confidential development feedback to our executives. Our executives have individual development plans based on that feedback that they actively manage.

   1   2   3   4   5

5. *Action-Oriented Learning:* Our executive learning experiences use active rather than passive learning methods to ensure learning by doing. Whenever feasible, we use some form of "action learning" whereby participants apply what they are learning to real, current business problems and opportunities.

   1   2   3   4   5

6. *A Strategy and System:* We have a strategy and long-term plan for executive development. Our programs and practices are part of a continuous system and process rather than stand-alone, ad hoc events.

   1   2   3   4   5

7. *Top-Down Implementation:* Whenever our executive and leadership development efforts are aimed at organization change, our top management attends the programs first as participants. Then the programs are cascaded down throughout the organization.

   1   2   3   4   5

8. *High-Potential Identification and Development:* Our organization has an effective process for identifying "high-potential" talent and accelerating its development.

   1   2   3   4   5

9. *Succession Management:* We have an effective succession-management system that ensures that we have the right executive in the right job at the right time. Seldom are we forced to hire from outside the organization to fill a key executive-level job opening as a result of not having a qualified internal candidate prepared.

   1   2   3   4   5

10. *Integrated Talent-Management System:* We have a well-integrated talent-management system (recruiting, succession management, external and internal executive education, leadership development, on-the-job development, coaching/mentoring, performance management, retention, etc.) rather than independent, stand-alone processes.

    1   2   3   4   5

11. *Measurement:* We set clear, measurable objectives when we create new executive development strategies, systems, processes, and programs. Then we measure the effectiveness and business impact using metrics that matter to senior management and communicate the results effectively.

    1   2   3   4   5

12. *Top-Management Driven:* Our top executives champion our executive development efforts. We have a senior executive advisory board. Our top executives attend the programs as participants so that they can role-model and reinforce what is being taught, and they also teach when appropriate.

    1   2   3   4   5

ABOUT THE AUTHOR

James F. Bolt founded Bolt Consulting, which specializes in strategic executive development. Prior to launching Bolt Consulting, Jim was the founder and Chairman of Executive Development Associates (EDA), and was also Chairman Emeritus of Executive Networks, the world's foremost constellation of HR-related executive peer networks. Earlier in his career, Jim spent more than 16 years at Xerox Corporation, including executive positions in marketing, operations, and human resources.

A writer and editor, Jim's *Harvard Business Review* article "Tailor Executive Development to Strategy" was the first to introduce the concept of linking executive development to business strategy; his book *Executive Development: Strategy for Corporate Competitiveness* chronicled how CEOs use executive development to shape and achieve their strategic agenda. His newest books include *The Future of Executive Development* and *Strategic Executive Development: The Five Essential Investments*.

Jim has been an online columnist for *Fast Company* and is the editor of the 2007 *Pfeiffer Leadership Development Annual*. He was selected by the *Financial Times* as one of the top experts in executive/leadership development, and Linkage, Inc., named him one of the top 50 Executive Coaches in the World. Contact Jim at www.boltconsulting.org and jbolt@boltconsulting.org.

CHAPTER 7

The Leader's Role in Growing New Leaders

➤ **Beverly Kaye**

Developing valued employees is particularly critical during periods of economic uncertainty. If organizations are to remain productive during a down cycle, leaders must commit to engaging and retaining the talent that is needed to simultaneously support the organization for the present and the future. This not only means the development of top leadership bench strength but the recognition and development of emerging potential leaders as well.

Although leaders will agree on the importance of this responsibility, they will also complain that they simply don't have the time to attend to this function, especially at the time of this writing, when everyone is forced to do more with less; and there is a belief that this kind of initiative takes time, and lots of it.

Although they don't mean to, leaders often take their top performers for granted. The focus is on the task at hand and the factors impacting the organization's productivity, with attention to people often taking a backseat. This is a natural response to tough times; after all, there's only so much time in a given day, and those hours have extended way beyond what they once were.

Sadly, the truth is that when the going is tough there is even more reason to focus on talent in the organization and to continually collaborate with employees on their development and growth. Great leaders know that they absolutely cannot put the development of the next generation of leaders on a back burner. This investment in the future is one that no organization can afford to ignore.

GROWING NEW LEADERS

Growing new leaders requires a conscious, public effort on the part of an organization's top leadership. Leaders set the pace in an organization: the organization's leaders have to behave in the same way as they expect everyone else to behave. As a leader in your own organization, the duty of growing new leaders is primarily yours.

You can personally participate in the process of growing new leaders in many different ways, but I have found that four basic skill areas are critical no matter what approach you take.

Pay Attention

Paying attention is not just hearing words, but *really* listening to what your employees have to say. Help your future leaders identify their career values, work interests, and marketable skills. Enable them to recognize the importance of taking the long view of their careers, and create an open and accepting climate for them to discuss any concerns they may have about their paths to leadership within their organizations. Help your employees understand and articulate exactly what they want from their careers.

Specifically:

➤ Encourage your employees to talk about themselves.

➤ Listen to the results of your employees' self-assessments.

➤ Ask questions to clarify employees' self-assessments.

➤ Give ideas on resources for further exploration.

Talk Straight

As Ken Blanchard once put it, "Feedback is the breakfast of champions."[1] Make a point of providing regular and candid feedback to your employees about their performance and how others perceive them within the organization. Be clear about what it will take for them to progress in the organization and for them to grow as leaders. Spell out expectations and standards, and point out the relationship between their performance and their future prospects with the organization. Make specific suggestions for how they can improve their performance and reputation.

Specifically:

> ➤ Establish clear standards and expectations.

> ➤ Give feedback with supporting evidence and rationale.

> ➤ Add information overlooked by the person.

> ➤ Connect performance to potential.

Provide Perspective

As a leader, you have a perspective that others in your organization do not have. Provide your future leaders with information about where your organization and the industry are going—be their eyes and ears. Show them how to locate and access additional sources of information that will allow them to keep their own fingers on the pulse of your business. Help them stay alert to emerging trends and developments that may have a direct impact on their career goals and on their own pathways to leadership. Explain the cultural and political realities of your organization and widely communicate its strategic direction.

Specifically:

> ➤ Give views about current organization problems and challenges.

> ➤ Offer ideas and input on opportunities.

> ➤ Provide awareness and insights on changes in your industry, field, and workplace.

Build Connections

Success is built on a firm foundation of personal relationships, and you are in a unique position to help your organization's future leaders develop a network of relationships that will serve them—and the company—well into the future. Take time to arrange contacts with people in other parts and at different levels of the organization and within your industry. Tell other leaders and managers about promising people on your team, and ask them to keep your people in mind for future opportunities. Work with people to develop detailed learning assignments and career action plans, and then connect them with the people and resources they'll need to implement them.

Specifically:

➤ Review your employees' development plans.

➤ Connect employees with others who have relevant organizational information.

➤ Debrief development plan assignments.

➤ Publicize your people's achievements.

No one ever said that growing new leaders is easy: there will always be a crisis to deal with, a problem to fix, or a fire to put out. But if you let these unavoidable realities of organization life distract you from investing time in your future leaders, you may not have potential leaders around when you ultimately need them.

MANY PATHS TO LEADERSHIP

Many people I talk to understand the importance of developing leaders at all levels, but they hold back because they are concerned about raising expectations they can't fulfill. They understand that as hierarchies flatten, most organizations have fewer upward paths than in the past. They are concerned that focusing on developing their people for leadership roles may ultimately lead to disappointment. What they don't understand is that although moving *up* is the obvious and traditional path to leadership, it is not the only path for future leaders to pursue. Five other paths are also open, and you ignore them not only at the risk of losing the best performance that your potential leaders have to offer but also perhaps actually losing these potential leaders to a competitor who is willing to take the time to develop their talents.

Lateral Moves

Moving across the organization may involve a change in a potential leader's job, but not necessarily in responsibility, pay, or status. As organizations cut back or downsize operations, these lateral moves become increasingly more frequent and more important. Lateral moves expand people's breadth of knowledge and skills while widening their network of contacts—both in and outside of the organization. These are all very valuable outcomes that will help to build and strengthen anyone's leadership skills.

Enrichment

Enrichment—or growing in place—occurs when you provide future leaders with expanded or changed responsibilities within their current jobs to build more relevant competencies. This requires your people to master new skills and to build new and productive relationships with customers and colleagues. By increasing your people's decision-making power, you make their jobs more challenging and give them the opportunity to deliver more value to the organization.

Exploration

Everyone reaches a point in his or her career when the best path to take isn't clear—or even that the right path exists within the organization. In this case, helping your people investigate possibilities that exist within your organization is not only the *right* thing to do, it may make the difference between whether a future leader decides to stay with the company or move on to greener pastures. When you offer short-term job assignments, temporary task force or project team participation, or other similar opportunities, you'll broaden your people's experience and network of contacts while giving them a measure of personal control over their careers.

Realignment

While realignment—or moving down in the organization—is often seen as a negative (or even career-ending) event, sometimes the best thing you can do for a future leader is to provide the opportunity to take a step backward to gain a better position for the next move. Whether as a result of an organizational downsizing or a decision to move someone into a less demanding position, realigning people can allow them to take on new challenges and opportunities while learning the skills they will need to become leaders in the future.

Relocation

If you and your employees have absolutely exhausted every possible option for them to move forward in their leadership journey in your organization—to no avail—then helping them move out of the organization may be the best option. Not only may such people become terrific ambassadors for your company, but also they may learn the leadership skills they need outside your organization and then return someday to a much better position.

* * *

Each of these paths can provide your people with the kind of unique experience and contacts that will be invaluable to them as they become leaders.

THE ART OF ENGAGEMENT

In my many years of watching leaders successfully grow new leaders, I have observed that three characteristics separate the winners from the also-rans. First, successful leaders have an attitude that supports learning and growth. They are continually on the lookout for ways to enrich and enliven work, and they get out of the way when future leaders take initiative and flex their own leadership muscles. Instead of keeping their stars under wraps, leaders link those stars with others in the organization who can help them along the pathways to leadership—coaches, mentors, colleagues, and other leaders.

Second, successful leaders provide feedback and tell the truth. Instead of beating around the bush or avoiding confrontation, leaders deliver feedback in a clear and tactful manner—addressing specific behavioral observations and aiming at continual learning and development—and they encourage people to give them constructive and frank feedback, too. By encouraging and welcoming feedback from their people, leaders set a very powerful example for future leaders to follow.

Finally, successful leaders create cultures that value inclusion, not exclusion, and they know that every person can make valuable contributions to the team when encouraged and given the opportunity. They support innovation and new approaches to familiar problems and opportunities, and they reward individuals and teams for a job well done. In this way, leaders create an environment that is both satisfying and meaningful, and they position their people to grow into successful leaders themselves.

CONCLUSION

The issue of development should always be a top concern of leaders whether the economy is bullish or bearish. At different times, development issues change, but their underlying principles do not. In a good economy with a tight labor market, managers need to work hard to recruit and retain the brightest and the best. During a down market, it must be a priority for organizations to continually develop their bench strength by conscientiously and continually growing leaders for the future.

ABOUT THE AUTHOR

Beverly Kaye is an internationally recognized authority on career issues and retention and engagement in the workplace. She was named a "Legend" by the American Society for Training & Development (ASTD) and one of North America's 100 top thought leaders by *Leadership Excellence.*

Dr. Kaye is founder and CEO of Career Systems International, which helps organizations worldwide maximize the strategic engagement, development, and retention of key talent and gain the Talent Edge™. The best-selling author of *Love 'Em or Lose 'Em: Getting Good People to Stay,* she has been a pioneer in addressing one of the most pressing workplace problems of the 21st century: retaining and engaging employees. Coeditor of *Learning Journeys* and author of numerous articles in both professional journals and popular publications, she is frequently sought by the news media for comment on workplace issues. Dr. Kaye is the recipient of numerous professional awards, and her clients have received Best Practice Awards. For more about Beverly Kaye, see www.careersystemsintl.com, www.keepem.com, and www.loveitdontleaveit.com.

NOTE

1. See http://thinkexist.com/quotation/feedback-is-the-breakfast-of-champi ons/348677.html, accessed April 24, 2009.

CHAPTER 8

Talent Pool or Talent Puddle: Where's the Talent in Talent Management?

➤ Marc Effron and Miriam Ort

These should be heady times for those in Talent Management (TM). CEOs fueled by good-to-great dreams are increasing their investment in building leaders. Companies fighting increased competition from China and India are recognizing that great talent is their only competitive advantage. Individual leaders are realizing that continually growing their capabilities is the only sure path to success. With talent issues like these dominating the agendas of nearly every organization, TM practitioners should be the new corporate "rock stars."

Instead, this enhanced focus on talent building has produced an ironic result. After years spent begging to be put in the game, many players in TM are underperforming on the field. Their promises to build leaders more quickly and effectively, if only given the chance, are showing little effect. Their practices still reflect the same bloated, impractical approaches that have long caused line managers' eyes to roll. Companies expecting their TM professionals to deliver superior results are discovering the sad, surprising truth: there's not enough talent in TM.

TALENT POOL OR TALENT PUDDLE?

A compelling metric of this talent shortage comes from those closest to the market. If you speak with leaders in the largest executive search firms, you'll hear an amazingly similar refrain: "There are very few people in this field to begin with and nearly none that we consider world-class talent." Or as stated another way by the head of the human resources (HR) search practice at one of the Big Three firms, "There are really only eight people in this field who are any good." Imagine that comment being made about finance, marketing, or any other function!

THE OPPORTUNITY OF A LIFETIME

One of the most troubling aspects of this TM talent shortage is that we're currently blessed with a once-in-a-lifetime opportunity. Executives are looking to HR and TM to deliver the leaders they need. If we achieve this goal, we offer the hope of redeeming HR's increasingly tattered reputation by producing something that executives truly value: more great leaders. If we do our job well, TM can single-handedly change HR's seat at the table from a high chair to an armchair.

Success will also establish us as the driver of the talent engine within our companies. We will shift our reputation from being the provider of assessments and tools to being the trusted adviser on the most important talent decisions. Most important, we will accomplish what most of us seek from this profession—a meaningful, positive impact on business results.

Our risk is as large as our opportunity. Failure to deliver will be seen by our organizations as yet another sign that HR doesn't work. TM will be dismissed as another HR fad, another failed quick fix brought to you by those folks who just don't seem to "get" the business. With the debate about HR's long-term value still raging, this would signal victory for those who feel that destroying HR is the best solution.

MAKING IT WORK

Here's the good news: *it ain't over yet.* While we do have a shovel in our hands, the hole's not very deep yet. We still have a chance to achieve the true potential of this field if we make some substantial changes, quickly. The solutions suggested next aren't intended to be simple, fast, or popular with the TM and HR community. They're intended to position us for long-term success as the preeminent group within HR—the true business partner whose contribution is clearly visible on the balance sheet.

First, let's be transparent about our challenges. We emerged from the soft side of a soft profession. Most of us in TM come from training, organization development, leadership development, and other fields not traditionally known for having a hard business "edge." Few of us have had accountability for a balance sheet or been responsible to make a payroll. We haven't always been as knowledgeable about business in general as we should have been. We don't always feel a burning passion for the commercial realities of our organizations.

Our solutions have been criticized as too complicated and too academic, and they've been rejected by our customers. Overall, we haven't consistently proved to our organizations that we add the value we know is possible. It's a healthy list of challenges and overcoming them requires making some fundamental and difficult changes in who we are and what we do. However, if our hopes for TM as a profession, and for ourselves as TM practitioners, are to succeed, we must:

➤ *Elevate practitioner quality.* We must improve our capabilities and business orientation, injecting an operations mentality into our TM practices. We must fall in love with business and help others to do the same.

➤ *Simplify our work.* We must radically simplify and simultaneously add value to the work we do. This means challenging every convention about how talent processes should be designed and, in many cases, starting from scratch.

➤ *Define the field.* We must define the boundaries of what we do, staking claim to those areas of HR where we have the greatest potential impact. We can't improve the quality of what we do until we agree on exactly what that is.

Elevate Practitioner Quality

The most difficult challenge we face is elevating the quality and capabilities of those who do this work. Let's start by stipulating that everyone in our field has good intentions, are good people, and genuinely have the best interests of the business at heart. With that said, the facts still suggest that there are meaningful gaps between what many TM practitioners offer and what our businesses need. Here's how we change that:

1. *Know the business.* We must understand the financial, operational, and strategic realities of business in general and our organization's business in particular. How do we get there?

   ➤ *Basic Business Literacy.* At a minimum, everyone in TM should have a degree of business literacy that includes the ability to understand company financial statements, the basics of how a good or service is produced, and an operative knowledge of at least one of the classic strategy models.

   ➤ *More MBAs.* It's possible to learn business fundamentals in many ways, but the MBA still provides the most broad-based knowledge of how business works. The rigorous business thinking and analytical skills that help engender love of the business are also most easily gained through this course of study. Additionally, it instills a discipline and toughness that help in making the critically difficult calls and trade-offs.

   ➤ *More Line Managers.* Even if we need to pay a 50 percent premium to get them, we need to attract more line managers into this field. We may only get them for a temporary assignment, but even a year or two in this area will deliver a bracing dose of reality into many TM practices.

2. *Love the business.* We should be fascinated by, and have a deep and unabiding curiosity about, business and how it works. Call it passion for business or intellectual curiosity or any other label that works for you, but acknowledge that it's a rare quality in this field.

   We can select for passion through a great interview process, but it's tough to say how we inspire this in others. One step might simply be thoroughly exposing those entering this field to the core business processes. Onboarding programs could go beyond a surface knowledge of the business and instead require that time be spent learning key organization processes. How much more successful would a new TM practitioner be if her orientation included a week in your research and development center, a week working on a new marketing campaign, a week in your factory, and a week with your sales force?

3. *Take a production mindset to building leaders.* The TM role is often seen as that of a craftsman—an individual tasked with helping each leader achieve his or her ultimate potential. So it's a challenging thought to many in our field that we should treat producing leaders like producing widgets. The reality is that TM

is a production job. We are responsible for turning out a specific number of leaders over a specific period of time with a specific set of capabilities. We are no different from a plant manager. Our responsibility is to deliver the most powerful element for the production of the goods or services in our company—qualified leaders.

Simplify Our Work

No less a challenge than changing ourselves is changing our approach to designing and implementing TM practices. One can barely identify what the core objectives are in much of the TM work being done today. Research, practice, and common sense tell us that TM practices are effective only if they are successfully implemented. So we must focus on designing our processes with successful implementation by managers as a primary goal.

We can achieve this by making two fundamental changes:

1. *Radically simplify our processes.* If implementation is the key to successful outcomes, then making processes simple is the key to successful implementation. Most managers will gladly use any HR tool or process that delivers more value than the effort required to use it. If we can redesign our processes to always meet this value/effort balance, we will see a marked increase in the effectiveness of our services. How do we get there?

   Here's where things get tough. To start, we must forget most of what we know about creating TM processes. This is tough because many of us have spent a lifetime acquiring knowledge and capabilities to achieve "expert" status in our field. We like to feel that we know the "best practices" in our area fairly well. But best practices according to whom? Where is the foundation, where are the facts, that justify how we design and implement TM practices?

   While there is significant research supporting what we do (i.e., assessment and feedback, coaching, performance management), there is no evidence supporting the complicated way in which we do it. Where is the evidence that a competency model with 8 headings and 15 descriptions under each helps anyone? Or that a goal-setting process involving anything more than just listing a goal and a metric improves the outcome? Or that providing 360-degree feedback on every possible leadership behavior actually helps to change any leadership behavior?

We have become so self-referential as a field that we are now all equally smart (or equally dumb) about how to make this work. We don't challenge the fundamental assumptions about the effectiveness of these practices. We don't ask, "Is there a radically different way to do this that would deliver better results?"

To achieve the value from TM practices, we need to approach the design and implementation of any process by asking the fundamental question, "What is the essential business goal of this process?" We then need to start with a blank slate and an open mind, and design the simplest possible process that uses the least amount of information necessary to achieve those results.

We started using that exact approach to redesign every talent process (e.g., performance management, development planning, engagement survey) we had at Avon. We started calling this approach "One Page Talent Management" because we typically found that we could fit the essential material on just one page. We applied this approach in creating new processes for performance management, development planning, and talent reviews, and in developing a new leadership capability model. Our success metrics were the only ones that mattered: managers successfully using these tools.

2. *Add value to each practice.* Taking work out of complex processes is one approach to improving TM effectiveness. Adding additional value to each practice is another. As an example, at Avon we applied our One Page Talent Management approach to both our new engagement survey and our new 360-degree assessment process. Both of these processes tend to present managers with overwhelming and complex information, with little practical advice about what to do next. In crafting our engagement survey report, we wanted to add value for managers without adding complexity. We thought that if we could "preanalyze" each manager's survey for him or her, providing specific advice about what to do, the survey would quickly become a useful tool.

Our "one page" solution provided managers with the essential information about their group's survey results, including *exactly which actions they could take to improve scores next year.* This last was accomplished through a proprietary algorithm that identified which questions were the significant drivers of engagement for each individual. Since almost every question was written in a way that suggested the activities required to increase it (e.g., "My manager provides me with frequent feedback about my performance"), increasing engagement scores was as easy as doing exactly what was said on that page. Avon's vice presidents are now held accountable, through their performance management plans, to annually increase their survey scores.

In short, anything we can do that simplifies a manager's ability to implement makes us more effective.

Define the Field

Finally, we need to establish the boundaries of our role in organizations. Our field is emerging without direction, without a common definition of what we do. Today, TM professionals might be responsible for any combination of talent reviews, succession planning, executive education, recruiting, and coaching, with performance management, employee engagement, and training often in the mix as well. Some focus exclusively on the "top 100" as defined in their organization; others have accountability down to the supervisory level.

The sooner we identify the key practices, processes, and outcomes we want to own, the faster we'll be able to start instituting the improvements we've discussed. A clearer definition will also help dispel the image of TM as simply a relabeling of HR, the next step after "Personnel." The bottom line is that until we agree on what it is we do, it will be difficult to achieve significant improvements.

TAKING CHARGE

While there's not enough talent in TM, we have the opportunity to both solve that problem and elevate this field to its rightful position in organizations. We know from our experience that when what we do works, the positive impact on individuals and companies exceeds any other organizational lever. We already possess many of the capabilities we need to succeed. We are a well-educated, well-intentioned, and experienced group. Our challenge is to address those vital few things that are missing—business knowledge and passion, a production mindset, and a commitment to simplicity. If we can successfully change how we do TM, the effectiveness of *what* we do will dramatically increase.

The good news is that we own this challenge and we control our future. If we set higher standards for ourselves and our teams, push down our egos just a bit to consider new ideas, and hold ourselves accountable for the success or failure of TM practices, we will move this profession to where it needs to be. And if we can't do that, maybe what they're saying about HR is true.

ABOUT THE AUTHORS

Marc Effron is Vice President, Talent Management, for Avon Products, Inc., in New York City. He is an author, a researcher, and a speaker on human resource issues. He can be reached at marc@effrons.com. A selection of his other articles and presentations is available at www.marceffron.com.

Miriam Ort is Senior Manager, Human Resources, for PepsiCo in Purchase, New York. She was a primary architect of the One Page Talent Management philosophy and tools while at Avon Products. She can be reached at miriam.ort@pepsi.com.

Marc and Miriam are coauthors of *One Page TM: Building Better Leaders, Faster* (Boston: Harvard Business Press, 2010).

REFERENCES

Deloitte Consulting. *Aligned at the Top: How Business and HR Executives View Today's Most Significant People Challenges—and What They're Doing About It.* Deloitte/The Economist Intelligence Unit (2007), http://www.deloitte.com/dtt/cda/doc/content/us_consulting_alignedatthetopsurvey_v2.pdf, accessed January 4, 2009.

Effron, Marc, Shelli Greenslade, and Michelle Salob. "Growing Great Leaders: Does It Really Matter?" *Human Resource Planning Society Journal* 28.3 (2005): 18–23. www.marceffron.com, accessed January 4, 2009.

Human Resource Competency Study Executive Summary. Provo, Utah: The RBL Group, 2007.

CHAPTER 9

The Cost of Investing in People Leadership Negatively Affects the Bottom Line: Fact or Fiction?

➤ Howard J. Morgan and Paula Kruger

One of the most significant, continuing debates facing business executives and human relations (HR) professionals is the perceived dichotomy between achieving business results and investing in people-leadership initiatives. Indeed, many business leaders believe that investing time and energy in HR leadership enhancement is an unnecessary cost and a diversion or distraction from achieving bottom-line results. This argument against "people investment" becomes particularly persuasive (and opportunistic) when executives face a groundswell of employee dissatisfaction. And if there is a negative impact on shareholder return when companies focus on people leadership, then organizations would be ill-advised to invest in leadership initiatives. This is particularly true in the challenging global economic environment that we currently face. What is the answer?

This question led to our analysis of Qwest Communications, a leading provider of voice, video, and data services, where leaders have demonstrated that, with rigorous attention to people-leadership development, cultures can be changed to achieve optimum business returns. The outcome is more satisfied employees, greater customer satisfaction, improved leadership, and bottom-line business results that all stakeholders are proud to achieve. In this chapter, we detail how Qwest Communications was able to achieve these results, demonstrating the benefits and value that a consolidated, strategic leadership approach can bring.

The culture of the "old" Qwest was an extremely challenging business environment: a long-term workforce with leaders who embraced "old school" thinking and who were highly resistant to change. In 2003, Paula Kruger joined Qwest Communications to become the head of Mass Markets, a division that has approximately 7,400 employees with an average tenure of approximately 14 months. Mass Markets was responsible for approximately 50 percent of the revenue at Qwest Communications and encompassed the call centers for the company, constituting about 15 percent of the employee base. When Ms. Kruger joined the organization, Mass Markets' performance was one of the lowest in the company and employee satisfaction with the organization was very low. This employee perception was well founded, given the well-publicized integrity issues of the former CEO, as well as mergers and challenging business problems resulting from decisions to abandon rights to cellular offerings.

Ms. Kruger's challenge was clear: make changes to the organization that would yield significant business improvements. As an accomplished executive, Paula has long believed that "true" leadership is the fundamental factor in driving business improvements through a more committed employee base. To enhance the effectiveness of her leadership team and drive the necessary cultural change, she engaged Howard Morgan of Leadership Research Institute to work with her to effect these changes. The challenge was not an easy one. Indeed, Mass Markets had become the division that talented employees moved away from rather than were attracted to.

People who have worked in call-center operations would attest that it is one of the most demanding work environments. Most call centers—regardless of industry—struggle both with retaining good people and with hiring strong employees. Despite this, Paula raised the bar. Rather than setting a goal that would convey a less-than-optimistic message, she was determined to create a world-class workplace. This standard necessitated the engagement of all people at all levels of the organization. While Ms. Kruger had the passion for what the organization could be, she knew it would not be possible without the commitment and efforts of her broader team. And she was asking for this commitment from people who had experienced many broken promises from former leaders and who were understandably skeptical.

To instill this cultural change—and drive for excellence—the first step was to find leaders who were as passionate as Ms. Kruger was in their belief that the vision was possible to achieve. To find these people, she spent the necessary time to determine if they existed in the current organization. (Often this requires searching for those individuals who have been held back—not the obvious choices—rather than the often easier option of recruiting external talent.) Key to driving the necessary changes was assembling a team with sufficient "diversity of thought" whose members would allow the executive team to work together respectfully while maintaining their unique styles and personalities. To this end, she created a team that had a commitment to achieving excellence, a willingness to take ownership for its businesses/functions, and an understanding of how to achieve the desired results.

Paula's next step was to provide the leadership team with both a clear vision of what was possible and the necessary skills to make it happen. To help achieve this, Howard Morgan developed a leadership development program that pushed the team to accomplish positive leadership growth—moving the team from past performance problems to a new standard of expectations and desired outcomes. The workshop included a confidential 360-degree feedback component that ensured the development and communication of an action plan to direct reports, peers, and managers.

This plan focused on the behaviors that would embrace and drive the future organization. Attendance was based on merit: the most respected leaders were the first to be invited to participate. Some would question whether it would have been smarter to send those leaders who were most "in need." However, Paula's goal was to encourage, value, and recognize the contribution of the organization's top performers. She wanted them to lead by example and demonstrate the merits of exemplary leadership to the rest of the organization. Also, it allowed the graduates to cofacilitate future programs and enabled the most respected and admired leaders to help transform the culture from the inside out. It was a key goal for all to be a part of the transformation, not simply relying on the senior leaders to provide their direction and wisdom from the top down.

Before revealing additional elements of Ms. Kruger's leadership strategy, it is important to ask: Did it work? Did the Mass Markets' business results change in a measurable way that would be unquestioned by internal and external shareholders? In the five-year period ending in 2008, the following results occurred:

1. Mass Markets achieved an extraordinary business turnaround. This achievement was measured through increased sales revenue, efficiency, and productivity, and rates of absenteeism were half that reported in 2004. Gross revenue per call center (GRPC) was up 32 percent for sales/service and GRPC increased over 200 percent since 2004. At the same time, adherence to schedule was nearly 90 percent compared to 60 percent in 2004.

2. Employee engagement scores increased from below average to among the best in the world. In fact, Mass Markets was awarded the Gallup Great Workplace Award in 2008.

3. The Mass Markets survey results were compiled from employee surveys and are shown in Figure 9.1. The "U.S. Working Population" results were collected by Gallup, Inc. Further, they define the terms: Engaged—psychologically committed; Not Engaged—not psychologically connected; Actively Disengaged—psychologically absent.

Figure 9.1 Mass Markets' Engagement Results

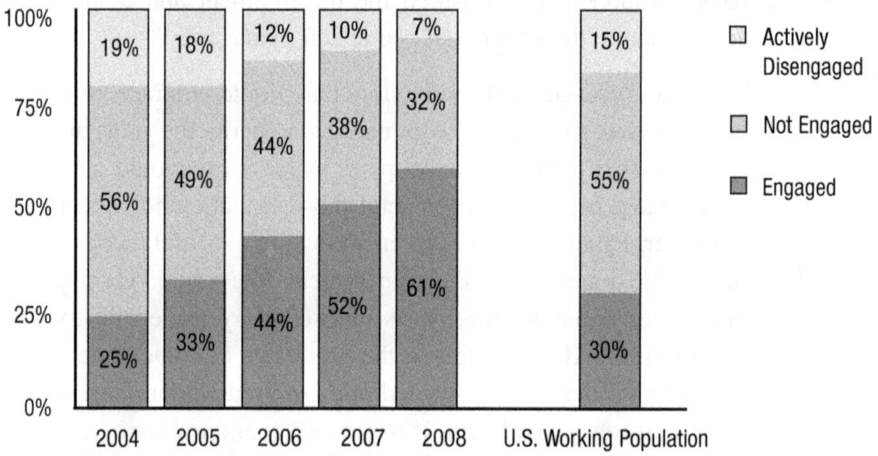

These results clearly establish both the viability and the benefits of a strategic approach to people leadership: leveraging results through people rather than simply defining the desired results and attempting to drive people to achieve them (a method that had failed at Mass Markets in the past and a situation found in many companies). There is little doubt that the speed, quantity, and quality of Mass Markets' positive results would not have been possible within the five-year time frame without the help of the collective leadership/employee base.

KEY LESSONS THAT CAN BE APPLIED TO OTHER ORGANIZATIONS

To accomplish the desired outcomes, what are the key lessons that can be applied to other organizations? Our thoughts are as follows:

1. *Engagement and leadership quality have to be the key strategic goal.* Most times getting to the strategic goal has a "people" component. The quality of employees and the leadership provided have to be a focal part of the solution, not just something "nice to do."

2. *Place the right people in the right jobs.* If all people were equal, great performers or poor performers would not exist. However, you can take a great person and put him in the wrong job or location and he can quickly become a less-than-average performer. You need to look at each person as an individual and ask yourself, "Is this the person who can get the job done?" If not, ask the question, "Does this person have the passion, desire, and talent that fit our organization, and if so, what is the best job fit for her?"

3. *Hold each leader/manager responsible for the level of engagement and performance for his or her organization.* That permits the workforce to be tailored to the individual characteristics of its geographic location and increases the responsibility of local leadership to the business outcome; simultaneously, it discourages the "I could not do anything with what I had" mindset.

4. *Although this will make many leaders cringe, performance reviews should be given on a regular and complete basis.* What does this mean? For employees to be challenged, they need to know where to focus. We too often take the position that a top performer will be satisfied with a statement like, "Everything that you are doing is great. I cannot think of anything that you need to change." Where is the challenge in this statement that will create the pride and feeling of accomplishment that your top performers require? Also, if you do not aggressively deal with people who are not performing, how can you expect them to change? In fact, the more serious concern is that you will start losing your most talented people—why would they want to work in an environment that is not energized and that has more than its share of nonperformers?

5. *Start looking for successors who embody the talent and capability to lead the change as others are promoted or removed from the organization.* Unless you give it proactive thought, most systems

reward loyalty or favoritism and do not encourage the innovative thinkers who will spearhead the transformation. Also, focusing on the traits that you are looking for will help clarify the desired behaviors for all.

6. *Develop a communication strategy that not only provides the vision but also contains the methodology and responsibilities for the journey.* In Qwest's Mass Markets, the messaging contained a number of integrated components: (a) Mass Markets' Web site; (b) monthly executive VP conference calls; (c) introduction of the "one team" concept; (d) best-practice manuals and Web sites; (e) podcasts that provided specific information on all dimensions of leadership.

7. *Provide funding for initiatives that identify, encourage, and build employee engagement, productivity, and loyalty.* These include items like building employee engagement progress reports into quarterly business updates, investment in leadership education, support for local performance-enhancement plans, and funding for recognition programs. When focusing on recognition plans, make them sincere and meaningful. In most organizations, such plans tend to be too complicated and do not reward behaviors that will transform an organization. The true test of a recognition/rewards program is what value your best employees give it. By keeping it at a local level, it puts the focus on the manager's "thank you" or small gesture that carries more meaning than the corporate-wide initiative. To accomplish this, Mass Markets focused on several types of recognition and reward: (a) formal events similar to those of many organizations; (b) local-level celebrations that relied on the judgment and knowledge of local leadership; (c) peer-to-peer recognition; (d) monthly "thank you" sessions.

    The resultant outcome was that employees' answers to the question, "In the last seven days, have you received recognition or praise for doing good work?" went from a mean score of 3.31 (out of a possible 5) in 2004 to a 4.26 in 2008.

8. *Create an awareness of the impact of putting the right people in the right jobs.* Give people the opportunity to do their best. The quickest ways to the greatest productivity improvements are by having engaged employees who are passionate about their business and the contributions that they make. If employees, at all levels, do not believe that their efforts and contributions make a difference, it will be almost impossible to get their best efforts.

9. *Make sure that employees have the right equipment and tools to do the job.* Years ago, behavioral innovators such as Abraham Maslow, Frederick Herzberg, and others identified certain attributes that are foundational to human performance. They argued that without these foundational essentials optimizing performance is impossible. It is difficult to ask talented people to take pride in their work and get the results that you want without giving them the basic equipment and methods to accomplish those results.

10. *Frontline input and ownership are essential.* All too often, frontline leaders are handed down solutions from senior management that they believe are unworkable for them and their employees. If they cannot understand and embrace the direction, it is unlikely that they will attain that result. Even if they try to accomplish the goal, their lack of passion will make the timeline much longer than it needs to be. We have a phrase that captures what we are saying here: "Involvement fosters commitment in others."

11. *Break down the silos or walls between units.* Many organizations strive for this goal, but too often the systems within their organizations run counter to what they are trying to achieve. To create an environment of collaboration, we would recommend the following steps:

    a. Clearly define expectations of how the various departments should interact with each other.

    b. Act quickly to eliminate unnecessary disputes between departments. Once bitter feelings have been allowed to develop, it is difficult to regain the peace.

    c. Clarify a mechanism that can help departments identify what they need from each other. This is common sense, since the customer sees the collective departmental structure as the company. Customers do not care about whether it is someone else's responsibility.

    d. Empower the department to do what is right for the customer. If it is not the best solution, tackle the issue of resolution later, but reward the initiative in meeting the customer's needs.

    e. Unlock the secrets between the various departments; there can be no secrets if the company is going to build trust.

    f. Create mutual appreciation across department lines to acknowledge the contributions that lead to success rather than foster competition.

12. *If you run a shift operation, make sure that people with the power to make decisions are working during each shift.* Empowering people requires that they be able to make timely decisions. This allows them to make the decision without concern about possible negative repercussions. It enables the behaviors that you want and goes a long way toward building an engaged workforce.

13. *Recognize the critical role that leadership plays in the transformation of the organization.* Leadership at all levels needs to believe that it is part of the business success, a vital contributor to developing goals, and rewarded when things go well. Work with the leadership to develop business/profit goals that are challenging, but not unrealistic. Engaged employees are driven by success and their role in it, not by meeting only 50 percent of the target.

14. *Make the message of attaining profitability and business growth part of the equation.* It is the blending of both of these with building a climate of committed, engaged employees that will enable the results that were achieved by Qwest. Everyone has to believe that he or she is linked and that each person is part of the necessary steps to attaining the goal.

It is our belief that the most sustainable, profitable results come when you have engaged, committed employees. Senior leaders can do only so much. While they are responsible for developing the culture and vision for the organization, it is the pride and efforts of the customer-interfacing level of the organization that truly defines success. If those who deal with customers on a daily basis are passionate about the company, the customer will want to deal with them. If customers want to deal with them, the number of customers and revenue per customer will increase.

As leaders, we are enablers of this outcome. We cannot do it ourselves; we must provide the vision and the tactics to allow others to buy into and attain our goals. Focusing on getting the numbers may be a great short-term action, but sustainable, long-term change and improved business results only come from investing in the effective leadership of people.

ABOUT THE AUTHORS

Howard J. Morgan, a Manager Director of Leadership Research Institute and 50 Top Coaches, has led major organizational change initiatives in partnership with top leaders and executives at numerous international organizations. He was named one of the world's 50 top coaches by Linkage, identified as one of five executive coaches with a "proven track record of success" by Executive Excellence, and has published several books. Contact Howard at howard.morgan@lri.com and www.50topcoaches.com.

Paula Kruger's line manager career focus has been on transforming large groups of employees into engaged employees in order to achieve revenue and expense targets. She spent almost 20 years at the senior-leader level in financial services at Citicorp and American Express. She has spent the last decade as an executive at Cablevision and Qwest Communications.

Engaging People

➤ The Force of Change

CHAPTER 10

Leadership's Silver Bullet: The Magic of Inspiration

➤ **John H. (Jack) Zenger**

Everyone recognizes that leadership is an extraordinarily complex phenomenon. Attempts to reduce it to one or two qualities or behaviors invariably are shown to be either incorrect or impractical, and ultimately fail. At the same time, it is also clear that not all behaviors that we have traditionally identified as being important elements of leadership are equal in their impact on key outcomes that we want and need leaders to produce.

Our organization collects data about leaders and their behavior. We have recently amassed over 150,000 360-degree feedback assessments pertaining to more than 11,000 leaders using a fairly standardized instrument. We know how leaders' behavior impacts the people who report to them. We also know what their subordinates wish their leaders did better. Additionally, we have extensive data about what drives the highest level of employee commitment and engagement.

This chapter describes one big "aha!" that comes from an extensive analysis of these mounds of data. Simply put, the discovery is that there is one leadership behavior that escalates to the top of the pack. It is the behavior described as: "Inspires and motivates to high performance." We have selected that behavior for a more intensive analysis, because it:

1. Best separates the top-performing leaders from those who are merely average, as well as identifies the leaders who are at the bottom of the distribution.

2. Is the most frequently selected by subordinates, often twice as frequently as the closest runner-up.

3. Is the behavior most correlated with the highest levels of employee engagement and commitment.

NOT THE ONLY IMPORTANT COMPETENCY

This is not to suggest that this one behavior is sufficient for a leader's success, because it is not. Combinations of skills make extraordinary leaders, especially when a few are done extremely well. It takes just three such behaviors at the 90th percentile to place a leader in the upper two deciles in most organizations. While "inspires and motivates" ascends to the top of the spectrum, we are not suggesting that it can exist all alone and be sufficient to define an outstanding leader.

THREE KEY QUESTIONS ABOUT "INSPIRES AND MOTIVATES"

Because one competency stands out so clearly above all the others, it raises some questions:

➤ What makes some leaders inspirational?

➤ Can this be learned or are people born with it?

➤ Why is this such an important behavior?

What Makes Some Leaders Inspirational?

What constitutes inspiring behavior? Despite the thousands of books and tens of thousands of articles on the subject of leadership, there remains an element of mystery about it.

While much of what leaders do can be objectively described, there seems to be a quality or characteristic that is off by itself. Often you will hear someone say, "That leader is charismatic." When pressed to explain exactly what this person does, the person providing the description is hard pressed to provide an answer. There is just something in this leader's manner, behavior, style, or skills that seems to set him or her apart. While some have tried, there is little agreement on exactly what constitutes this elusive quality we label "charisma."

My colleague Joe Folkman and I decided to approach the question in a slightly different way. We had extensive data about the 11,000 leaders mentioned earlier. One of the dimensions that we had measured was the degree to which they were perceived as being "inspiring and motivating." This enabled us to separate those with the highest scores from those with average to low scores. There were a relatively large number of behaviors or competencies that were highly correlated with "inspires and motivates."

We want to quickly acknowledge that because two things are correlated, that does not prove one causes the other. For example, being married has a relatively high correlation with happiness. It would be easy to conclude that in general being married causes people to be happier. But the fact of the matter is that the opposite could be true. Possibly happy people are more inclined to get married.

Some have wondered if inspiring behavior isn't simply a collection of clever tactics or tricks that some leaders acquire. Is it possible that inspiration merely consists of the following?

> ➤ Pushing or provoking people

> ➤ Pleading for higher performance

> ➤ Shaming by comparing one group to another

> ➤ Cheerleading

> ➤ Rewarding or bribing

> ➤ Appealing to higher motives

> ➤ Instilling fear

> ➤ Creating competition

> ➤ Invoking peer pressure

> ➤ Praising

As we examined the data, we saw that not one of these was described by subordinates as the behavior they sought from their leader. With but two exceptions—praising and appealing to higher motivates—we deem these "negative behaviors." Both our own and other research evidence clearly demonstrates that positive behaviors are far more inspiring than negative ones.

Indeed, our analysis revealed that there were 10 "competency companions" (or as my colleague Joe Folkman suggested, "behavioral buddies"), clustered in three areas. First, there were three behaviors that appeared to describe a leader's willingness and ability to understand and fully accept what it means to be a leader. Realizing that you are constantly a role model, 24 hours a day and seven days a week, whether you like it or not, is a key part of accepting that role. Acknowledging that you are now responsible for the organization's progress and its ability to make change, and that it is your initiative that will drive a great deal of that change, are the other parts of this cluster of "fully accepting the role of leader."

Second, there is a multidimensional cluster that we've labeled "emotion." This encompasses a leader's understanding of the role of emotions in how people behave, as well as his or her willingness and ability to both be aware of and comfortably use emotion. Jack and Suzy Welch wrote, "Real leaders touch people. They get under their skin, filling their hearts with inspiration, courage and hope. They share the pain at times of loss and are there to celebrate the wins."[1] There is no escaping the fact that how people are feeling about their work and their employer plays an enormous role in the success of their work. If you want to be more inspirational, understand that you have to become more comfortable in the world of emotions, feelings, and moods.

The final cluster of competency companions has six behaviors that leaders use. These six specific behaviors appear to be like batteries in a battery pack: they can be interchanged, used in many different combinations. And just as with batteries, the more that are used to fire the action, the greater is the power injected into the system.

Can Anyone Learn to Be Inspirational?

Though the behaviors that are described as competency companions may come more naturally to some than to others, and some people may perform them with far greater skill and finesse, there are no behaviors we have described that are reserved for a special few uniquely talented or blessed people.

Unlike some child prodigies, one is not "born" with the ability to inspire. However, when it comes to behaving as a leader, it helps to be extraverted. There is clear evidence that highly outgoing people exert more influence over others than do those who are introverted. It also helps to have a high energy level and to be comfortable making presentations before large groups.

Why Is This So Important?

There are a host of reasons why inspiration is so important in the leadership process. In terms of his or her subordinates, an inspiring leader can:

> ➤ *Enhance self-esteem.* People perform at their best when they feel confident. Inspiring behavior from a leader directly enhances people's feelings of self-worth and self-efficacy.

> ➤ *Give new meaning to work.* The inspiring leader is able to inject a higher meaning to work. There is a classic story about a bystander who asks two workers, "What are you doing?" One worker replies, "I'm cutting stones"; the second worker says, "I'm building a cathedral." Then the bystander watches the care and the quality of work done by each of them and quickly understands why the second worker produced such quality artisanship and the first did not.

> ➤ *Increase cooperation.* Inspiring leaders create a culture of cooperation rather than one of competition and rivalry.

> ➤ *Encourage higher goals.* Inspirational leadership encourages people to set their sights at a much higher level.

> ➤ *Heighten creativity.* Inspirational leadership can foster a greater willingness in people to attempt new behaviors and to seek ingenious new ways to accomplish tasks.

> ➤ *Increase risk taking and exploration.* Inspirational leadership frees people to take greater risks, to explore different ways of accomplishing a task.

> ➤ *Create higher productivity.* An inspiring leader elevates the standard of productivity, how hard people work, the hours they put in, and their willingness to overcome any obstacles.

> ➤ *Provide stronger identification with the organization.* The leader's emotional connection with the team members creates a stronger bond between the organization and its people.

Inspirational leadership behavior provides a powerful "glue" between the leader and the group. The culture of the organization is fundamentally transformed and people are motivated to work longer, harder, and with greater focus than before.

KEY POINTS

➤ Inspiration is not a collection of simple tricks, wall posters, or locker-room speeches.

➤ The big secret about leadership is that there is no one "big secret"—inspiring leadership comes from many elements working together.

➤ Inspiration has primarily to do with the relationship between the leader and the group.

➤ Emotion has the power to inspire. Emotions are extremely contagious.

➤ Inspiration is a by-product of sound leadership practices. It calls for goals to be stretched, a clearly defined vision, excellent communication, collaborative working relationships, efforts to develop people, and openness to innovation.

➤ The companion behaviors with the highest correlation to inspiration and motivation involve a leader's willingness to fully accept the responsibilities that come with the role.

➤ The best results come when leaders implement several activities at once; that is, there is a multiplier effect when the leader implements more than one behavior at a time.

➤ While the behavior to inspire is contagious, negative behavior is also contagious and long-lasting. A boss's emotions and behaviors have an exponential effect—that is, leaders cannot afford to have a bad day without doing a great deal of damage.

ABOUT THE AUTHOR

John H. (Jack) Zenger is the cofounder and CEO of Zenger Folkman, a professional services firm providing consulting, leadership development programs, and implementation software for organizational effectiveness initiatives. He is considered a world expert in the field of leadership development, and is a highly respected and sought-after speaker, consultant, and executive coach.

Jack's career has combined entrepreneurial, corporate, and academic activities, including cofounding Zenger-Miller, being president of Provant and Vice President of HR Syntex, and being a faculty member of the University of Southern California and Stanford Graduate School of Business. Among other awards he has received, Jack has been inducted into the Human Resources Development Hall of Fame and received the "Thought Leadership Award" in 2007.

Jack has authored or coauthored numerous articles, and is the coauthor of books on leadership, productivity improvement, and teams, including *Results-Based Leadership,* voted by the Society of Human Resource Management (SHRM) as the Best Business Book of 2000, and the best-selling *The Extraordinary Leader: Turning Good Managers into Great Leaders.* For a more complete explanation of the power and makeup of inspiration, see his book (coauthored with Joe Wheeler) *The Inspiring Leader: Unlocking the Secrets of How Extraordinary Leaders Motivate* (2009).

NOTE

1. Jack Welch and Suzy Welch, "The Welchway," *BusinessWeek,* June 25, 2008, p. 86.

CHAPTER 11

Create Awareness; Create Change

➤ **Judith M. Bardwick**

It's very strange: In the roughly four years that I've been speaking to management about the hundreds of studies clearly demonstrating that high levels of employee commitment and engagement *predict* financial success, I've consistently found that virtually no one in the audience has heard of these studies. So, here is a small sample of data supporting the idea that when employees feel positively about the place where they work and the work that they do, tangible success is achieved, as measured by financial results:

➤ Companies consistently rated as the "Best to Work For" are run by people who hold two goals in mind simultaneously: (1) to achieve their business targets and (2) to uphold the welfare of their employees.[1] These organizations have higher market value, growth, return on assets, and return to shareholders than do peer organizations that don't value and involve employees.

➤ The worldwide consulting firm Watson Wyatt administered surveys of the Human Capital Index (HCI) to 51 organizations in the United States and Europe.[2] When the HCI scores were compared with each corporation's five-year total return to shareholders, companies with a low HCI score averaged a 21 percent total return, companies with medium HCI scores achieved a 39 percent total return, and those with high scores had a 64 percent return.

➤ When customers give a company high marks, that organization earns a 160 percent five-year return to shareholders when compared with the Standard & Poor's (S&P) Index. When both customers and employees give a company a high rating, that company's five-year return to shareholders is 320 percent of the S&P.[3]

➤ Vanderbilt University and human resource consultants Hewitt Associates studied the financial results of *Fortune*'s "100 Best Companies to Work For" from 1998 to 2003. "Best Companies" cumulative stock returns averaged 50 percent above the market average. The publicly traded companies on *Fortune*'s 2007 list of "Best Companies" consistently beat the market over the preceding 10 years.[4]

Over the last 20 years, numerous studies involving millions of people in many nations and industries have overwhelmingly demonstrated that when people feel positive about their job and their workplace, these feelings of commitment and engagement *predict* positive financial results. When employees are committed to their organization and find their work challenging and important, that company will, on average, achieve 30 percent higher profits and a share price two to three times higher than a peer company whose employees are neither committed to the organization nor engaged in its work. The reason is simple: companies in which employees are really involved retain their employees and their customers.

The reverse is also true. When companies see employees only as costs and not as key assets, and use massive layoffs as the first tool to raise money and increase profits, employees reciprocate with powerful negative feelings. People then come to work although in their minds they've already quit. They withhold discretionary effort, fear prevails, innovation disappears, and teamwork is only a slogan. That's a route to failure.

In the great majority of organizations, decision makers don't know that the single most important route to success is to make commitments to valuable employees so that employees reciprocate with strong feelings of commitment to the organization. Ignorance of these facts leads to callous practices toward employees, who become too scared for either their own or the organization's good.

THE MESSAGE

A critical leadership task is to create widespread awareness of this information throughout an organization as a first step in reinstating employees as stakeholders and as assets. The key message is simple: *When employees are viewed and treated as critical resources, and commitments are made to them, financial success is probable.*

People need to know that commitment and engagement are powerful variables, not just substitute words for the weak variables of morale and satisfaction. Commitment and engagement measure passion: How strongly, negatively or positively, do you feel about your organization and your work? Where employees are committed to their organization and find pride in being a member of it, and they are fully engaged in their work because it fulfills their need to do work that matters, motivation, innovation, retention, discretionary effort, and financial outcomes are all very high. When these are the prevailing feelings, customers enjoy doing business with that organization and, like employees, they stay. Replacement costs for employees and customers are low, positive feelings prevail, and sales and profits rise.

One way to think about this situation is to realize that there are three stakeholders in every company: shareholders, customers, and employees. Success requires that all three constituencies are satisfied. The reverse is also true: when employees are treated as costs and not as assets, they feel abused and frightened (for good reason!). When people are neither trusted nor respected, and their work is not regarded as significant, they are neither committed nor engaged. Instead, they become preoccupied with their negative feelings about their organization, their boss, and their job. The real cost of a nonengaged employee—or worse, an actively disengaged employee—is enormous because that person alienates customers and customers leave. So do sales and profits.

When management is ignorant of these facts, the decision makers don't know that the surest path to success involves creating high levels of positive feelings in their members. In fact, the most prominent current practices regarding employees essentially guarantee high levels of negative feelings and low levels of commitment and engagement—a sure route to failure. Indeed, the most prominent current practices regarding employees involve large layoffs and outsourcing *in the absence of a crisis*. Thus, most executives are unwittingly making choices in regard to employees that will almost certainly ensure employee alienation and business failure.

What might account for this widespread executive ignorance? Perhaps the reason is that these studies strongly disagree with the most widespread current policies regarding employees.[5] In practice, employee welfare is frequently disregarded even when the enterprise is profitable. While drastic cuts in employee-related costs may well be appropriate and necessary when the organization is in financial crisis, when red ink is *not* flowing and the goal is increasing profits and share price, these practices inevitably increase nonengagement and active disengagement.

When people feel there is no way for them to achieve any level of control over their lives, when there's no way to gain reasonable security, fear prevails. Even when the economy was good, about half of all employees felt vulnerable economically and psychologically. I call these feelings a "psychological recession"—the feeling that "while the present is awful, the future will be worse." Prolonged fear and depression invite failure because scared and worried people can neither concentrate nor focus.

The first task for change makers is to create real awareness at every level of an organization that (1) these practices create serious problems with powerful negative effects that impede success, and (2) there are policies that make success much more likely. In order to have an impact, the message must resonate with people—it must be an honest, simple, brief, and focused message. It must begin with a sense of alarm that is based on the organization's reality, and then move to the idea that when the core issues are faced, the right changes can be made and then success and a better future become likely. Experience teaches us that this message will need to be repeated often.

CREATE CHANGE

When I speak to employees who are not executives, they always relate to these facts and ideas. I am, after all, describing what they've experienced and how most of them feel. So it is not surprising that they always ask, "Have you talked with our executives and upper-level managers? If you have, what was their reaction? Are they even aware of what's going on? Are they concerned enough to do anything different now that they know how people feel? What can I do to make change happen?"

My answer begins with this caution: don't try to create major change unless you feel strongly that achieving change is of vital importance, because the effort will be much harder and take much longer than you expect. In other words, you have to really care. And you mustn't begin a change effort before you're convinced that at least some success is possible. In the majority of change efforts, the program is announced with great fanfare and then, as other things become more important, executives lose interest. Repeated fizzles of change efforts are about as dispiriting as outright failure.

The most visible leader in an organizational change effort is usually a top executive. But core change does not happen until and unless an aligned leadership develops throughout the organization, at all levels. Success in creating major change ultimately has to involve the majority of people.

Therefore, I'm answering the essential question, "What can I do?" in terms of you. Your first task in trying to create basic change is to get the facts and master them. Every person involved in creating change has to be able to describe those facts easily and, more important, clearly and simply. The majority of people in the organization have to believe that you are telling the truth and not manipulating them. You must also convince them that you are guided by a deep sense of unease, the conviction that current practices are putting the organization's and every person's well-being in jeopardy.

The next task is to be able to describe the problem and the solution in "elevator speech." That means you have less than a minute to get your views across. To achieve this, you need a great answer to the question, "What really matters?" In some ways, crafting this message is the hardest task of the entire effort. It's relatively easy to talk a lot; it's hard to be brief, right on point, and convincing.

Never forget that feelings are much more important than facts in getting a buy-in to change, and core change is always unsettling. You must create the fear that not changing is much more dangerous than changing. Then, it is time to create hope. Your message must be, "If we pull together and we all get on the train, while it won't be easy, we can do it! Count me in!"

MAKE CHANGE HAPPEN

Generating the motivation for change and the specific ideas about how to succeed are only the starting points. Operationalizing anything—actually making things happen—is at least equally difficult.

The task is to regain the perspective that people are a major asset and we must behave in ways that tell employees they are valuable and important. Ideas, attitudes, and behaviors must be aligned, converging on the single idea that making commitments to our people and gaining commitment from them is the only way we can succeed. When most people share that value and agree on that goal, lots of ways to reinforce commitment and engagement will be generated.

Now that the economy is in serious difficulty, it is more important than ever for employees to be able to earn some forms of job security. Some versions already exist: time and funds for retraining; information about future areas of growth and investment; shared jobs; cutting salaries and bonuses before lay-offs. The most effective and mutually fair policy to increase and sustain employee commitment, engagement, and performance during both hard and good times is "conditional commitment." This means that employees are expected to perform at sustained high levels and keep their skills and knowledge at the cutting edge. If that is the case, and the organization needs them and can afford to pay them, employees have a job. Conditional commitment involves mutual responsibilities, obligations, and respect. It is, by far, the better path.

No one, not even the CEO, can make things happen alone. To make things happen, you must gain power. There are two relevant kinds of power; the first involves role power—people at the highest levels in the organization who are responsible for making decisions in the business of the business. In corporations, those are the people who have the major profit-and-loss responsibilities. These positions have the greatest authority and, frequently, the highest influence and political power. *Anyone who has access to these people is also seen as powerful, simply because he or she has access to these people.* It is the responsibility of change agents to learn which of these decision makers is already in basic agreement with the view that people are a critical asset. The task is to identify these people in order to gain powerful allies as quickly as possible.

The second kind of power lies in numbers. When many people in an organization believe the same thing and are calling for change, their message has greater importance than if it were from only a few top decision makers.

Top executives' responsibilities require that they see the forest and not the trees. As a result, they don't and shouldn't have frequent interactions with the many employees who are in the middle and lower levels of the organizational pyramid. But middle managers and supervisors are especially important in issues related to employee feelings and behaviors, because they interact directly and daily with subordinates. And, if employees listen to and trust anyone in the organization, it will be their bosses. So the large number of supervisors and middle managers is a ripe source of allies, as they are in a position to really know how their subordinates are feeling and behaving and how strong the feeling is that management doesn't give a damn.

In terms of numbers, the middle and lower rungs of the organization are your potential sources of the greatest supporters. There are leaders everywhere; they are simply people whom others trust, respect, and want to listen to and follow—having less education is not a barrier to becoming a leader, for example. Change leaders must find these potential allies wherever they are: at entry level, in blue- and pink-collar positions, in the collarless jobs of sole professionals, and in the different generations.

And now, with a firm understanding of the problem and a clear message of alarm and hope, and with allies who are in fundamental agreement with you, how do you make change happen? Complex plans diffuse focus and are usually less effective in terms of making things happen, so you need a fundamental plan that is so direct and focused that it fits on a single page.

A plan starts with some simple but difficult questions: Where are we and what is getting in the way of our succeeding? What do we need to achieve in terms of our core business? Who are our potential leaders—the people who favor core change and are models of the values, attitudes, and behaviors we need? Which people spew poison and need to go?

THE CHANGE PROCESS, IN STEPS

1. Open the books. Speak the unspeakable. Step up to face the real, major problems.

2. Identify the core business and whether it is a cash cow or a high-risk, high-growth business. Create the essential strategy based on competitive advantage. If there is no clear competitive advantage, revisit the question, "What is the business of this business?"

3. Identify the most important goals and those that are easiest to accomplish. Balance the goals of importance and ease. Limit the number of goals at one time to three and identify the due dates.

4. Identify the organization's few core values. For example, for the U.S. Marines, they are honor, courage, and commitment. This is critical because it is values, not rules, that are the true guides of behavior.

5. Create simple, honest, and direct communications to gain understanding and buy-in. Never assume that your message has been heard. Go into the field and find out what people think has been said.

6. Have organizational units and individuals create line-of-sight goals from the organization to their own, with due dates.

7. Reward the angels and fire the snakes. Distinguish thrivers—people who are eager to make and lead the changes—from survivors—fence-sitters, cynics, and strugglers or failures who oppose the changes. Move thrivers into leadership roles.

8. Fire troublemaking strugglers.

9. Fire chronic nonperformers.

10. Start again. Murphy's law, "If anything can go wrong, it will," is bedrock truth.

The most poignant sound in the midst of major upheaval and basic change is the question, "What is going to happen to me?" While that question can't be answered absolutely, anxiety and fear can be reduced by opening the books and telling people the truth about what is known and what might happen, by being clear and specific about what people are expected to do, and by making as many people as possible part of the change process. And everyone must be working toward goals that are achievable and that directly increase the possibilities for organizational success. Never forget that nothing motivates people more than succeeding.

People who are free from strong negative feelings of fear, depression, and hopelessness are able to feel committed to their organization and be engaged in their work. As a result, they are the most motivated, productive, and innovative employees, and the organization's success is a direct result of their sustained excellence. It is patently clear, and factually true, that it is in the organization's best interest to act in ways that increase the numbers of these people.

ABOUT THE AUTHOR

Judith M. Bardwick has been called one of the great management thinkers of our time. She is a highly regarded writer, speaker, and management consultant, specializing in the psychology of the corporate environment. For more than two decades, Dr. Bardwick has combined cutting-edge psychological research with practical business applications to optimize organizational performance, change organizational views and values, and help managers achieve financial and personal success. IBM, Hewlett-Packard, Johnson & Johnson, and 3M are among her many clients.

Dr. Bardwick is the author of one of the top 25 best-selling business books of the last decade, *Danger in the Comfort Zone* (AMACOM, 1995). Her latest book, *One Foot Out the Door* (AMACOM, 2007), was selected as the #1 Human Resources/Organizational Developmental Book in 2008.

Judith Bardwick earned a BS from Purdue University, an MS from Cornell, and a PhD from the University of Michigan. She lives in La Jolla, California. Contact Dr. Bardwick at jmbwick@san.rr.com and Judithmbardwick.com.

NOTES

1. Catherine Fox, "Best Employers 2003," *Australian Financial Review BOSS* (March 2003): 20–27.

2. Watson Wyatt Worldwide Research, "Human Capital Index: Linking Human Capital and Shareholder Value" (Watson Wyatt, 2002): 1–12.

3. Neil Woodcock and Michael Starkey, "Enterprise IG Case History for Customer Loyalty," *Futures UK,* July 8, 2004.

4. Study by Vanderbilt University and Hewitt Associates, 2000. http://www.workfamily.com/Work-lifeClearinghouse/UpDates/ud0043.htm, accessed November 26, 2008.

5. Judith M. Bardwick, *One Foot Out the Door* (New York: AMACOM, 2007), see especially chap. 4, "Bad Management Is (Really) Expensive," pp. 35–44, and chap. 5, "Good Management (Really) Makes Money," pp. 45–62.

CHAPTER 12

I Really Do Care!

> **Joseph Folkman**

Chris had been appointed manager of an IT group for the past year. When he was an individual contributor, he was dissatisfied with his manager. The manager seemed to float above everything. All this manager seemed to care about was taking the credit for everyone else's good work. Performance declined and so did morale. When Chris was given the job of replacing this manager, he made a commitment to himself that he would be a different kind of leader. He was concerned about all of the employees in his group, but he also knew that there were some critical deadlines that needed to be met.

The first day in his new position, Chris met with his new boss and was informed that he needed to get a critical project done, "or else." It was clear that if the project did not get done, Chris would be looking for another job. It took a little time and some pushing on his part, but within two months the project was on track, and Chris was feeling proud. After a meeting with Randy, one of his direct reports and a good friend, Chris asked for some honest feedback on how he was doing as manager.

Randy seemed uncomfortable with the question, but finally looked at Chris and said, "You don't care about us; all you care about is getting this project done and keeping your job." After Randy left the office, Chris thought about the feedback he received. In reality, Chris *did* care about his team, but if the project did not get completed he was not the only person who would lose his job. "Why can't they see that I care?" Chris lamented to himself.

Chris was frustrated with the perception that he did not care and he wondered how he could communicate his caring and concern to his direct reports.

There is not an objective measure to show how much a person really cares. As a result, we all have learned to make educated guesses about how much a person cares, based on a set of observable behaviors. Likewise, people make assumptions about which behaviors most show others how much they care. These observations and assumptions may be correct or incorrect.

Rather than guess which behaviors best show that you care, wouldn't it be helpful to research the topic and identify, say, the top 12 behaviors that do just that?

12 KEY BEHAVIORS THAT SHOW YOU CARE

To better understand these key "caring" triggers, our firm studied 100,000 360-degree assessments from 12,827 leaders in hundreds of companies, both domestic and international.[1] Bosses, peers, direct reports, and others were asked to rate a leader's effectiveness, shown via a broad set of behaviors. We then measured the extent to which leaders were perceived as caring or concerned about others based on these behaviors. Some of the named behaviors may seem fairly obvious, while others may surprise you.

Builds Trust

It is difficult for leaders to communicate that they care about others when there is a lack of trust. When trust is missing, everything that is said or done is subject to question.

Feelings of trust between people are built over time and, likewise, can be destroyed over time. Trust is built in different ways. First, leaders can engender trust by becoming aware of the concerns, aspirations, and circumstances of others. The reality is that we tend to trust our friends more than our enemies—trust is the foundation for positive relationships.

In addition to building positive relationships, leaders need to be aware of what is happening in the lives of others. A leader can know everything about what is happening in his or her department and yet know nothing about the people working in it. It's the little things that count here: remembering names and being aware of someone's personal challenges at home. But the concern must be genuine. When people suspect an ulterior motive for a leader's actions, they will distrust that leader.

Trust is also built through knowledge and expertise. People trust leaders who show expertise and deep knowledge of the matter at hand, because they project confidence in their ability to make informed decisions.

A third way trust is built is through consistent behavior. When our behavior, our decisions, or our actions change from day to day, people cannot predict what will happen and feel unsure of the situation. When leaders are consistent and predictable, however, others acquire confidence in them and trust them.

Finally, trust is built by a leader's rock-solid honesty and integrity. When direct reports know that they will never be told anything that is not 100 percent accurate, they can trust that leader. Consistency is the key to building trust via honesty.

Leaders need to assume that direct reports are always on guard, that they rarely place significant trust in their bosses. So, building trust helps others sense leaders' concern for them, but also brings other positive benefits.

Respects Others

This behavior seems fairly obvious. Most people know that disrespecting others communicates a lack of caring. While many leaders understand this principle, they lack awareness that their behavior is disrespectful. Some actions that can communicate a lack of respect are:

- ➤ Cutting people off in conversations
- ➤ Treating some people differently from others
- ➤ Acting arrogantly
- ➤ Being unwilling to listen
- ➤ Being unsupportive of diversity

➤ Not valuing the contributions of all employees

➤ Being unwilling to do particular "lower-level" jobs

➤ Lacking awareness of the difficulties employees face at work or at home

➤ Being overly critical

➤ Being unfriendly

➤ Being unavailable

➤ Being out of touch with how organizational changes might impact individual employees

Take the time to look at your actions and ask yourself if they might appear disrespectful to others. Sometimes leaders make efforts to be more respectful, but their approach only seems to have the opposite effect—that is, they appear condescending or fake. It is critical for leaders to gather feedback from others, not only to show respect but also to understand if their actions are having the intended positive impact.

Is Approachable and Friendly

Nothing says "I don't care" more than a leader who never says "hello" or constantly appears to be in a bad mood. Leaders need to be aware that others take their cues from the mood and atmosphere that they, as leaders, bring to the workplace. New research by James H. Fowler and Nicholas A. Christakis shows that happiness spreads through social networks much like a cold—that there are clusters of happy and unhappy people whose moods reinforce one another.[2] The bottom line is that if you have close friends who are happy there is a substantially higher likelihood that you also will be happy.

Leaders can and do set the tone for their workplace. We have observed employees who frequently delay meetings to ensure that the manager is in the best possible mood for making critical decisions. Do others monitor your mood before approaching you? Consider the following questions and see how you stack up:

➤ Am I easy to get along with?

➤ Does everyone feel that I am approachable?

➤ Do I relate well to people at all levels of the organization?

➤ Am I accessible?

➤ Do I show "grace under pressure"?

➤ Am I smiling and in a good mood 90 percent of the time?

➤ Do I say hello to everyone I meet?

➤ Do I go out of my way to ask others how their day is going?

➤ Do others withhold information because they are afraid of how I will react?

There is tremendous power in a smile and in setting a positive atmosphere.

Is Fair

Lack of fairness is one of the most significant negative triggers of caring that is associated with leadership. Employees keep score: when their peers receive something they don't, they notice. Similarly, most parents with more than one child are acutely aware of how quickly unequal treatment gets noticed. Leaders need to continually ask themselves, "If I do X for person A, how will it be perceived by others?"

Encourages Input and Involvement

Too many leaders believe in the "mushroom theory" of management, which compares a way to manage people to the way that mushrooms are grown— that is, by keeping them in the dark and feeding them lots of manure! Not surprisingly, this approach to management communicates a lack of caring. Instead, encouraging input from every person on the staff and asking for their involvement in important decisions communicate that the leader cares for and values them and their ideas. In order for this to work successfully, however, leaders need to do more than just ask for input—they must actually *want* it. Asking for input but then ignoring what is offered does not convey caring. Of course, when leaders involve others, not all of the input is valuable, but some of it is often exceptional. Other people offer perspectives and experiences different from those of the leader and those insights can lead to better decisions. So, ask yourself:

➤ Is there good two-way communication in your work group?

➤ Is everyone kept well informed about changes and new developments?

➤ Do people feel safe to voice their opinions?

➤ Are people willing to share bad news with you?

➤ Are you a good listener?

Builds Unity

Leaders who encourage cooperation and collaboration among employees and between groups in the organization are perceived as much more caring than those who compete internally for people, equipment, and resources. When team members observe a leader being overly competitive with other teams and individuals in the organization, they quickly recognize that the tables can be turned and their own disagreements with that leader may lead to similar treatment. Organizations that compete internally tend to foster feuds and disagreements between individuals. Leaders who have the ability to unify and collaborate send the message that everyone in the organization is important, not just the team. To some extent, leaders who see others as competitors lack the self-confidence to cooperate; they feel that they need more credit and they worry that if one group does well, other groups (including their own) will look bad. Consider this on an international scale. Do countries that promote conflicts, wars, and disagreements have the best needs of their citizens at heart? Typically, the answer is no.

Gives Honest Feedback

Many leaders seek approval from others, telling them what they *want* to hear rather than what they *need* to hear. Delivering tough feedback is often difficult and it can strain relationships; nevertheless, giving honest feedback ultimately shows caring.

It is interesting that, in our analysis, employees who indicated that their leaders really cared also felt that they delivered honest, straightforward feedback. That is, leaders told people what they really needed to hear, and they delivered the negative feedback in a way that encouraged those employees to improve their performance. A leader who truly cares will tell others the truth about their performance. Most people can think of a personal experience when they received some difficult feedback from a leader who was genuinely concerned about their development and improvement. Most people view this as a positive experience. While that feedback is difficult to receive, they recognize that it is necessary.

Develops Others

It is hard to think of a much better gift than to help another person learn a new skill. When leaders work with employees and push them to develop new skills and abilities, they are truly showing their concern for those employees. Employees become higher performing and more promotable. Leaders who are effective at developing employees are thrilled by the success of others, while leaders who are more concerned with their own personal success are rarely effective at developing others.

When we consider those who have acted as our coaches or mentors, we inevitably have positive feelings toward those people. One way an organization develops is when leaders create a learning environment in which people are encouraged to learn from their mistakes and to analyze their successes to understand what went well. There is an abundance of feedback in a solid learning environment, and it flows both up and down the organization.

Resolves Conflicts

In 1964, Kitty Genovese was murdered while 38 people either watched or listened for 35 minutes—not one person called the police. The *New York Times* ran a story about the tragedy that shocked the nation. People assumed that this was an isolated incident, but when researchers ran controlled experiments, they found that bystander apathy was quite a common phenomenon.

Most people assume that others will help in a difficult situation and therefore rationalize their apathy. Similarly, leaders frequently see conflicts occurring and often assume that the individuals will work out the problems on their own. This, however, is just another form of bystander apathy. Instead, leaders need to acknowledge these conflicts and work to get them quickly resolved.

Walks the Talk

Leaders whose actions match their words are more likely to be perceived as concerned and caring. Leaders can be tough-minded in their views and strict about rules, as long as they consistently enforce those standards. They are role models.

A key attribute for a leader who wants to be a role model is assertiveness. When leaders fail to speak up or don't take action to deal with others who ignore the rules, other people assume the leader's implied agreement or complicity. But leaders who are willing to speak up and take a stand when they see inappropriate actions are viewed as "walking their talk."

Is Open to Feedback and Willing to Change

A forceful way to show that you care about others is to be willing to change your own behavior, based on feedback. Leaders who are open to feedback from their direct reports and are willing to work on personal improvements are perceived as caring individuals.

In a recent study, Zenger Folkman looked at data on executives who had been asked to leave an organization because of poor performance. One key difference between these leaders and more successful leaders was that the former were resistant to accepting feedback from direct reports. Indeed, two profiles emerged for those who resisted feedback: (1) arrogance, in that some leaders assumed they were doing fine and refused any feedback to the contrary; and (2) insecurity, in that these leaders were afraid of feedback and felt that it would demoralize them. There is an assumption made by these leaders that if the feedback is never provided, it must not be true. Nothing could be further from the truth! The feedback is already out there; everyone in the organization recognizes this is true except the leader who resists hearing it.

Gives Recognition

It is often interesting to watch people being recognized for their accomplishments. Many insist that they do not need to be recognized, but as recognition is given, they generally seem pleased. The truth is that most accomplishments mean very little until other people notice; recognition by others increases the value of those accomplishments.

In a meeting with a group of leaders, not one could recall encountering a leader who recognized others too often! Leaders will never be hurt by finding more opportunities to recognize and reward others for their contributions. Sometimes this can be just a sincere "thank you" or a pat on the back. Sometimes a personal note or an e-mail is more appropriate. In other instances, recognition should be public.

Several years ago we studied an organization's rewards and recognition program. The organization had a number of regional groups, each of which used the same recognition program with the same monetary rewards. But we found that one group had substantially more positive ratings for the recognition program. In interviews with leaders and employees from that group, we discovered that while the basics of the program were the same, the administration of the program made all the difference. One employee described the annual awards dinner as "a bigger deal than the Oscars." In fact, people would accept their awards with tears in their eyes. The size of the reward was the same from one region to another, but the greater intrinsic value of the reward made all the difference.

HELP OTHERS TO SEE HOW MUCH YOU CARE

When considering all of the behaviors just discussed, most people would rate themselves as better at some than others. It is important, however, for leaders to assess all behaviors that they consider problems or do very poorly. Getting some input from others may help to more accurately assess significant weaknesses and that could create the impression of not caring. As a leader, it is critical that you address those behaviors first; you do not need to move to make it a profound strength, but you do need to move it from negative to at least neutral.

That is, to substantially improve the extent to which others perceive you as caring, you don't need to be exceptional in every behavior. Select the two or three that will have the greatest impact in your situation, and plan to improve them. Many of these behaviors can be improved just by your paying attention to others and developing good listening habits.

We encourage you to make a list of the behaviors you would like to change and then create an action plan for making that change. If you work on improving your concern and caring for other people they will take notice. Others will say, "That person really cares." But a more interesting phenomenon may also occur: you may find that you actually *do* care more.

ABOUT THE AUTHOR

Joseph Folkman is cofounder and President of Zenger Folkman, a firm specializing in leadership and organizational development. He is a highly acclaimed keynote speaker at conferences and seminars the world over. His topics focus on subjects related to leadership, feedback, and individual and organizational change. As one of the nation's renowned psychometricians, he focuses his extensive expertise on survey research and change management. He has more than 30 years of experience, consulting with some of the world's most prestigious and successful organizations.

Joe Folkman holds a master's degree in organizational behavior and a doctorate in social and organizational psychology from Brigham Young University. He is the author or coauthor of seven books: *Turning Feedback into Change* (Novations Consulting Group, 1996), *Making Feedback Work* (Executive Excellence Publishing, 1996), *Employee Surveys That Make a Difference* (Executive Excellence Publishing, 1999), *The Extraordinary Leader* (McGraw-Hill, 2009), *The Handbook for Leaders* (McGraw-Hill, 2007), *The Power of Feedback* (John Wiley & Sons, 2006), and *The Inspiring Leader* (McGraw-Hill, 2009).

NOTES

1. For more information on research done by Zenger Folkman, go to
   www.zengerfolkman.com.

2. James H. Fowler and Nicholas A. Christakis, "Dynamic Spread of
   Happiness in a Large Social Network: Longitudinal Analysis over 20 Years
   in the Framingham Heart Study," *British Medical Journal* 337 (42): a2338
   (2008).

CHAPTER 13

The Real Legacy of Leadership: Aligning Rhetoric with Reality

➤ **Albert A. Vicere**

Whether you lead a global organization or a small team, success depends on instilling in your followers a clear, shared image of the purpose and aspirations of the organization. In times of change and uncertainty, people look to their leaders for inspiration and confidence. Skilled leaders reflect a sense of purpose and perseverance; those less skilled reflect a sense of confusion and desperation.

This chapter explores the boundaries between inspiration and desperation, between organizational effectiveness and ineffectiveness, between skilled and less skilled leadership. The focus of our exploration is on the critical need for leaders to ensure that their rhetoric and that of their organization match the reality of the organization's operating environment and culture—that is, that the organization actually is what its strategy and mission statements say it aspires to be. Our discussion will show that when leaders achieve that objective and align purpose and aspirations with focus and activity, they create the foundation for a high-performance organization.

THE CHALLENGE

Mission and strategy statements may define an organization's direction and aspirations, but the reality of economic and competitive environments can easily shift a company's focus from lofty goals to short-term survival.

People and organizations have a choice: either they continue to learn and evolve as circumstances around them shift, or they fall victim to changing environmental pressures. Great leaders reflect a sense of focus and purpose that not only adds meaning to work but also helps make organizations more dynamic, decisive, and adept at responding to change.

High-performing organizations stay vital by resisting decay. As they mature, their leaders successfully manage the tension between adaptation—perfecting and improving existing products, services, and processes—and innovation—doing things differently, offering unique products, or changing the rules.[1] These leaders realize that the healthiest organizational cultures maintain a balance between these two perspectives: they continually strive to get better, yet remain open to new ideas and new ways of thinking. They do this by ensuring that the organization retains a sense of purpose and meaning along with a relentless drive for performance.

THE CONTEXT

Scan typical corporate mission statements and you will note that most companies aspire to be some combination of innovative, customer driven, market leading, employee focused, performance oriented, and of course, profitable. Although admirable, most leaders would agree that living up to those traits consistently over time is incredibly demanding and extremely difficult. That is not to challenge corporate aspirations, but simply to make an obvious observation: declaring aspirations is much easier than actually achieving them.

My research, coupled with my years of experience as a consultant, has convinced me that the key to resolving this perplexing challenge is rooted in the ability of leaders to reconcile the rhetoric of corporate aspirations with the reality of the corporate operating environment. Organizations need aspirations, and as Jim Collins reminded us in his book *Built to Last: Successful Habits of Visionary Companies* (HarperBusiness, 2004), people seek the exuberance of being part of an organization with "Big Hairy Audacious Goals." But if the organization's declared purpose and aspirations are out of synch with its operating environment, if people within the organization experience a culture that is very different from its stated purpose and aspirations, the organization is headed for disaster.

Consider an example. Imagine you worked for the Bank (it could be any type of business) and it had recently created a new strategy and mission statement extolling its position as a market leader, its focus on innovation and customer service, and its support for employees. The Bank further commissioned a new advertising campaign that emphasized those very characteristics, complete with TV and radio ads, billboards, print ads, and so on.

Imagine that as an employee, however, you experienced each day a very different operating environment within the Bank. The Bank seldom launched new products or services unless in response to competitor initiatives. The operating norm for employees was to follow the rules and not challenge the status quo. Customer complaints were ignored. And unless you were in a senior leadership position, you were treated as if you had been hired merely as a set of hands.

Given that situation, how likely is it that the Bank will achieve its aspirations of market leadership and so on? Moreover, might the mismatch between the rhetoric of the Bank's strategy and the reality of its operating environment contribute to cynicism and discontent among employees? And if you and your fellow employees became cynical, would you likely be exuberant supporters of the Bank? And could that mismatch of rhetoric and reality, coupled with the employee and eventual customer cynicism it inspired, be a sign of the eventual demise of the Bank? Oftentimes, it is.

All of that leads to a reiteration of the main premise of this chapter: a key factor in the ability of an organization to execute its strategy and achieve its aspirations is the capacity of its leaders to ensure that the rhetoric matches the reality, that the organization actually is what it says it aspires to be.

I doubt that many leaders would take issue with that premise. Yet, it almost seems inevitable that an organization will lose the capacity to maintain alignment between rhetoric and reality and eventually fall victim to time. *Fortune* magazine reported that fewer than 20 percent of the original Fortune 500 companies were still in existence in their original form in 2004 when it published its issue celebrating the 50th anniversary of that venerated list.[2] In reality, organizational life spans tend to be relatively short.

THE CAUSE

To consider the nature of the potentially dire fate for organizations, think of the organizational life cycle—the stages companies go through as they evolve over time. They begin at the start-up phase when an often "crazy" idea becomes the germ for an organization. The small band of believers in the idea put their hearts and souls into bringing the organization and its aspirations to life. If the crazy idea catches on, the company experiences growth: the business develops, demand begins to exceed capacity, and the new company begins to expand. Growth invites competitors and imitators. Eventually, maturity sets in and growth slows down. Unless the organization takes action to revitalize—to revisit and reinvigorate its purpose and aspirations—it begins to decline. Absent dramatic action, a crisis hits, decay sets in, and the company is on its way out.

Before you panic, realize that it is possible for companies to manage this cycle. Just look at 3M, Johnson & Johnson, Proctor & Gamble, and countless other companies that have stayed relevant and effective for decades. But it's rare that a company will survive unscathed once it moves into decline and decay. Under CEO Lou Gerstner, IBM revived itself with a massive restructuring and an expanded business focus. But for every successful turnaround like IBM's, there are examples like Digital Equipment Corporation, Westinghouse, and many other formerly great organizations that have fallen victim to their inability to adapt to changing times.

My research suggests that what actually gets an organization into trouble early on is not incompetence or ineffectiveness but, rather, the organization's past record of success. Over time, the very elements of a business model that enabled that organization to grow and become successful can become the seeds of the organization's self-destruction. As it faces competitive and performance pressures owing to a changing external environment, rather than evolving its business model while retaining its aspirations and sense of purpose, it shifts into a "performance-at-all-cost mode" in which it is driven by the mantras of maintaining market share, margins, and profitability. Metrics and reward systems drive short-term thinking. Leaders emphasize short-term performance. Employees are shaped to consider only bottom-line impacts. The purpose of the organization becomes that of perpetuating current operating processes and objectives with a goal of meeting short-term financial objectives.

Imagine now that environmental pressures subside, performance targets are met, and the organization is ready once again to move into the marketplace and grow. Yet employees have been shaped to view the purpose of the organization as short-term performance. Metrics and reward systems reinforce a short-term, bottom-line mentality. Leaders have been trained to think only about expense control and performance at all cost.

So a new strategy statement is released. The organization is going to grow by being innovative, a market leader, customer focused, and employee oriented. The new direction sends conflicting messages, to be sure. What's an employee to do? The safest (and maybe smartest) thing is to hunker down and make your numbers while you figure out what all this new rhetoric really means. And if the focus and behavior of senior leaders stay the same, if metrics stay the same, if performance criteria remain as they've always been, then there is no compelling reason for any employee at any level to change behavior.

I suspect we've all experienced this phenomenon, on both a personal and an organizational level. Regardless of the strategy statement or CEO speeches, the way an organization's leaders actually behave, coupled with the things they ultimately measure and reward, shapes employee thinking and behavior across the organization. In effect, they shape what I call "organizational DNA."

Just as human DNA contains the complete set of instructions for making a person, organizational DNA contains the complete set of instructions for how and why organizational members think the way they do, and how their thinking impacts motivation and performance.

THE RESEARCH

Preliminary results from an ongoing study involving leaders from a wide variety of major corporations, government agencies, and not-for-profit organizations around the world help shed light on how organizational DNA is related to the challenge of maintaining alignment between an organization's rhetoric and the reality of its operating environment.[3]

The critical dimensions of organizational DNA have been broken down into the set of measurable components depicted in the Direction and Alignment (DNA) Model in Figure 13.1. The model is based on a visual metaphor, the DNA double helix, which is made of a backbone—the two intertwining strands that frame genetic character. These strands are connected by a four-letter code comprising the instructions for a person's genetic profile. Each letter of the code contains essential chemical elements that combine into sets of base pairs within which one's genetic code resides.

In the Direction and Alignment (DNA) Model, the backbone of organizational DNA comprises two intertwining strands: an organization's Roots, or its

Figure 13.1 The Direction and Alignment (DNA)® Model

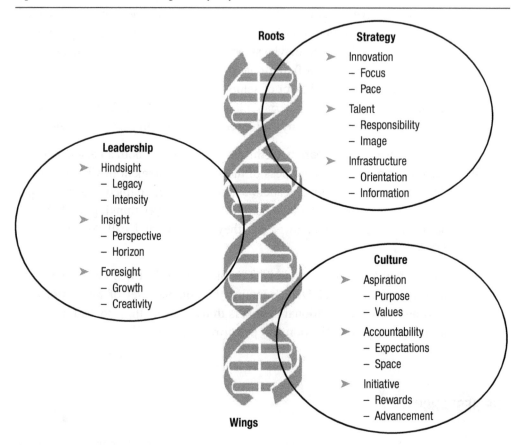

history and operating capabilities, and its Wings, or its ability to change and innovate. Those two strands are connected by a three-letter code, SLC, denoting Strategy, Leadership, and Culture. Each letter of an organization's genetic code contains three essential elements. *Strategy* consists of innovation, talent, and infrastructure. *Leadership* consists of hindsight, insight, and foresight. *Culture* consists of aspiration, accountability, and initiative. As indicated in Figure 13.1, each of these nine essential elements can be defined by a set of "base pairs," or essential viewpoints held by leaders that guide their interpretation of organizational strategy, leadership, and culture.

THE ASSESSMENT

The DNA Model has been operationalized in a survey instrument entitled the Strategy, Leadership, Culture Questionnaire (SLCQ).[4] Survey respondents indicate their perceptions of their organizations with regard to each set of base pairs. The data generated by the SLCQ reveal what organization members think about strategy, leadership, and culture, and the potential impact those perceptions have on member behavior, organizational performance, and strategy execution.

The SLCQ has been used by a variety of major organizations and in a number of settings over the past six years, resulting in a database of over 11,000 respondents representing all organizational levels (though the vast majority are in middle- through senior-level leadership positions). An analysis of the database paints a compelling picture of the challenges faced by leaders as they attempt to align their organizations with a desired future state.

THE PROFILE

Over the period that data have been collected using the SLCQ,[5] the database has generated a "typical" or average profile of an organization that has remained consistent over time, despite economic fluctuations and changing business conditions.

In terms of *Strategy,* respondents indicated that their organizations were followers/perfecters slow to develop new ideas or approaches to business, staffed by take-charge people complemented by technical experts, who were trying to work together but felt like they were operating in silos.

In terms of *Culture,* they indicated that their organizations were prospecting for/reacting to opportunities in order to generate improvements, for the purpose of extracting as much return as possible from their current asset base.

In terms of *Leadership,* they indicated a passion for their organization, felt challenged by their jobs, and were energized by their work situation; however, over 30 percent perceived that their organization's reward system was not tied to job performance and that there was little certainty about pathways for personal advancement.

It is worth repeating that this general profile emerged early and has remained consistent over the years that we have collected data. Individual organizations can vary dramatically from this norm, but the norm itself has remained consistent. Respondents indicate that the "typical" organization is exactly as described.

THE CHALLENGE REVISITED

I believe that the "typical" profile reflects our previous discussion of organizational life cycles. The vast majority of respondents to the SLCQ have been from large, established companies.[6] As those companies have grown and become successful, their culture—as defined by focus, metrics, and rewards—has evolved from the creation of new products, services, and business models to a focus on maintaining share and margins and driving profits. The typical organization is profiled as having limited openness to new ideas and making limited effort to divine new opportunities for growth and development.

If that's the case, how likely is it that a new strategy statement, even one rolled out with town meetings, speeches, and training programs, is really going to make an impact on the way respondents think and behave on their job? It's a safe bet that respondents will keep working as they always have until leaders not only generate the rhetoric of a change in focus and emphasis but also take steps to align that rhetoric with the reality of the operating environment by changing metrics, adjusting rewards, modeling new behaviors, and demonstrating that the organization actually means what it is saying.

THE RESPONSE

I believe that the true legacy of leadership is directly related to the ability of leaders to align the rhetoric of the organization with its operating environment. Leaders who are able to achieve and maintain that alignment are in a better position to prevent track records of growth and success from becoming blinders to an organization's continual need to adapt and evolve to a changing environment.

Take the example of Allied Waste Industries, until recently the nation's second largest solid-waste disposal company. Allied grew through acquisitions that left it highly leveraged, with a driving focus on short-term performance in order to deal with the challenge of paying down debt and generating profits for shareholders.

When John Zillmer became CEO of Allied in 2005, he saw more opportunity and potential for the company. With environmental sustainability emerging as a core social value and business challenge, solid-waste companies had an opportunity to create far more value than just hauling away trash; they stood poised to become experts and advisers in the green movement.

Zillmer, along with President and COO Don Slager, EVP and CFO Pete Hathaway, and HR EVP Ed Evans, made a decision as Allied's top leadership team to move the organization forward. They created a strategy statement, but did so with the help of key leaders throughout the company. They built a strategy, not by hiring consultants to do the analysis and make recommendations, but by involving dozens of leaders from throughout the company in the analysis and decision-making process. They established training programs for leaders and employees at all levels, but they did not just delegate the training to HR and outside resources; they actively participated in the training as sponsors, mentors, and teachers. They changed business metrics to drive not just financial performance but also customer focus and organizational development. They adjusted employee competency models, compensation, and assessment processes at all levels to support the new Allied. In short, they took pains to ensure that the rhetoric of the company increasingly matched the reality of its operating environment.

At the beginning of this effort, the SLCQ was administered and a DNA profile created. Allied's profile looked much like that of the "typical" company described previously. As the process unfolded and we conducted subsequent analysis, Allied's profile began to evolve. Respondents perceived that the company was looking for opportunities to grow, that employees were more engaged and networked, that emphases on customer focus and top-line growth were gaining in parity with profitability and performance, and that the company was committed to employee development and success.

During the three-plus years prior to its 2008 merger with Republic Services, Allied made significant progress in revenue growth, profitability, employee recruitment and retention, and customer service. I don't think that it was any coincidence that the more employees perceived a match between the rhetoric of the organization and the reality of the operating environment, the more Allied's overall performance improved.

I've seen similar patterns in numerous companies across many industries. When the reality of the organization's operating environment is aligned with the rhetoric of the company's strategy, intensity, performance, and morale invariably improve. Organization members seem better able to see where their company is headed, identify opportunities in the marketplace, understand how and why the organization needs to change, and grasp their role in the future of the business. When there is misalignment, members can become frustrated and cynical, often disengaging from the organization. Matching rhetoric with reality is often the difference in an organization's ability to execute a strategy and its failure to achieve defined objectives and aspirations.

THE LEGACY OF LEADERSHIP

Like many key elements of leadership and strategy, it may seem like common sense that to achieve organizational performance and longevity, leaders must align the rhetoric of an organization with the reality of its operating environment. Yet my research and experience suggest that, for most organizations, this connection is fleeting at best. That's why the true legacy of leadership is the ability to maintain that alignment, ensuring that the organization retains a sense of purpose and meaning along with a relentless drive for performance. It's about giving the organization both a set of roots and a pair of wings. It's about ensuring that an organization not only gets better at what it does in order to be profitable but also is able to evolve in order to stay relevant in a changing world.

ABOUT THE AUTHOR

Albert A. Vicere is Executive Education Professor of Strategic Leadership for the Smeal College of Business at Penn State. He also serves as President of Vicere Associates, Inc., a consulting firm whose clients span the globe. Dr. Vicere has published over 80 articles; his books include *Leadership by Design* and *The Many Facets of Leadership*. His article "Leadership in the

Networked Economy" (*The Many Facets of Leadership,* FT Press, 2002) was awarded the Walker Prize by the Human Resource Planning Society. In addition to a number of MBA teaching awards, he has received the Institute for Management Studies' Distinguished Faculty Award, was named one of the "12 Gurus of Executive Education" by *Business Horizons,* and was listed among the 10 top leadership development coaches in the book *The Art and Practice of Leadership Coaching* (eds. Marshall Goldsmith, Howard Morgan, Phil Harkins).

NOTES

1. A. A. Vicere, "The Strategic Leadership Imperative for Executive Development," *Human Resource Planning* 15, no. 1 (1992): 15–31.

2. Julie Schlosser, Ellen Florian, et al., "Amazing Facts," *Fortune* 149, no. 7 (April 5, 2004): 152–159.

3. An overview of the assessment process and theoretical underpinnings can be found at http://www.vicere.com/documents/SLCQDesc-nos.pdf.

4. Ibid.

5. Ibid.

6. Ibid.

CHAPTER 14

What Do Leaders Need to Know About Generation Y in Order to Lead Successfully?

➤ **Paul Hersey**

They're talented, educated, tolerant, sociable, collaborative, and oriented toward achievement, but they haven't been tested yet. What happens when they are faced with a world in economic crisis that won't support the lifestyle they've grown accustomed to? Will they pout and think, "Somebody's got to fix this," or will they take on the responsibility as their own? The members of Generation Y certainly have the courage to ask for what they want and are more civically involved in the world than their predecessors, but do they have the leadership skills to take on the responsibility of running the world?

Consider that when I went off to college on a basketball scholarship my father handed me a one-way bus ticket and said, "Good luck" as he shook my hand to say good-bye. When my grandson went, he drove his own SUV followed by his parents in two other vehicles packed with stuff. When they got there, his mother felt that the mattress and desk chair weren't good enough so they went shopping while his father stood in line for him to get his meal card.

Who did the planning? The organizing? The motivating? For this generation, that responsibility has been placed on the parents, nannies, coaches, and teachers—in fact, anyone but the kids. All they have to do is show up and perform to be praised. Granted, they have better skills than earlier generations, but it remains to be seen if they've lost something even more important. Have adults taken away their opportunities for leadership, creativity, and responsibility? Have we sheltered them and deprived them of the chance to experience and deal with life? Or have we armed them for battle by setting the example?

Leading today is a tougher, more demanding job than ever before. The obstacles are more numerous and the stakes are higher. Time is running out. Leaders are retiring in record numbers, and the young are called to lead long before we asked that of generations before them. They have days to learn what others were granted years to perfect. It is critical that leaders take the time now to train, guide, and mentor Generation Yers—to leave a legacy.

GENERATION Y

The Generation Y workforce comprises those born roughly between the second half of the 1970s and the first half of the 1990s. These are the children of the Baby Boomers. They have come of age in a politically and socially tumultuous period—the country is at war and people they know are losing their jobs and homes as a result of a recession. All of this they experience instantaneously via technology.

Demographers indicate that the first major events that older Generation Yers are likely to remember are the 1986 *Challenger* explosion and the fall of the Berlin Wall in 1989. They also witnessed the collapse of the Soviet Union and the first Gulf War. What is different for this generation, though, is that these children didn't just read about these events after the fact; technology brought them images of history-in-the-making as these events unfolded. They saw and heard the Columbine school shooting and other incidents of school violence; they watched uncensored and terrifying images of the 9/11 terrorist attacks and heard the screams of people running from the destruction. It wasn't just empathy or simple compassion that they felt for nameless, faceless victims; these children grieved. They felt shock, then anger and sadness over events like the Iraq War, Hurricane Katrina, and the Indian Ocean tsunami because they witnessed their effects on humanity. It wasn't just events that shaped this generation; it was also how technology allowed them to experience those moments.

GROWING UP

This newest addition to the workforce grew up heavily immersed in the digital world. They have an understanding and knowledge of technology that the generations before them could not. More important, Generation Yers keep up quite well with technological advances. They view change as desired, not dreaded, as cause for excitement, not anxiety or stress.

Technology also brought this generation the Internet, where a wealth of information is available in just seconds. Generation Yers have grown accustomed to the fact that if they do not get what they want from one source, they can immediately go to another. They know that there are other options out there if they are not satisfied with the answers.

Generation Yers have grown up in a culture of praise, raised by active, involved parents who often interceded on their behalf, protecting them and ensuring that they were treated well and grew up safely. They have been brought up in the most child-centered generation ever, even though over half of all families in the United States have divorced parents, one in four children lives in a single-parent household, and three in four children have working mothers. The parents of Generation Yers view the child as the center of the family and spend more time with their children than did those of the previous generation, despite doing so in dual-income and single-parent families. These children are not left to make key decisions on their own like the latchkey kids of the previous generation; the parents of Generation Y are very hands-on. They are involved in the daily lives and decisions of Generation Yers by helping them plan their achievements, taking part in their activities, and demonstrating behaviors that indicate a strong belief in their child's worth. Their children actually *like* them, as opposed to the resentment and teenage angst experienced by the previous generation. Generation Yers have been programmed and nurtured to expect to be told how they're doing and to think anything is possible.

The secure feeling attained by strong parental involvement makes the members of the Y Generation believe they can accomplish most anything. Here's the thing, though. If they don't accomplish what they want in the time frame they have in mind, they can always go back home and get help and support. They have a safety net. Generation Yers take jobs because they want to, not because they have to. In fact, more than half of Generation Y's new graduates move back to their parents' homes after collecting their degrees, and that cushion of support gives them the time to pick the job they really want or leave one that isn't meeting their expectations. What's interesting is that they hop from job to job when they see no other choice, when they don't think they can grow fast enough in their current job. They don't leave for the sake of leaving. They're more practical than that. They usually leave to do something that they could have done if their current employer hadn't made it so difficult for them to transition. Parental coddling has often deprived them of learning the face-to-face social skills necessary for dealing with difficult people or situations.

Many have noted a strong sense of entitlement with regard to Generation Y, citing the perhaps overindulgent praise they received growing up as the cause. As a group, Generation Yers are driven and ambitious, and tend to set high expectations for themselves and others. They seem to want the best and think that they deserve it. When they enter the workforce, they appear to want to start at the top, or at least be climbing the corporate ladder by their sixth month on the job. Their behavior has been interpreted to mean that they believe that they deserve the position they want, whether experienced or not. The situation can be further complicated by the fact that members of Generation X, who had to pay their dues to get where they are, don't see the same willingness on the part of Generation Y to perform those same menial tasks associated with entry-level positions.

It is a mistake, however, to believe that Generation Y is against hard work. This is not a lazy generation, just one that expects immediate gratification owing to a childhood of receiving it. They won't wait for an annual review for feedback on their accomplishments. They want to do the work better and faster than their coworkers and they need to know their progress in real time. It is an expectation born of the technology age with its instant access to information and nurtured by active parenting and continual praise. Being competitive with themselves and others is in their nature, as is not trusting the system to take care of them in the long run.

This generation remembers Enron. They look to their immediate boss to take care of them in the short term, right now. It's not that they don't want a long-term relationship with a company; they want to be able to trust that whomever they work for *really* wants a long-term relationship with them. It comes down to trust. Why should they pay their dues if they can't trust the company to be there in the long run to reward their performance? That is not entitlement; that is practical and sensible and based on a skepticism born of the environment in which they came of age.

Generation Y is one of the most ethnically diverse demographic groups, with one in three not being Caucasian. In fact, it is likely that with the growing diversification of the population, the word *minority* may no longer have meaning to this and future generations. Members of Generation Y are very tolerant of the diversity around them. Great care was taken to teach them both at home and in school to be inclusive and tolerant of other races, religions, and sexual orientations. They see value in making sure that no one is left behind; this has engendered a sense of collaboration that supports their preference for being organized into teams. Working and interacting with people outside of their own ethnic group is the norm, and acceptable. It is likely that this generation will get along better with the Baby Boomer generation than Generation X did owing to this greater tolerance for the views of others.

CHARACTERISTICS OF GENERATION Y

Consider the following:

- ➤ *Tolerant.* They're racially and ethnically diverse. They're used to adapting to and being comfortable in various situations. They were taught to be inclusive and tolerant of other races, religions, and sexual orientations.

- ➤ *Collaborative.* Friendship is such a strong motivator for them that Generation Y workers will choose a job just to be with their friends. They're used to being organized into teams and making certain that no one is left behind, but prefer to do so virtually through technology rather than face-to-face.

- ➤ *Educated.* They are one of the most educated generations yet, and they love to learn. They may lack experience, but they do have confidence in their ability to learn what is necessary to get the job done.

- ➤ *Confident.* They were raised by parents who believed in the importance of self-esteem and praised them liberally, leading them to consider themselves ready to overcome challenges regardless of related knowledge, experience, or skill. It's a "can-do" attitude that can be unsettling to some. They are still young. They have a "seen it all, done it all" air about them, as is normal with young adults, but their lack of life experience means that they do not know everything yet. They are aware of this, though, and are not afraid to ask questions or challenge the status quo.

➤ *Questioning.* They believe that it is better and more time-saving to ask questions than to waste time trying to figure something out. They grew up questioning their parents and take that trait with them into the workplace. Some of this behavior has been interpreted to indicate that they don't know when to shut up. "Do it and do it now" won't work because most are in the no-fear category— not motivated by threats and punishment or firing. They are willing and unafraid to challenge the status quo.

➤ *Interdependent.* They learned to be interdependent on family, friends, and teachers to fulfill the needs caused by divorce, day care, single parents, and latchkey parenting, and often used technology to accomplish that. Unlike their predecessors, Generation X, these are not latchkey kids, forced to be independent and using technology as an escape from that reality. These kids know that their parents are behind them, and rely on them for personal and financial support even into adulthood.

➤ *Civic minded.* They were taught to think in terms of the greater good. They have a high rate of volunteerism.

➤ *Impatient.* They are addicted to change and were raised in a world dominated by technology and instant gratification. Waiting is a waste of time to these multitaskers.

➤ *Blunt and expressive.* Self-expression is favored over self-control. It's critical to them to make personal statements about themselves with their image; making their point is most important. They believe in their own worth and value enough that they're not shy about trying to change the companies they work for.

➤ *Skeptical.* They don't expect to stay in a job or even a career for too long—they're skeptical when it comes to such concepts as employee loyalty. They don't like to stay too long on any one assignment, either. This is a generation of multitaskers capable of answering e-mail on BlackBerrys while talking on cell phones while surfing the Internet.

WHAT DOES THIS MEAN FOR LEADERS?

This may be the most high-maintenance workforce in history, but it also has the potential to be the most high-performing if leaders take the time to give them what they need. It comes down to how ready they are to perform the tasks you give them. Consider it a blessing that Generation Yers want to do everything better and faster and they are confident in their ability to do so. You can't teach that kind of willingness, and it can be difficult to inspire. What they need is knowledge, experience, and the chance to practice their skills. These are things that can be taught.

As a leader, you need to:

> ➤ *Encourage their values.* Find ways to show appreciation for their individuality and let them be expressive, even if it seems a little silly. It will keep them around. Allow them to have input into the decision-making process when you can. They want to be heard and respected. They want to work with friends and have a little fun.

> ➤ *Be flexible.* The busiest generation ever isn't going to give up its activities just because of a job. Many feel that as long as they get the work done, when they come in and when they leave should be up to them. It takes time to come to find that middle ground where both parties feel fairly treated. Give what you can when you can as long as performance doesn't suffer and they do get the job done. More important, have valid reasons when you can't be flexible. "Because I say so" won't cut it with Generation Y.

> ➤ *Praise them when they earn it, when they meet expectations, and not before.* If you offer too much praise too soon, it loses its motivational effect and makes Generation Yers feel like they are performing to an acceptable standard when they aren't.

> ➤ *Train them.* This is the most education-oriented generation in history. If you want a job well done, tell them how to do it, give them the tools and resources to do it, but don't forget to also share why. They *need* that.

> ➤ *Mentor them.* They want to add to your company, not own it. Do not be afraid to give feedback, positive or negative. Keep it about performance. Be honest and timely. Earn their respect.

➤ *Make their work valid.* Don't just give orders; give the reasoning behind your requests. If you want them to do something, tell them why in a way that lets them know the importance of the task to the company. If they ask why, try not to get frustrated or take it as a challenge to your authority. If you start believing that they don't know when to shut up, you may resort to a "Do it and do it now" leadership style. This won't work, because Generation Yers reside in the no-fear zone—most aren't motivated by threats and punishment or firing because they have parental safety nets.

➤ *Provide full disclosure.* Generation Y values fairness and ethical behavior, while also being skeptical. If they feel that you are not being truthful, they will not be satisfied. That is no way to earn loyalty.

➤ *Provide access to technology.* It's not about having the newest and best technology but about having the *right* technology. Capitalize on their expertise and involve them in the process of choosing and implementing technology. This creates a sense of ownership in them that can foster not only their respect, but also their loyalty.

Generation Yers feel empowered as a result of overindulgent parents. They have a sense of security and are optimistic about the future in a very practical way. They expect a workplace that is challenging, collaborative, creative, fun, and financially rewarding, and they expect pay commensurate with what they are doing, not promises that may or may not come true.

On the other hand, there is a whole group of Generation Yers coming of age separate from the experience so far discussed. Sixteen percent grew up or are currently being raised in poverty. The schism, termed the "digital divide," is about technology, which has had a profound impact on the personality of Generation Yers. Never has the gap between the haves and have-nots been so great. It is entirely possible that this will result in a generational subculture that has yet to be defined and certainly has the potential to have an impact on leadership.

ABOUT THE AUTHOR

Paul Hersey is an internationally renowned behavioral scientist, recognized by business leaders around the world as one of the outstanding authorities on training and human resource development. His research at the Center for Leadership Studies led to the development of the Situational Leadership Model. This approach to leadership has been used to train more than 14 million managers, including those in some of the most well-known Fortune 500 companies. The model reminds us that it is not enough to describe your leadership style or communicate your intentions. A Situational Leader assesses the performance of others and takes responsibility for making things happen.

Founder and Chairman of the Board of the Center for Leadership Studies, Dr. Hersey's current passion resides with online training. For more about Dr. Hersey and the Center for Leadership Studies, go to www.situational.com.

Facilitating Change

➤ The Leader's Role

CHAPTER 15

What Is an Effective Leader?
The Leadership Code and Leadership Brand

> **Norm Smallwood and Dave Ulrich**

If you Google the word *leader,* you get more than 300 million hits. On Amazon, there are 480,881 books today whose topics have to do with leaders. It doesn't help to go to Wikipedia to get a clearer definition because, right off the bat, 11 different types of leaders are named, from bureaucratic to transformational to laissez-faire. In the field of leadership there are as many opinions as there are writers, and there is also a lack of common language and tools.

So it's no wonder that if you ask any roomful of leaders or potential leaders what effective leaders need to be, know, or do, you get as many answers as there are people in the room. Leaders are authentic, have judgment and emotional intelligence, practice the Seven Habits (Stephen Covey), and know the 21 Irrefutable Laws (John Maxwell). They are like Lincoln, Moses, Jack Welch, Santa Claus, Mother Teresa, Jesus, Mohammed, and Attila the Hun. So with all of this information, what does it really mean to be an effective leader and why are we writing yet another chapter on the topic?

We believe it is time to bring together decades of theorizing about leadership: we need to simplify and synthesize rather than generate more complexity and confusion. Faced with the incredible volume of information about leadership, we (along with Kate Sweetman, our colleague and coauthor of our most recent book, *The Leadership*

Code: 5 Rules to Lead By) turned to recognized experts in the field who had already spent years sifting through the evidence and developing their own theories. These "thought leaders" had each published a theory of leadership based on a long history of empirical research on effective leadership. Collectively, they have written over 50 books on leadership and performed well over 2 million leadership 360-degree feedback assessments.[1]

In our discussions with them, we focused on two simple but elusive questions:

1. What percentage of effective leadership is basically the same? Are there some common rules that any leader anywhere must master? Is there a recognizable leadership code?

2. If there are common rules that all leaders must master, what are they?

To the first question, responses from the experts were varied, estimating that somewhere in the range of 50 to 85 percent of leadership characteristics are shared across all effective leaders. The range is fairly broad, to be sure, but consistent. As one of our interviewees put it, "I think . . . that 85 percent of the competencies in various competency models appear to be the same. I think we have a relatively good handle on the necessary competencies for a leader to possess in order to be effective." Then the expert added something of equally great significance: "But there are some other variables that competency models do not account for. [These] include . . . the leader's personal situation (family pressures, economics, competition, social, etc.); internal influences, such as health, energy, vitality, resilience; the intensity of effort the individual is willing to put forth; ambition and drive, willingness to sacrifice."

THE LEADERSHIP CODE

From the body of interviews we conducted, we concluded that 60 to 70 percent of leadership effectiveness would be revealed in a code—if we could crack it! Synthesizing the data, the interviews, and our own research and experience, we emerged with a framework that we simply call the Leadership Code.

An analogy guided our thinking. How different is a luxury Lexus sedan from a Chrysler minivan? If you are like most people, you likely view the two vehicles as very different from each other, perhaps even opposites. The

Lexus appeals to people interested in comfort and prestige, while the mini-van is a perfect vehicle for an active family on a budget. You may love to drive either one and not want to be caught dead in the other, believing them to be different species.

But are they really? Beneath the obvious external characteristics, they share more in common than they differ. First, they are both forms of individual (versus mass) transportation. They both get you where you need to go. They each do that by sharing an important set of core elements: wheels, engine, drive train, crankshaft, brakes, alternator, and battery. In fact, when you add it up, the degree to which any two cars share fundamental similarities is much greater than their differences.

As we listened to leadership experts, we felt that the same logic would apply. Does an effective leader at Wal-Mart in any way resemble an effective leader at Virgin Airlines? Does an effective leader in a bootstrapping nongovernmental organization in any way resemble one at the famously bureaucratic United Nations? Does an effective leader in an emerging market resemble one in a mature market? Does an effective leader in organized crime in any way resemble one in organized religion? Does an effective leader in a Swiss pharmaceutical company share any underlying characteristics with an effective leader at Google?

In an effort to create a useful visual, we have mapped out two dimensions (time and focus) and placed what we call "personal proficiency" (self-management) at the center as an underlying support for the other two. Figure 15.1 synthesizes the Leadership Code and captures the five rules of leadership that make up leadership DNA.

The Five Rules of Leadership

1. *Shape the future.* This rule is embodied in the *strategist* dimension of the leader. Strategists answer the question, "Where are we going?" and they make sure that those around them understand the direction as well. They figure out where the organization needs to go to succeed; they test these ideas pragmatically against current resources (money, people, organizational capabilities); and they work with others to figure out how to get from the present to the desired future. Strategists have a vision about the future and are able to position their organizations to create and respond to that future. The rules for strategists are about creating, defining, and delivering principles of what can be.

Figure 15.1 The Leadership Code

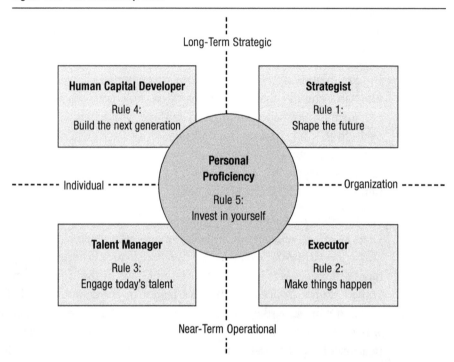

2. *Make things happen.* Turn what you know into what you do.
   The *executor* dimension of the leader focuses on the question,
   "How will we make sure we get to where we are going?"
   Executors translate strategy into action and put the systems in
   place for others to do the same. Executors understand how to make
   change happy, assign accountability, know which key decisions to
   take and which to delegate, and make sure that teams work well
   together. They keep promises to multiple stakeholders. The rules
   for executors revolve around discipline for getting things done and
   the technical expertise to get the right things done right.

3. *Engage today's talent.* Leaders who optimize talent answer the
   question, "Who goes with us on our business journey?" *Talent
   managers* know how to identify, build, and engage talent to get
   results now. They identify what skills are required, draw talent
   to their organizations, engage these people, communicate
   extensively, and ensure that employees turn in their best efforts.
   Talent managers generate intense personal, professional, and
   organizational loyalty. The rules for talent managers center on res-

olutions that help people develop themselves for the good of the organization.

4. *Build the next generation.* Leaders who are *human capital developers* answer the question, "Who stays and sustains the organization for the next generation?" Talent managers ensure shorter-term results through people, while human capital developers ensure that the organization has the longer-term competencies required for future strategic success; they ensure that the organization will outlive any single individual. Just as good parents invest in helping their children succeed, human capital developers help future leaders be successful. Throughout the organization, they build a workforce plan focused on future talent, understand how to develop that talent, and help employees see their future careers within the company. Human capital developers install rules that demonstrate a pledge to building the next generation of talent.

5. *Invest in yourself.* At the heart of the Leadership Code—literally and figuratively—is *personal proficiency.* Effective leaders cannot be reduced to what they know or what they do. Who they are as human beings has everything to do with how much they can accomplish with and through other people.

    Leaders are learners: from success, failure, assignments, books, classes, people, and life itself. Passionate about their beliefs and interests, they expend enormous personal energy on and give great attention to whatever matters to them. Effective leaders inspire loyalty and goodwill in others because they themselves act with integrity and trust. Decisive and impassioned, they are capable of bold and courageous moves. Confident in their ability to deal with situations as they arise, they can tolerate ambiguity.

Over the last few years that we have worked with these five rules of leadership, we have come to some summary observations:

> ➤ *All leaders must excel at personal proficiency.* Without the foundation of trust and credibility, you cannot ask others to follow you. While individuals may have different styles (introvert/extrovert, intuitive/sensing, etc.), an individual leader must be seen as having personal proficiency to engage followers. This is probably the toughest of the five domains to train and some individuals are naturally more capable than others.

➤ *All leaders must have one towering strength.* Most successful
leaders assume at least one of the four roles in which they excel
and most are personally predisposed to one of the four areas.
These are the signature strengths of your leaders.

➤ *Each leader must be at least average in his or her "weaker"
leadership domains.* It is possible to train someone to learn how
to be strategic, execute, manage talent, and develop future talent.
There are behaviors and skills in each domain that can be
identified, developed, and mastered.

➤ *Leaders must be able to grow.* The higher up the organization that
the leader rises, the more he or she needs to develop excellence
in more than one of the four domains.

WHAT ELSE IS NEEDED? THE LEADERSHIP BRAND

We describe the Leadership Code as a synthesis of what it takes to be an
effective leader. According to our thought leaders, it also explains about 60
to 70 percent of the leadership puzzle. So, what's the other 30 to 40 percent?

Think of giving Richard Branson, Chairman of the Virgin Group, and Jeff
Immelt, CEO of General Electric (GE), a Leadership Code 360-degree feedback assessment. We bet that both would score very high! Both are strong
strategists; they both know how to execute and to get their ideas implemented by others, they are both high in personal proficiency, both are talent developers, and both are concerned about the next generation of talent and act as
human capital developers. So, according to our 360, they are both effective
leaders. They have the core competencies according to the Leadership Code.
But they are also very different from one another.

In terms of personal style, Immelt tends to be more corporate looking than
Branson. He wears his hair shorter, is clean shaven, and most of the time
wears a suit and tie; we're not sure if we've ever seen the shaggy-haired
Branson in a suit, much less a tie. Branson is playful, while Immelt comes
across as conservative and businesslike. Immelt speaks in an articulate manner and Branson tends to use "colorful" language to make his points.
Branson seems more fun loving while Immelt seems more authoritative. So,
they have some differences in their style and perhaps some important other

differences as leaders. The Leadership Code 360 does not pick up what we call "leader differentiators," so what are *leader differentiators* and how are they different from the fundamentals of the Leadership Code?

In our book *Leadership Brand: Developing Customer-Focused Leaders to Drive Performance and Build Lasting Value* (Harvard Business School Press, 2007), we focused on these dual aspects of leadership and derived a simple formula, also reflected in Figure 15.2:

Leadership Code × Leadership Differentiators = Leadership Brand

Rather than derive leadership differentiators from interviews of successful and less successful leaders (a traditional approach used in most competency models), we suggest that leadership differentiators for any organization may be derived from the firm's identity, or *firm brand*. The firm brand is the way the company wants to be described by its target customers. Typically, the firm brand descriptors are the firm's customer value proposition along with how the company wants its target customers to experience that value proposition. For example, Southwest Airlines' value proposition is "low price." However, Southwest also wants its customers to experience the low-price value proposition in a different way from other low-price airline competitors—it wants Southwest customers to see it also as "on time" and "fun." These three phrases—low price, on time, and fun—are Southwest's firm brand identity in the minds of its best customers. Defining leadership from the outside in by starting with customer expectations ensures that leadership behavior inside a firm drives the customer experience.

Figure 15.2 The Leadership Brand

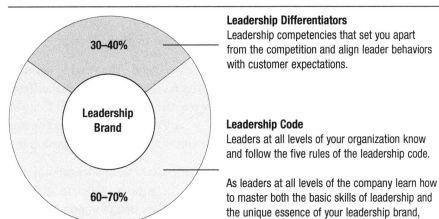

Leadership Differentiators
Leadership competencies that set you apart from the competition and align leader behaviors with customer expectations.

Leadership Code
Leaders at all levels of your organization know and follow the five rules of the leadership code.

As leaders at all levels of the company learn how to master both the basic skills of leadership and the unique essence of your leadership brand, they will establish sustainable value.

The next step is to translate these firm brand descriptors into unique leadership differentiators—that is, the unique leadership competencies that make the firm brand real to customers whenever they interact with employees of the firm. These leadership differentiators are always outside in; they bring the customer mindset to the table. In the Southwest Airlines example, the best firm leaders make sure that whenever a customer flies on Southwest, the individual has a fun experience. Founder Herb Kelleher (perhaps one of the few leaders on the planet who makes Richard Branson look conservative) personifies "fun" at Southwest. It's easy to find pictures of Herb in drag, in a tutu, or celebrating key milestones for his company in other outrageous (think "fun") ways. On down through the ranks, Southwest selects "fun" leaders, rewarding people who improvise ways to have fun with customers that customers enjoy, and celebrates their success. As a result of a culture that is reinforced by leaders at every level, most customers find flying Southwest to be a unique experience that they quite enjoy—even if they do not get a first-class seat or a free meal.

Let's revisit Immelt and Branson now. Jeff Immelt personifies GE's firm identity. He is a role model to other GE leaders about how the firm should be seen by outside stakeholders. GE's firm identity is about organic growth and innovation, with a lot of measurement and accountability going on. In contrast, Virgin's firm identity is about fun, irreverence, and challenging the status quo—and that's exactly what Richard Branson is continually doing. He lives on an island and seems to enjoy the high life in ways that the rest of us can only dream of. He personifies the leadership style of the Virgin brand.

When GE or Virgin or Southwest can develop leaders at every level who have their own style that fits within the context of the differing firm identities, the company has a leadership brand that is appreciated by customers and employees and is rewarded by financial markets as an envied capability.

At a personal level, you are your own brand. You need to define and become the leader you want to become. You need to create personal differentiators that distinguish you from others. By mastering the Leadership Code and developing differentiators, you establish your identity and personal brand, and you can align it to create or complement your organization's leadership brand.

Remember, it's not about Leadership Code versus leadership differentiators. It's about building leaders who have both. Leaders need to have the Leadership Code to be effective, and they need to know their organization's unique brand in terms of how it delivers the desired customer connection.

Effective leaders know and practice the fundamentals of both the Leadership Code and the leadership differentiators. It's not easy to be an effective leader, but achieving clarity amid the confusion about what leadership entails is a good start.

ABOUT THE AUTHORS

Norm Smallwood is cofounder of The RBL Group, a firm of well-known and broadly experienced management educators and consultants. Prior to The RBL Group, Norm cofounded the Novations Group and was managing partner from 1985 to 1999. Before that he was an HR professional at Proctor & Gamble and Esso Resources Canada Ltd.

Norm is coauthor of six books, including the recently published *The Leadership Code: 5 Rules to Lead By* (Harvard Business School Press, 2008). He has published more than 150 articles in leading journals and newspapers, and has contributed chapters to many books. He was selected as one of the top 100 Voices in Leadership by *Leadership Excellence* magazine in February 2005, 2006, and 2007.

Dave Ulrich is a Professor of Business at the University of Michigan and a partner at The RBL Group, a consulting firm focused on helping organizations and leaders deliver value. He studies how organizations build capabilities of speed, learning, collaboration, accountability, talent, and leadership through leveraging human resources. He has helped generate award-winning databases that assess alignment between strategies, human resource practices, and HR competencies.

Dave has published more than 100 articles and book chapters, as well as 15 books, including most recently *The Leadership Code: 5 Rules to Lead By* with Norm Smallwood and Kate Sweetman. He edited *Human Resource Management* from 1990 to 1999, and served on the editorial board of four other journals, on the Board of Directors for Herman Miller, and on the Board of Trustees at Southern Virginia University. He is also a Fellow in the National Academy of Human Resources. Among many other honors and awards, Dave was ranked the no. 1 most influential person in HR by *HR Magazine,* he received the Lifetime Achievement Award from American Society of Training and Development (ASTD), and he was listed in *Forbes* as one of the "World's Top 5" business coaches.

NOTE

1. These generous thought leaders included Jim Bolt (working on leadership development efforts), Richard Boyatzis (working on the competency models and resonant leadership), Jay Conger (working on leadership skills as aligned with strategy), Bob Fulmer (working on leadership skills), Bob Eichinger (working with Mike Lombardo to extend work from Center for Creative Leadership and leadership abilities), Marc Effron (working on large studies of global leaders), Marshall Goldsmith (working on global leadership skills and how to develop those skills), Gary Hamel (working on leadership as it relates to strategy), Linda Hill (working on how managers become leaders, and leadership in emerging economies), Jon Katzenbach (working on leaders from within the organization), Jim Kouzes (working on how leaders build credibility), Morgan McCall (representing Center for Creative Leadership), Barry Posner (working on how leaders build credibility), and Jack Zenger and Joe Folkman (working on how leaders deliver results and become extraordinary).

CHAPTER 16

Leading the Emotional Side of Change:
The New 21st-Century Leadership Capability

➤ Robert H. Rosen

Leaders have always had to deal with tough times, weather economic storms, and adapt to unforeseen circumstances. Change is nothing new. What *is* new is the fact that the current pace and complexity of change are outstripping many leaders' ability to reinvent themselves and their companies.

Too many leaders are blindsided by unanticipated events, falling too far behind to catch, let alone surpass, their competition. Their long-term plans are being overtaken by short-term fixes. They are facing problems that are too big and too complicated to solve with one-dimensional solutions. Their insular systems are woefully inadequate to track transactions in the global business environment. And their companies' stock values, no longer contingent on national economies alone, are rising and falling with every change in markets halfway around the world.

Let's face it: Leadership used to be about creating certainty. Now it is about leading through uncertainty. Leaders have little time to respond to one change before the next wave crashes down. The need to survive seems to have replaced the drive to thrive. Constant change has become the new norm, with anxiety its constant companion.

Unending uncertainty places everyone in a continual state of transformation. Many leaders find this unsettling or intimidating. They feel vulnerable, uneasy, or even helpless as they struggle to close gap after gap between where they are and where they want to be, between their companies' current reality and their desired future. But leading people across these gaps is the biggest—and newest—challenge of leadership today. It calls for a dramatic reassessment of leadership values and beliefs. It requires a new leadership capability.

I have had a front-row seat to observe the changing demands on leaders. Over the past two decades, I've interviewed or worked with more than 250 top business leaders, from companies such as Johnson & Johnson, Northrop Grumman, Intel, New York Life, PricewaterhouseCoopers, Boeing, and ING. From my perspective as a psychologist, entrepreneur, and CEO adviser, I've seen that the increased speed of change today requires unique leadership skills beyond those honed by leaders not that long ago.

Leaders need to master two equally important capabilities to lead change in the future. The first capability is *cognitive*. It involves clarifying the organization's vision, values, strategy, and goals to help people focus on what's important. It's all about thinking things through and selecting the most promising pathway through the changing landscape. Many leaders are good at this.

The second capability is *emotional*. It involves facing the unknown with courage and confidence, inspiring and challenging people to do their best, and mobilizing human energy. It's all about channeling anxiety into productive action while remaining responsive to the inevitable twists and turns that appear unexpectedly. This capability is the one that most leaders still need to master. Those who don't will continue to lose to the competition, or risk losing their companies, as they attempt to deal with unpredictable change after change.

Leading the emotional side of change requires the ability to embrace change and uncertainty as facts of life, to feel at home in uncharted territory. This, in turn, requires the ability to make friends with the anxiety that change creates, and use it in positive ways. It is this ability to harness and direct anxiety—to create *just enough anxiety*—that will enable today's leaders to master the emotional side of change.

What is just enough anxiety? It is the right level of anxiety—at any given moment in time—that drives people forward without causing them to resist, give up, or try to control what happens. It unleashes creativity and enables people to stretch beyond current reality into their desired future, closing the gaps that change creates—gaps between who they are and who they wish to be and between where their organizations are and where they are headed.

Just enough anxiety is the essential new tool for leading the emotional side of change. To master its use, today's leaders must *reframe* their (1) view of change and uncertainty, (2) beliefs about themselves in the world, (3) understanding and use of anxiety, and (4) perspective on key leadership qualities. Let's take a closer look at each of these reframes.

REFRAMING ONE'S VIEW OF CHANGE AND UNCERTAINTY— FROM CRISIS TO OPPORTUNITY

Change and uncertainty are constants in today's fast-paced world. Leaders who want things to stay the same or who believe constancy is a sign of success are certain to resist these facts. To them, threats to the status quo must be fought and vanquished. Yet, by being attached to the ways things are, they sabotage their ability to live with uncertainty. They end up denying reality— and forfeiting their capacity to handle change—if they become attached to pleasure and try to avoid discomfort, if they become attached to praise and try to avoid criticism, or if they become attached to getting what they want and try to avoid losing what they have. They spend too much time looking backward, longing for the ways things were, instead of accepting and exploring the terrain where they are.

The desire for stability is warranted in areas such as personal values, commitments, and spiritual beliefs. It helps keep leaders grounded in the midst of uncertainty. But craving continuous stability in all areas of their lives causes leaders to magnify or suppress their anxiety when circumstances start to change, as they always will. Only by learning to allow themselves to feel their insecurity, discomfort, and confusion can they make the most of change. Only when they acknowledge where they are can they begin to move in a new direction.

This can be a tough task to master. But, if you want to build an organization responsive to change, you must give up any notion that you can protect yourself from pain or predict the future based on the past. You must let go of your desire for permanence and accept new ideas, especially those that contradict or expand what you think you know. You must be willing to think outside the box—or to invent a new box, if necessary. This will help you reframe how you look at change and uncertainty, *from* a crisis to be avoided *to* an opportunity to learn and grow.

REFRAMING ONE'S BELIEFS ABOUT SELF IN THE WORLD—
FROM SELF-DEFEATING TO SELF-AFFIRMING

When faced with change, many leaders hold self-defeating beliefs that make it hard for them to lead the emotional side of change. Some think they have to know everything in advance, handle everything on their own, or achieve predictable results. Some believe that they have to avoid conflicting ideas to be accepted or admired, or that they will be seen as incompetent if they can't answer every question or if they make a mistake. Others believe their anxiety is a sign of weakness, rendering them powerless to act in the midst of uncertainty. These self-defeating beliefs become self-fulfilling prophecies. They determine what makes people anxious, the amount of anxiety they feel, and what they choose to do. And they lead to individual failures and the inability of organizations to navigate change.

Uncovering deep-seated self-defeating beliefs is at the heart of leading the emotional side of change. As a leader, you need to uproot and replace the beliefs that sabotage change efforts. You might, for example, need to replace the needs to be right, avoid conflict, or do everything on your own with the willingness to learn from your mistakes, use conflict to build bigger and better solutions, or collaborate with others. In this way you can reframe what you believe about yourself in the world, *from* self-defeating *to* self-affirming.

REFRAMING ONE'S UNDERSTANDING AND USE OF ANXIETY—
FROM DESTRUCTIVE TO PRODUCTIVE

For our primitive ancestors, anxiety was a lifesaver. It signaled the need to fight or flee. But 21st-century challenges are too numerous and complex to consider all anxiety as a precursor to danger, something to be avoided or overcome. There are three basic levels of anxiety: too much, too little, and just enough. It's easy to recognize leaders who operate on each level (see Table 16.1).

Leaders with *too much anxiety* are compelled to take charge. Consummate fighters, they focus their personal power on making things turn out their way. But their take-charge demeanor masks deep-seated insecurities and fears— of inadequacy, failure, or insignificance. They are frequently held hostage by their emotions—particularly anxiety, anger, sadness, and fear. Yet they wear their feelings on their sleeves. Their emotional transparency is the problem: they bring their inner chaotic energy to everyone around them.

Table 16.1 Levels of Anxiety

Too Much Anxiety	Too Little Anxiety	Just Enough Anxiety
Comes from negative thinking and emotions. It causes you to resist, attack, or avoid change to ease the pain it might produce. Too much anxiety creates discomfort, tension, and frustration.	Grounded in contentment. It is based on an unrealistic belief that all is well, and an unfounded expectation that good times will continue unabated, with no need for change or improvement. Too little anxiety leads to complacency, boredom, and stagnation.	The emotional charge that tells you you're ready to take action—your signal for learning and growth. At the organizational level, just enough anxiety unleashes human energy and creates hope and momentum.

Leaders with too much anxiety often attack change and push themselves and others through gap after gap to achieve their goals. Their preoccupation with success keeps them focused on problems often to the point of exhaustion. Some get so overwhelmed that they become unable to take action of any kind. Others keep going well beyond reason and judgment. There's no time for rest and relaxation. But, since much of their energy is negative, these leaders end up sabotaging their organization's achievements.

Leaders with *too little anxiety* strive to avoid discomfort. They are driven by one or more fears—of their own emotions, of not being successful, or of being imperfect or disliked. Lacking emotional honesty with themselves, they shy away from emotional honesty with or from others. They prefer to sweep anxiety under the rug or run away from it altogether.

Not surprisingly, leaders with too little anxiety tend to live in a bubble. It's like they are wearing a self-imposed blindfold that keeps them from having to face difficult problems and limits their ability to learn. It makes them falter in the face of adversity. These leaders stay stuck in old ways of doing things or reach for quick fixes that they think will shorten or lessen their anxiety.

But leaders who hold *just enough anxiety* within themselves are able to use that anxiety to face uncertainty, conquer change, and perform their best. They do this not only for themselves but for the people in their organizations as well. They understand that either too much anxiety or too little anxiety shuts down learning, growth, and performance, making it impossible to move from where they are to where they want to be. They know that only when the distance between "here" and "there" is big enough to make people stretch, yet small enough to be surmounted, can it lead people through change and uncertainty.

Finding the right level of anxiety to drive an organization forward is more art than science. It sits on the softer side of the leadership fence. Just enough anxiety can differ from person to person and company to company, and change with time and circumstance. Leaders who learn to monitor anxiety levels in themselves and their organizations can turn the heat up or down as required.

As a leader, you are the steward of anxiety inside your organization. You need to manage your own anxiety before you can help others manage theirs. If you display too little anxiety, people will lose their enthusiasm. Their level of engagement and productivity will decline. If you display too much anxiety, people will lose their focus. They will begin to make mistakes and bad decisions. But if you bring just enough anxiety to the table, people will feel excited, hopeful, and challenged to do their best. This will enable you to help others reframe their understanding and use of anxiety, *from* destructive *to* productive.

REFRAMING ONE'S PERSPECTIVE ON KEY LEADERSHIP QUALITIES— FROM ONE-DIMENSIONAL TO PARADOXICAL

The world is too complex for one-dimensional solutions. Even the much anticipated 2008 and 2009 bailouts of financial institutions by the governments of many countries were not sufficient, in and of themselves, to turn around volatile global markets.

Leaders limit their options and shortchange their organizations by trying to lead from a single perspective or follow a simple course of action. The best leaders, especially those who lead with just enough anxiety, exhibit seemingly opposing qualities simultaneously. They are adept at demonstrating paradoxical leadership traits that, in combination, become more powerful than either trait is on its own.

There are three sets of paradoxical traits that enable top leaders to create just enough anxiety in themselves and others: realistic optimism, constructive impatience, and confident humility. Let's look at each of these contrasting qualities.

Realistic Optimism

Telling the truth about the present while dreaming about the future signifies *realistic optimism*. It is the way to keep moving forward in a world that keeps changing. It involves living "here" and "there" simultaneously. When leaders do this, they heighten their organization's focus, instill a sense of common purpose, and create a clear mental image of success.

If you are realistic, you are neither afraid of the truth nor cynical about it. You're good at assessing the current situation and are problem-oriented, fact-based, and a great short-term thinker. You face problems and opportunities head-on and look at all sides of an issue—seeing things as they are, not as you want them to be. You know that being honest with yourself and others is an act of courage, and the only way to run a business in a world of uncertainty.

If you are optimistic, you are all about envisioning the future. You're imaginative, solution-oriented, and a great long-term thinker. You believe that tomorrow will be better than today, and that people are capable of doing more than they think they can. You see the glass half full. And you know you can refill it, even if it appears to be leaking.

TIPS FOR BEING REALISTIC AND OPTIMISTIC

> ➤ Be focused and flexible about what you want.

> ➤ Balance achieving goals with discovering them.

> ➤ Be aware and wary about what you know.

> ➤ Balance facts and figures with imagination.

> ➤ Be practical and magical in what you do.

To be both realistic and optimistic, you need to learn to live in the present *and* the future simultaneously. This will allow you to create just enough anxiety to thrive in uncertainty, while closing the gap between your current reality and desired future, for yourself and your organization. When you find the right balance between realism and optimism, you discover the secret to providing focus. With realistic optimism, your vision grounded in reality and hopeful about the future, you instill a sense of common purpose and a clear mental image of success.

Constructive Impatience

The ability to build a positive, supportive environment while instilling in people a drive for results defines *constructive impatience*. It involves learning to be comfortable with discomfort and balancing a sense of urgency with compassion and patience. When leaders do this, they foster people's hunger to get ahead and challenge them to stretch their capabilities while providing them with what they need to succeed.

If you're constructive, you are predictable and credible, honest and open. You foster participation and learning by helping people feel good about themselves, their work, and their organization. You create an environment in which it is safe to take risks and express conflicting opinions.

TIPS FOR BEING CONSTRUCTIVE AND IMPATIENT

➤ Balance compassion with a drive for results.

➤ Challenge people to perform in a supportive environment.

➤ Balance setting stretch goals with getting buy-in.

➤ Know when to move forward and when to stay put.

➤ Balance winning with win-win.

If you're impatient, you focus on performance and results. You set audacious goals to stretch people beyond their comfort zones. You see people bigger than they see themselves.

Leading with constructive impatience is a lot like pulling a rubber band. If you pull too hard, you break people's spirits. If you don't pull hard enough, you fail to maximize their potential. But if you find the right tension, amazing things happen. You engage people's hearts and minds and create just enough anxiety to stretch them to their limits—and beyond where they imagine these limits to be.

Confident Humility

The ability to lead with power and generosity at the same time is the mark of *confident humility*. It involves being sure of yourself, while openly listening and learning from others. When leaders do this, they build trust, develop productive relationships, and create high-performing teams.

Confidence is an attitude. It's about believing in yourself and your ability to master your environment. It is also about believing in the people around you. It's being sure that your organization can meet challenges head-on, solve problems, and win in the marketplace. You can't build a winning team without it.

If you are confident you exude confidence in yourself and express confidence in others. You know and share yourself, talk about your life, and are open about your fears and aspirations. You live your values personally and professionally, and you encourage others to do the same. This makes you predictable and trustworthy.

TIPS FOR BEING CONFIDENT AND HUMBLE

➤ Share your strengths and shortcomings.

➤ Listen to and learn from others.

➤ Empower people to succeed.

➤ Respect others' values.

➤ Build mutually satisfying relationships.

Being humble involves admitting that you don't know everything and not feeling like you have to. Humility is essential in today's complex world. It entails listening deeply to others and being eager to learn something new. It also involves giving of yourself in service to others—being generous with your time and attention.

If you are humble, you are generous in your compassionate and respectful attitude toward others and in your gentle and accepting attitudes toward yourself. You realize that nobody can have all the answers and that people need each other to thrive in a world of change. You use humility to build mutually rewarding relationships that are catalysts for success. This can make your life more fulfilling and your organization more competitive.

Confident humility is born from a positive self-image and compassionate respect for others. It grows with the development of personal power and generosity of spirit. And it blossoms with lifelong learning, strong values, and a desire to share power and serve others. Leading with confident humility helps you take bold actions without becoming arrogant and to maintain a healthy ego without feeling self-important. You feel at ease with your own power. You also readily share power and are adept at empowering others.

* * *

These four reframes enable great leaders to create just enough anxiety within themselves and the people around them. With just enough anxiety, individuals and organizations can survive, and even thrive, in the midst of uncertainty.

Just imagine how the economic roller-coaster ride of the past couple years might have been different if mortgage lenders, mortgage holders, and the Securities and Exchange Commission had anticipated and planned for change. If they had not believed that the bubble would never burst. Or if Bear Stearns, Lehman Brothers, and AIG executives had identified and reframed their beliefs that everything would work itself out without any efforts on their parts. Or if stock traders had understood and used their anxiety in productive ways and we, as a people, had been more comfortable with a little discomfort. What if leaders at all levels of business and government had told the truth about what was happening, admitting the probable consequences of their actions, while painting a vivid picture of a positive future; had created a safe environment for people and organizations to stretch into new and better versions of themselves; and had acted with confidence while inviting and empowering others to participate in solutions that benefited all parties?

To the leaders who did these things, we should be grateful. They are the ones whose companies are surviving and who helped, or are helping, the global economy regain its balance. They show us that it's possible to weather even perfect economic storms with confidence, courage, and commitment.

Seasoned veterans of leading the cognitive side of change, they have also mastered the new 21st-century leadership capability. They see change as opportunity; hold self-affirming beliefs about themselves in the world; use anxiety as a productive and positive force in their lives and their organizations; and willingly embody paradoxical leadership qualities—simultaneously realistic and optimistic, constructive and impatient, and confident and humble. These just-enough-anxiety leaders are exceptional role models for leading the emotional side of change.

ABOUT THE AUTHOR

Robert H. Rosen is an internationally recognized psychologist, best-selling author, researcher, and CEO adviser to world-class companies. He is the founder, Chairman, and CEO of Healthy Companies International (HCI), a Washington, D.C.–based research, education, and consulting firm whose mission is to partner with CEOs and executive teams in building healthy, high-performing organizations. HCI supports and advises CEOs on large-scale transformational change and delivers hundreds of leadership and performance tools, via the Internet, around the world.

Bob is the author of *Global Literacies: Lessons on Business Leadership and National Cultures* (Simon & Schuster, 2000); *Leading People: Transforming Business from the Inside Out* (Viking, 1996); *The Healthy Company: Eight Strategies to Develop People, Productivity, and Profits* (Putnam, 1991); and *Just Enough Anxiety: The Hidden Driver of Business Success* (Portfolio/Penguin, 2008). He is the coauthor of *The Catalyst: How YOU Can Become an Extraordinary Growth Leader* (Crown Business, 2009). For more information visit www.healthycompanies.com and www.justenoughanxiety.com.

CHAPTER 17

Adjusting the Political Temperature of Your Team

➤ Gary Ranker and Colin Gautrey

Political activity—the behaviors that people use as they seek to influence others—is inevitable among any group of human beings. The desire to influence is built into the human psyche. At its most basic level, we all have a need to be accepted by those around us. As we mature and start our careers, the desire grows with our ambitions, vision, and plans for success.

The extent to which this political activity is positive or negative depends on the individual. Some people are so focused on their own gain that they will stop at nothing to get what they want. Others have more altruistic dispositions, and once their basic needs have been met, they are able to work for the good of the organization. They recognize and respect the needs and desires of those around them.

When people work together they bring with them their unique mix of beliefs, attitudes, and motivations. People with high levels of motivation for success—either for their own gain or for that of the organization—will put a great deal of energy and effort into their political activity. The intensity, or the *temperature,* of the political activity will vary depending on the strength of motivation expressed by each individual in the team. It can also be affected by the team leader.

The challenges that arise from the current business climate make it essential that political temperature be heightened so that organizations can stretch their thinking, develop new innovative strategies, and implement plans swiftly. The teams that succeed will feature vigorous internal competition during the strategy-formulation phase. This will maximize the prospect that only the best will survive—that is, the ideas that are most likely to help the organization thrive. Once the decisions have been made, the team members will need to pull together so that they can execute the strategy rapidly. The rules of the game need to change, so that it becomes a team competing together against external competition. At this stage, the political temperature needs to be reduced to allow the organization to benefit fully from the implementation.

The ability to adjust the temperature of political activity of a team is a critical yet neglected leadership task. Usually this is left to chance or the natural inclinations of the leader. A leader who thrives on competition will tend to foster that trait in his or her team; the opposite will also be true. The danger is that these natural inclinations may not suit the situation that the team is facing. The risks associated with ignoring this dynamic can be huge—and the benefits of its prudent consideration immense.

Our purpose here is to explore the risks and benefits of high and low political temperatures. This will help you to understand more about where your team is at the moment and will start to provide ideas about the temperature level required for your team's situation. We will then conclude with some ideas about how you can start to adjust the temperature to suit the context. Rather than leaving it to chance, your conscious management of the political activity within the team can yield significant bottom-line benefits. Our suggestions will stimulate your ideas about the practical steps you can start to take immediately to usher in a more productive team dynamic.

HIGH POLITICAL TEMPERATURE BENEFITS

When the temperature is high, the internal challenge is tough and relentless. Team members compete to find the winning idea. The creative tension this causes will yield increased innovation and a radical search for new strategies. With chaotic environmental changes, organizations need strong and robust strategies in order to win. They need to look around every corner as they attempt to predict which will succeed and which will fail. Internal competition helps bring these ideas forward.

Once the great ideas emerge, they will be subjected to vigorous inspection. The flaws will be quickly discovered, the downsides and drawbacks brought out into the open. This will give the team a great opportunity to pressure-test proposals and allow the organization to overcome faults and improve strategy still more. Healthy internal competition will give the team the best opportunity to make the right choice. The prize to be gained from high temperature is increased performance. Great results are always needed, but now more than ever.

When the decisions have been made, the chances are quite high that the key advocates will already be in a strong position to drive forward their advantage. They will have already set the wheels in motion to capitalize on their success, making their moves to secure the territory gained. For the organization, this provides a welcome boost to the initial implementation of the new strategy.

HIGH POLITICAL TEMPERATURE RISKS

Despite its benefits, the high temperature needs to be monitored closely. Because we each play the game based on our own set of beliefs and standards, leadership needs to take care of the pitfalls that this competition can produce—and there are many!

If the internal competition is set up to win, there are going to be losers along the way. This can encourage unscrupulous behaviors that sometimes breach ethics or the law. Those hell-bent on success may stop at nothing to win. Their actions could include sabotage, threats, and even blackmail, all designed to hide the vulnerability inherent in their ideas and avoid the rational debate that could expose those weaknesses.

As the embattled team members take stock, they may become increasingly defensive of the territory they hold. At times they will decide that if the prospects for winning are remote, better to at least save some ground and protect their own jobs and turf. All of this tends to lead to silo mentality and erosion of trust. The right ideas can win only if trust and appropriate honest debate are allowed.

Other side effects of high levels of political temperature include rising levels of fear and stress—perhaps even derailment. There is also a high risk of duplication and failure to synthesize implementation plans. This leads to unnecessary costs that erode the financial benefits of the winning strategies.

High political temperatures must be managed carefully to avoid excesses, maintain integrity, and avoid harmful side effects.

LOW POLITICAL TEMPERATURE BENEFITS

When the temperature is low, the team works well together. Open and honest dialogue flourishes. Individuals are sympathetic to the positions of their peers and seek to harmonize their plans so that they can all win together. In effect, they are all playing for the same team and being selfless in their pursuit of organizational goals.

With everyone invested in the same strategy and direction, the team's attention is focused; team members are working hard to implement the chosen course and make sure that the expected performance is delivered. The low level of conflict that this culture exhibits will minimize the potential for disruption, stress, and derailment. At best, the team will help those who are struggling to perform and will share the results.

From the organization's perspective, performance will be robust because everyone is working together. The combined energy, enthusiasm, and motivation can be harnessed. Resource utilization will be optimized because everyone knows the what, the why, and the how. This clarity also offers a strong and durable approach to implementation.

LOW POLITICAL TEMPERATURE RISKS

When the temperature is low, organizational pace suffers. Because of the desire for consensus and buy-in, change and implementation could be dogged by committees. Likely to be large and cumbersome, these committees may take far too long to make decisions, owing to the number of people involved and the time it takes to arrange meetings. Add to this the potential for individuals' vetoing the decisions, and the delays can become extreme.

There is also a significant risk of innovation being stifled. When someone has a great idea, the individual may have to jump through too many hoops to gain acceptance by the team. As with any good idea, the potential for disrupting a well-ordered and disciplined organization could be too great for anyone to risk saying yes. There are also well-documented concepts such as "risky shift" and "groupthink" to be mindful of.

Overall, the negative effects of low temperatures cause a drag on organizational performance. During certain phases, this can be fatal.

CHOOSING THE TEMPERATURE

In many regions of the world, temperature changes with the seasons. So, too, does the political temperature in organizational life. At certain times during the economic cycle or competitive market phases, particular temperatures are optimal for success. Being able to determine the correct temperature as a leader will help you to maximize performance and minimize risk as you take the team and the organization forward.

Every situation is unique, but the following will help you to choose which temperature is appropriate for your team at a particular time.

High Political Temperatures Are Beneficial When:

➤ Organizational performance is sliding.

➤ A significant strategic challenge or change emerges.

➤ New and strong external competition threatens.

➤ Credit crunches and similar chaos exist in the marketplace.

➤ Markets are fast paced and change rapidly.

➤ Innovation need is high.

➤ Ideas for strategic direction are diverse.

Low Temperatures Can Be Great When:

➤ Clear strategic decisions have been made.

➤ Successful implementation is critical to survival.

➤ Cost management is the top priority.

➤ An organizational crisis has arisen.

➤ Significant leadership changes are under way.

➤ Organizational performance is growing strongly.

➤ Market conditions are stable.

ADJUSTING THE TEMPERATURE

If, as a leader, you recognize that the temperature needs to change, you need to take consistent action over a period of time. You need to integrate the steps into the systems that exist in the organization and also instill those measures in other leaders who can have an impact. In particular, you must be ready and willing to change your behaviors and habits to succeed.

The temperature controls need active management. Monitoring the results of your actions will give you valuable insights that you can use to make further adjustments. Here are some suggestions to stimulate your own thoughts on how best to adjust the political temperature of your team.

Turning the Temperature Up

➤ Make individual goals public.

➤ Regularly review goals in team meetings.

➤ Focus on end results rather than actions.

➤ Speculate openly about who will hit his or her goals.

➤ Ask individuals how they think they are performing compared to their peers.

➤ Ask individuals how they think others are doing.

➤ Introduce "winning," "being the best," and "survival of the fittest" phrases into your dialogue.

➤ Review your reward structure; focus on individual rather than team performance.

➤ Make success public and failure noticeable.

➤ Review succession plans and let people know you're doing that.

➤ Be clear about decision criteria for succession plans—and make them stretch!

➤ Tell people frankly that they will get ahead by outperforming others.

➤ Hold small and frequent ad hoc meetings where decisions get made.

Turning the Temperature Down

- ➤ Encourage teamwork.

- ➤ Ask people how their plans fit with others' plans.

- ➤ Establish quorum decisions at meetings.

- ➤ Remove veto power.

- ➤ Have management reports include impact assessments on others.

- ➤ Insist that key stakeholders sign off on proposals.

- ➤ Incorporate "working together" and "winning team" terms into your dialogue.

- ➤ Build an external succession plan.

- ➤ Schedule regular team social events.

- ➤ Reward collaboration and teamwork.

- ➤ In meetings, focus on team goals rather than individual goals.

- ➤ Design projects that require the team to work together.

As you consider these ideas, pay careful attention to what will work in your organizational culture. Making a sudden shift in the temperature is unlikely to work; it is far better to begin making gradual changes as you turn the heat up or down. Some of these suggestions may also challenge your natural style and approach; you need to consider how well you may be able to implement the idea of adjusting the temperature and perhaps consider getting some coaching to help you become more comfortable with this new skill.

The Bottom Line

Teams vary in their political intensity as a result of a wide variety of factors, from the leader's personality to the climatic conditions in which the team operates. In addition, there are so many dynamics affecting temperature that it varies over time—it is not static. Some teams are highly competitive by nature; others hold collaboration as a central value. Both can be good news for an organization's performance, but only if the culture is appropriate to the context in which the team must deliver.

It is an important aspect of a leader's role to monitor and manage the political temperature of his or her team. Making sure that the right level of internal competition and/or collaboration exists is a delicate task and not for the fainthearted. As you start to pull the levers to adjust the temperature, you will get a mixture of positive and negative responses. That is natural because you are changing the rules of engagement for your team. There will be some who will benefit and some who will find it harder. Staying attentive to these reactions and managing the risks are critical to success.

You will also have to be careful not to move to the extremes. A highly competitive culture can quickly turn into bitter rivalry that harms not only the organization but also those working there. At the other extreme, dropping the temperature too low can cause the organization to freeze. There will also be a time lag between your actions and when the full effect is felt, so use caution as you explore this new dimension of leadership.

Diligent and careful action on the temperature controls can usher in a new phase of corporate performance. It can help you address the needs of the team and the organization more appropriately in your role as a leader. You will become a far more effective and versatile leader with greater results!

ABOUT THE AUTHORS

Gary Ranker is cited by *Forbes* as one of the top five executive coaches. *Financial Times* nominated him as one of "50 Global Thought Leaders." Dr. Ranker specializes in coaching senior executives and lecturing about how to succeed in cultures where corporate politics is a major factor. Having worked and lived on four continents, Gary brings a valuable global mindset to his coaching relationships and seminars. He is the coauthor of *Political Dilemmas at Work*. Dr. Ranker can be reached at www.garyranker.com and gary@garyranker.com.

Colin Gautrey is an internationally recognized thought leader in the practical use of power and influence in the workplace. He is coauthor of *21 Dirty Tricks at Work* and *Political Dilemmas at Work* and has written many articles and chapters in books. Colin works as a coach and facilitator with executives, teams, and leading business schools in various countries around the globe. His focus is helping people to become more influential and achieve greater success. Contact Colin at www.siccg.com and colin@siccg.com.

CHAPTER 18

Making Successful Transitions: The Leader's Perspective

> Patricia Wheeler

Job security in the executive suite may be more tenuous than ever. The rate at which executives move or are moved from one organization to another, and the frequency at which they transition from one role to another inside the organization, are at an all-time high. According to a study by Booz Allen Hamilton in 2007, global CEO turnover was at roughly 15 percent—the highest it had been since 1997.[1] In January 2009, amid the global economic crisis, this had not changed. Challenger Gray & Christmas, a Chicago-based executive recruitment firm, estimates that 1,484 CEOs transited out of their jobs in 2008. This is the equivalent of five CEO transitions every business day.[2]

Yet, even as the number of executive transitions and the complexity of executive roles increases, the chances of failure appear to be increasing as well. Studies point to 40 percent of new leaders failing within the first 18 months.[3] Aon Consulting reports a 50 percent chance that an executive will quit or be fired within his or her first three years.[4] A new study reports that almost one in three senior-level executives coming aboard from other organizations will fail by the two-year mark; this number is one in five for corporate leaders who are promoted from within the company.[5]

Failed transitions mean significant loss of opportunities for the leaders and are quite costly to organizations. Therefore, for the benefit of both the leaders *and* the organizations, a significant part of leading in the new world of business is learning how to maximize success when transitioning to new roles.

THE NEW LEADER

Leaders today face high expectations that go beyond being an expert in one primary line of business, one principal role, or one segment of the organization. In an environment of mergers, acquisitions, divestments, and sell-offs, it is not unusual for the organizational context to change quickly during the leader's tenure, requiring the leader to (1) come up to speed quickly and (2) broaden his or her sphere of influence and experience across the organization in order to be successful. In addition, with the increasing level of globalization and movement into new markets, such as Brazil, Russia, India, and China (BRIC), organizations are increasingly moving their U.S.-based talent to expatriate assignments, requiring leaders to have a global perspective and broader experience across geographical areas. And finally, the amount of information leaders have to manage is staggering as the rate of technology hits warp speed. Leaders in new roles have to assimilate and integrate enormous amounts of information. And, even the most seasoned executives require time to assimilate and process so much information.

THE EXECUTIVE TRANSITIONS SURVEY: TRENDS AND IMPLICATIONS

In 2007 and 2008, the Institute of Executive Development and Alexcel Group conducted a market study to examine transitions that the seniormost leaders (those executives in the top 5 percent of their organizations) make, as well as the roadblocks they encounter as they attempt to successfully transition into new roles. Participants included approximately 150 executives and talent professionals from more than 100 organizations in 12 countries and 21 industries. Participants took an online survey consisting of 18 multiple-choice questions, plus a number of deep-dive interviews, specifically on the subject of internal and external transitions, how many fail, and why they fail. *Failure* was defined as when the leader failed to meet his or her organization's criteria for success by the two-year mark. This did not mean that all leaders who were considered "failing" were fired or moved out of their roles—just that they had not met expectations by the two-year mark as defined by their organizations.

What is notable about the Executive Transitions Survey is that it targeted only transitions of the top 5 percent of an organization's leaders. Additionally, we sought to differentiate between the failure rate of externally hired senior leaders and leaders taking new senior roles within their existing organization.

We found that 30 percent of senior executive external hires failed to meet their organization's criteria for successful performance within two years. In other words, almost one in three externally recruited and hired senior leaders failed. Our numbers are consistent with and perhaps even better than those of some other studies, particularly those that focused on the entire executive population, not just those at the top.

What was even more noteworthy was our finding that 21 percent of internally transitioning senior leaders failed to meet their organization's criteria for successful performance. Worded differently this means that 1 in 5 senior leaders taking on new roles within their existing organization failed. This is the statistic that brings looks of surprise and dismay to the faces of leaders and talent management professionals as we share our results.

These findings squelch the assumption that what has made a leader successful in one role in the organization will continue to drive his or her success in the next role. In fact, senior leaders transitioning within their own organizations must prepare themselves to expect significant obstacles to success.

Why did so many of the senior-most leaders, internal and external, fail to make successful transitions? The top two reasons for executive failure cited by the organizations we surveyed were lack of interpersonal skills and lack of personal skills. (Each survey respondent could choose to cite more than one cause of executive failure within his or her organization.) Only 15 percent of respondents reported that leaders within their organization failed owing to technical capabilities or business skills, whereas a significant percentage, 68 percent, reported that leaders within their organization failed owing to interpersonal leadership skills and 45 percent reported that failure occurred owing to poor personal skills, including the leader's need for better focus and self-management (see Figure 18.1). The implications for leaders who wish to be successful in new roles are clear: obstacles to success in new roles are more often connected to what many organizations consider "soft" skills—those that focus on the quality and quantity of relationships the leader crafts and maintains.

Figure 18.1 Reasons Cited for Senior Leader Failure

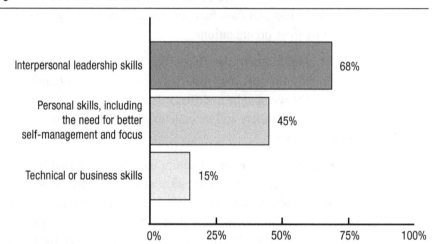

Now let's consider how long it takes senior leaders to reach full productivity in their new roles. Current theory tends to focus on creating 90- to 100-day action plans; however, our results suggest that the length of time to full productivity, particularly when a new leader comes from another organization, is considerably longer. Within our sample, fewer than 1 in 3 organizations said that senior leaders transitioning from within reached full productivity within 90 days, and fewer than 1 in 10 externally transitioning leaders were fully productive by this time. For external transitions, it appears to take six to nine months for new leaders to reach full productivity; for internal transitions, between three and six months. Leaders must be clear about keeping a transition plan in action for at least six months to maximize the chances of success (see Figure 18.2).

How do organizations help transitioning leaders? There is an increasing emphasis on onboarding programs (perhaps we reference Aberdeen research here), but we know that the content and rigor of new leader assimilation and onboarding programs vary from organization to organization. Table 18.1 lists the resources survey respondent organizations currently provide to transitioning executives, and which resources the organizations deem to be effective in maximizing senior leader success.

In interviews with talent management professionals, we hear that many programs that they deploy beneath their onboarding umbrella have to do with familiarizing transitioning leaders with policies, procedures, and paperwork and are clearly more positioned toward external hires. The relative lack of effectiveness of preemployment activities and executive orientations suggests

Figure 18.2 Learning Curve: Internal Transfers vs. External Hires
"How many months does it take in your organization for a senior executive in a new role to reach full productivity?"

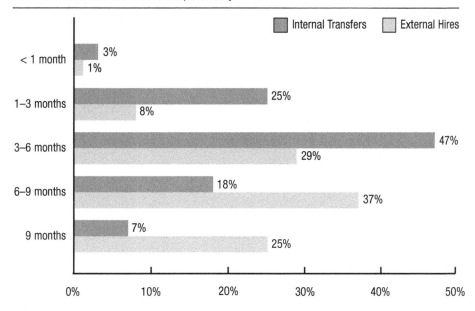

Source: Alexcel Group and the Institute of Executive Development, 2008.

Table 18.1 Type and Effectiveness of Organizational Support

Resources Provided	Internal		External	
	What's Done	What Works	What's Done	What Works
Preemployment activities	n/a	n/a	26%	8%
Orientations with other new executives	22%	11%	46%	19%
Mentoring/informal "buddy" networks	47%	30%	48%	46%
Executive coaching	33%	43%	28%	36%
Customized assimilation plans	33%	38%	33%	38%

that these efforts are necessary but not sufficiently robust to drive success. Creating mentoring relationships and informal networks with other executives were the support modalities that were perceived as most effective in assisting new senior external hires. Customized assimilation plans and executive coaching were also seen as helpful.

The responses tell a different story for internally transitioning leaders. The supports perceived as most helpful to internally transitioning leaders were executive coaching and the creation of a customized assimilation plan. This speaks to how important it is for leaders to create a network of people who will help them differentiate the demands and needs of their old roles from those of their new roles.

FIVE KEY SKILLS FOR MAKING SUCCESSFUL TRANSITIONS

Unsuccessful transitions in the executive suite tend to occur most frequently due to the lack of critical interpersonal and personal skills that lead to success in senior positions. That being the case, what can leaders do to ensure that their transition is successful? Leaders must clearly take responsibility for the success of their own transitions, no matter what support the organization does or does not offer. Following are five critical skills that focus on interpersonal and personal development. Practicing these skills will help position leaders for successful transitions.

1. Identify and upgrade your personal skills.

2. Know and manage your derailers.

3. Gather intelligence.

4. Practice Feed*Forward*.

5. Work your plan.

Identify and Upgrade Your Personal Skills

It is essential to understand that the *person* is the basic engine of how work gets done. We all have "default settings": those styles and patterns that we revert to when we're not paying attention to our behavior. To lead successfully, you should know your "default setting." Ask yourself the following question: How would I and others describe my leadership style? Because different interpersonal skills will be needed in the many different roles you will undertake in your career, self-knowledge is critical to (1) deciding when and how to make a transition and (2) ensuring the success of that transition. For instance, if you are a creative, rock-the-boat-and-make-waves type of leader, and you are asked to take on the position of CEO in a company known for its by-the-numbers approach, you may have a significant challenge on your hands. As a matter of fact, failure is a distinct possibility unless you understand your own style and how it interacts with the styles of other stakeholders and then craft an ongoing dialogue to manage the differences and disagreements that will occur. Ask yourself: How often do I pause and reflect on my behavior and its consequences?

CASE STUDY
EXTERNAL TRANSITION (LIN)

Lin was hired in her first vice president role within a Fortune 500 consumer products company. She was charged with streamlining processes and increasing performance within their North American business. One of her key tasks was to turn around an underperforming team in an "old" established culture of loyalty, in which less productive and talented workers had for years been given good performance ratings in the absence of results. She was on track to take her boss's global position within three years—if she was able to streamline and upgrade her team while still keeping it engaged and motivated.

Lin was nine months into her role when I was brought in as her coach. There was no formal assimilation plan in place when she took the role. A bright woman with several graduate degrees and a mind like a steel trap, she tends to speed up when she's agitated or excited. She loves learning new things and has little patience with others who do not share her passion for continual improvement. This characteristic helped her connect with the few "A" players on her team, but led to trepidation and a great deal of back-office conversation among her employees whom she saw as less talented (and with whom she spent significantly less time and energy). Lin was seen as a great contributor and a "breath of fresh air" by senior leadership, but experienced as dismissive and impatient by direct reports. When several of her key employees left the company, her behavior was seen as a major factor in this talent drain, and senior management was worried.

It was clear that Lin's interpersonal style was causing her to lose traction with her team. Part of Lin's coaching plan involved becoming a better listener to her direct reports, allowing them to develop as leaders (in other words, supporting them rather than merely directing them). Although this seemed at first like a simple task to her, it was much harder than it seemed. In the midst of business urgency, she needed to calm the fear within her team, and Lin's default setting was to deal with business first and people second.

She managed to strike a good balance between her boss's urgency for results and the need to gain the trust and engagement of her team. One year later, she is still on track as her boss's successor, and she has successfully developed the leadership abilities of some of her direct reports.

Know and Manage Your Derailers

In his book *What Got You Here Won't Get You There,* Marshall Goldsmith discusses some of the most common strengths and behaviors of successful leaders.[6] We know that when our strengths are taken to excess or used in the wrong situation, they quickly become derailers. At this point these behaviors move from valuable traits that assist the transition to obstacles that hinder our progress and may ultimately cause us failure. As stress increases, derailers are more likely to emerge.

For example, many successful leaders are opinionated and passionate. When taken to excess, however, being opinionated quickly morphs into steamrolling others and behaving dismissively. It's easy to see how this trait taken to excess can quickly destroy any chances of a successful transition. Another strength often attributed to successful leaders is being confident and driven to "win." Taken to excess, the leader with this quality is viewed as arrogant and self-promoting. For more qualities of successful leaders that become derailers when used to excess, see Table 18.2. And be aware: We all have them!

Gather Intelligence

The third skill that will assist you in making a successful transition is gathering intelligence from others—about yourself, your team, your organization, the expectations you face, and the support you'll get to meet those expectations. Following are some key questions transitioning leaders can ask themselves to ensure a smoother and perhaps better executed transition. Consider these questions before you take on a new role as well. Having this knowledge fresh in your mind will help you to decide if (1) you are suited to the new role and (2) the new role is suited to you.

Table 18.2 Strengths Taken to Excess

Strength	To Excess
Opinionated, passionate	Poor listener, dismissive
Eager to please	Conflict avoidant
Plays "devil's advocate"	Cynical, distrustful
Conscientious, detail oriented	Perfectionist, micromanager
Confident, drive to "win"	Self-promoting, arrogant
Craves independence	Distant and disengaged
Intense and energetic	Moody and overreactive

➤ *About you:* What situations do you shine in? What situations lower your morale? What are your strengths? What are the values you embrace most strongly? What are the strengths and challenges of your leadership style? What sorts of people do you work well with? What sorts of people do you have difficulty with? How directive are you? How do you typically influence people over whom you lack authority? How much and in what way do you communicate when you are setting expectations or making changes?

➤ *About the team:* What is the history of the team you are inheriting? What do the team members need that you may not normally provide? How will you need to stretch and change your style to lead these people, in this situation, toward a particular end? What sort of experience did your team have with your predecessor?

➤ *About your organization:* How would you and others describe the organization's culture? What are the stated and unstated rules? Remember, there are always ways that the unstated culture is different from the stated culture. For instance, the stated message may be: "We are a fair and equal opportunity employer"; however, you may notice that those promoted are by far members of one "in group." How do the unstated rules manifest themselves?

➤ *About the organization's expectations of you:* What challenges face you? How reasonable are the expectations? Give careful consideration to what we know about ramp time for new executives, keeping in mind it can take as long as six or nine months for an external hire to reach full productivity. As we've found, it is just not realistic to believe a new executive will be up to speed in 90 days. New executives need to create a clear picture of the "real job." Bear in mind, what you hear during the interview and hiring process may not match the reality of your new role.

➤ *About how the organization supports people and to what degree:* Does the organization invest in coaching and mentoring? Having a coach is an invaluable resource to an executive entering a new role. A coach can help outline key actions and deliverables to focus on first and help fine-tune leadership behaviors. Given so much internal movement in some organizations, some companies have a pool of internal and external "onboarding coaches" to ensure consistency and accountability. At the same time, don't overlook the power of mentoring and the role that current executives, retired executives, and board members can play in helping to assimilate you into a new role. Consider finding a mentor for yourself and be mindful of which stakeholders will be crucial to your success.

Practice Feed*Forward*

Most of us have taken part in a feedback process. Feedback is helpful in telling us where we can improve. However, because we can't change the past and that is the focus of feedback, it can be and often is a negative experience. We can, however, change the future. Feed*Forward,* a process developed by Marshall Goldsmith, is a quick and proven method for helping successful people be even more successful. The practice of Feed*Forward* requires a disciplined approach to following up with important stakeholders, which research has shown is the key ingredient to successful change.[7] This process of follow-up, though an important component of transition success, is often neglected by many transitioning leaders. Here is a brief description of how transitioning leaders can utilize the Feed*Forward* process to accelerate success in their new roles.

1. Make a list of stakeholders with whom you must collaborate in your new role, and with whom forming an effective working relationship will be a key component of your success in this role. Potential stakeholder categories are manager(s), direct reports, peers, other senior leaders, and external stakeholders such as customer groups or business partners.

2. Before or immediately after entering the new role, engage in dialogue with these stakeholders. Ask them what they need from you in your new role, as well as from the team you will be taking over, that will be helpful to them in their role. Keep a log of these stakeholders and the issues you will need to craft an ongoing dialogue.

3. Make sure that your conversation is directed toward suggestions for the future. While it is important to understand the history of the position you are taking and the leader you are replacing, you want the conversation going forward to be primarily about the past or what *not* to do.

4. Ask open-ended questions. Yes/no questions like "Any suggestions for me?" will yield much less information than questions such as "What suggestions do you have for how our business units can collaborate even better?"

5. Craft an agreement with your stakeholders to give you ongoing Feed*Forward* and decide on how frequently you will check in with them for the first six to nine months of your new role.

6. Write down their suggestions and thank them for their input. You may also wish to tell each stakeholder that while you can't make all the changes that are suggested you will take the input seriously and take action on some of them.

7. Ensure that you have brief regular check-ins with these stakeholders, which is particularly important during the first 9 to 12 months of your new role. During check-ins, remind stakeholders what you are trying to improve, ask them how they think you are doing on that improvement agenda, and gather one or two suggestions for future action or continued improvement. Regular check-ins should take just 5 or 10 minutes of a leader's time per stakeholder, and are an investment well worth making.

    Don't skip this step if you are transitioning to a new role within the same organization! Even if you have previously worked with the same stakeholders, your role with them will always shift, at least to some degree.

CASE STUDY
INTERNAL TRANSITION (PETE)

Pete was a talented engineer who was a senior director with a Fortune 500 technology company, where he had worked for more than 10 years. He had been my client a few years earlier when he participated in his division's high-potential program. During our work together, he worked to move from an "individual contributor" mentality to a more collaborative mindset.

Pete called me two months after taking a new position, and he was worried. His new job was not going well. His boss, who was also new to his position, rarely spent time with him and seemed to lack focus about what the most critical priorities were. As time went on, things got worse. For the first time in his life Pete began experiencing bouts of severe anxiety, beginning after a poor first quarter's results that brought scrutiny from leaders several levels up. Pete was distraught and asked me to help.

We gave Pete a leadership-style assessment, to take an even deeper look at what was derailing him in this position. His strengths included being very conscientious, detail-oriented, and eager to please. However, despite his self-assured and easygoing exterior, he tended to overworry when he did not get clear feedback from those in authority. And when he worried, he tended to keep his distance and keep his office door closed. We also focused on his tendency to end conversations when the technical part was over, and how he did not usually spend the needed time building relationships with those who could be important stakeholders in his success. The most important revelation to him was that he had always selected jobs based on their technical demands—he had never really evaluated how important the fit with his boss was.

Pete found another director-level position within the company as soon as he could. This time, he and I took a close look at the boss before he accepted. Inwardly, he thought his shot at a VP-level position was lost owing to his previous failure. An important part of his transition plan involved building relationships across the company with other leaders whose input he needed in order to be successful in this role. He created a comprehensive contact plan (on an Excel spreadsheet) to keep him on track—and he did a great job, both with keeping in contact and with achieving results. So great, in fact, that within a year, other leaders began calling him to find out if he was available for an even bigger role in the organization. Pete got his vice president position and we are currently working on his transition into this role.

Work Your Plan

Currently, the vast majority of companies provide only low to moderate support for transitions. While this fact may be surprising, it is nonetheless true; to be successful, leaders must be proactive in developing and working a transition plan. Practicing the other 4 key skills will help you develop a clear plan for what you need to know to maximize your success. If you are transitioning to a role within your same organization, ask yourself, How is my new role similar to the position that I came from, and how is it different? How are my relationships with the same people going to change? How might my transition fail? And, most important, what steps will I take to manage the challenges before me so that I maximize the probability of success?

CONCLUSION

Leaders today must manage multiple job transitions throughout their careers, much more so than in the past for a number of reasons, including the rapid rate of corporate change and the increasing level of globalization. It is not unusual for the context of the organization to change dramatically during the employee's tenure there and executives are expected to come up to speed ever more quickly. Even though many organizations are moving toward developing robust transition programs, leaders entering into new senior roles must take charge of their own destiny, and craft and execute a clear plan to maximize their success. Even very successful leaders can and do fail in new senior roles.

During times of transition, continuing to monitor and develop personal and interpersonal skills is absolutely critical to success. Derailing behaviors are often strengths taken to excess; and failure is rarely caused by a lack of technical or business skill. It takes longer than 90 days to reach full productivity in a new organization, generally even when taking a new role within the same company.

As we continue to coach senior leaders in transition and explore what helps executive transitions succeed, we will continue to gather further survey, interview, and case study data on the most effective ways that leaders can meet the increasing challenges and complexity of their new roles, and how they can best develop the skill sets and strategic perspectives that will position them for success in future roles.

CASE STUDY
INTERNAL TRANSITION (MARK)

Mark had been with his organization, a Fortune 100 manufacturing division, for 14 years. He moved around to a number of positions so that he could understand how all the parts came together, and he was eventually named general manager of one of its largest plants. Mark was moved from this position into a vice president within the corporate office; this move coincided with an overall reorganization in which his division was aligned more closely with the global parent company. In this role, he needed to rapidly form relationships with his new stakeholders, many of whom he knew from afar, but with whom he had never worked closely.

In his 20-year career, Mark had worked for three different organizations. This was his 12th position in his current company. Until this transition, he had never participated in a formal program designed to help him assimilate into a new role. First, we reviewed the 360-degree evaluation generated for his former position. As seen by others, his strengths included his clear ethics, dependability, ability to collaborate with others, and his easygoing manner. His primary leadership challenge was his tendency to be too easygoing with employee communication and feedback; we decided that in his new position, he would focus on giving clear, ongoing feedback (and Feed*Forward*) to his team and challenge himself to adopt a greater sense of urgency about results.

We crafted a transition process that included an "all-hands" meeting, with Mark and two levels of his direct reports. In advance, Mark was asked to organize his thoughts around issues affecting the team, including:

➤ Team vision and expected results for the first six months

➤ Key customers

➤ First impressions of his role and of the team

➤ Expectations of the team

➤ Plan for ongoing review of progress

An advance meeting with the team focused on a few key questions, including:

➤ What did Mark need to know about the history of the team and the current challenges it faces?

➤ Who were the most important stakeholders outside the team whom Mark needed to form relationships with?

➤   What were their first impressions of Mark and the reputation that preceded him?

➤   What questions did the team have about Mark and his leadership style?

➤   What results did the team expect within the first six months?

The team meeting involved a facilitated dialogue around the questions and issues generated by Mark and the team. My continued role as coach was to help Mark stay aware of his leadership style, leverage his strengths, and manage around potential derailers. He created a contact plan to help him identify and reach out to key stake-holders in his new role, so that he kept on track with the emerging need to eliminate silos and create an effective matrix-based organization. He also generated checklists that helped him hold himself accountable for giving ongoing Feed*Forward* to his team, boosting both its performance and engagement scores.

Two years later, Mark continues to be successful in his role. Comparing his previous transitions to this one, he credits the transition process to saving at least six month's worth of wasted time, false starts, and "watercooler talk." Forming key relationships quickly and creating a platform by which these relationships are maintained and deepened is, according to him, the most valuable benefit of the assimilation program.

ABOUT THE AUTHOR

Patricia Wheeler is a leadership development expert and executive coach who helps smart executives become better leaders. As managing partner for the Levin Group LLC, she has spent 25 years working with senior leaders and their teams. Dr. Wheeler is also managing director of the global coaching alliance Alexcel.

Patricia is a former assistant professor at the Emory University School of Medicine and serves as guest lecturer for the Robinson School of Business at Georgia State University. She publishes the executive resource *Leading News* with Marshall Goldsmith. Articles by and about her have appeared in *Forbes, BusinessWeek, Capital Magazine, Healthcare Executive,* and other publications. You may contact Patricia at Patricia@TheLevinGroup.com and sign up for *Leading News* at LeadingNews.org.

NOTES

1. "CEO Turnover Remains High at World's Largest Companies, Booz Allen Study Finds," May 22, 2007; http://www.boozallen.com/news/36608085, accessed February 18, 2009.

2. Nic Paton, "CEO Turnover Hits New High," *Management Issues;* http://www.management-issues.com/2009/1/16/research/ceo-turnover-hits-new-high.asp, accessed February 18, 2009.

3. Center for Creative Leadership, as cited by Anne Fisher, *Fortune,* June 22, 1998.

4. See http://aonrpoconsulting.wordpress.com/2008/11/24/executive-coaching, accessed June 7, 2009.

5. The Institute of Executive Development and Alexcel Group conducted a market study in 2007 and 2008 to examine the transitions that top executives make into and through organizations, and the roadblocks that can occur in the process, along with the organizational roles and processes that may facilitate such transitions and change. Participants included approximately 150 executives and talent professionals across a variety of companies and industries, who participated in an online survey consisting of 18 multiple-choice questions.

6. Marshall Goldsmith, *What Got You Here Won't Get You There* (New York: Hyperion, 2007).

7. Marshall Goldsmith and Howard Morgan, "Leadership Is a Contact Sport: The 'Follow-up Factor' in Management Development," *Strategy + Business* (Fall 2004): 71–79.

CHAPTER 19

A Question of Leadership: What Does the Organization Need Me to Do?

> John Baldoni

One of the questions that all of us engaged in leadership development have been asked at one time or another is basic: What does it mean to be a leader? For years my standard answer has been that being a leader means that you do what is right for the organization and put people into positions where they can succeed and benefit themselves and the team. This explanation still works, but I have come up with a much shorter statement—actually it is a question—that may be more precise and actionable. As a leader, what does the organization need me to do?

Leadership by nature is straightforward; putting it into practice is much tougher, especially when you are confronted with two equally attractive propositions, or "rights." Harvard professor and business ethicist Joseph Badaracco has written and taught about this duality for years.[1] His insights are relevant to leaders at every level.

The example that comes to mind is choosing whom to promote, especially when the field of candidates is well qualified. The easy answer is to put the best person for the team in charge—but what if you have two "best" people? What do you do if one is male and the other female? Or one is a minority and the other is not? Many organizations opt for diversity, and an organization that puts its qualified minority candidates into positions to influence and lead demonstrates meritocracy. On the other hand, is that fair or just to those candidates who are not chosen?

These are tough questions that will require tough answers. The application of our question (What does the organization need me to do?) may help shape the ultimate and workable answer. The person who answers the call and takes action is the person we call a *leader*.

Our question can be applied to a host of issues. For example, how do you manage? If you are someone who likes to exert a high degree of control, then you may be getting things done, but at what price? You may be logging ungodly hours and wasting energy that you need for new projects, not to mention unexpected crises. Worse, you may be stifling your team members and preventing them from doing for themselves. By asking "What does the organization need me to do?" it becomes clear. Ease up and hand over the reins!

By contrast, our same question may prompt a different response in another situation. Let's say your company just bought a new manufacturing plant in another country. If you are the operations guru, you will have to get on a plane and ensure that the transition is smooth and that the new plant management understands from the outset your company's standards for operations, quality, and employee behavior. These tasks cannot be delegated; the operations chief must be present.

The beauty of this question is its simplicity: it assumes ownership of an issue by a leader and in turn what the leader will do to effect change or maintain course. It squares the leadership proposition with the action steps and in the process serves to create alignment around vision, mission, and values.

In determining what the organization needs you to do, it may be useful to take a step back and ask a few more questions. Answering a question with a question is something that was bred into me by eight years of Jesuit education, a tradition that extends back to the ancient Greeks.

ANCIENT WISDOM, CURRENT TRUTHS

One notable seeker of truth was Socrates; he made liberal use of questions. By raising questions, Socrates was able to gain information, provide alternate points of view, and even poke fun. Managers can employ questions in the same way. Asking employees what they are doing and why, and then engaging them in conversation, demonstrates interest. Like Socrates, make certain the questions are not used to bludgeon but, rather, to illuminate, thereby bringing new understanding to the issues at hand.

Asking reflective questions and pausing long enough for an honest reply is part art and part discipline. The art comes in crafting questions that get to the heart of the situation; the discipline comes from the practice of doing it, but also having the guts to listen to less-than-flattering replies.

Socrates was by nature one who did not accept things at face value. He was both a debater and an explainer. And as Thomas Cahill explains in *Sailing the Wine-Dark Sea: Why the Greeks Matter,* Socrates' chief tool was his ability to raise questions.[2] Socrates used questions like an artist uses a brush to apply color—in ways that illuminate with light, shade, and perspective. Above all, Socrates was a seeker of truth, someone who sought meaning and pursued it to the *n*th degree. His example is one from which managers today can learn much.

Managers say that they want their people to think and act strategically. That's a statement that many up-and-coming executives discover in their performance reviews. Issued as an imperative, it connotes the need to shape up and start thinking like a strategist! As a result, many executives find themselves flummoxed as to how to acquire and develop a strategic mindset. While the topic is taught in most business schools, the focus is most often on analytics. In reality, strategic thinking is a leadership proposition, too, and so the urging to "be more strategic" prompts the question, "How? With my boss, with my team, or with my choice of perfume or aftershave?"

Thinking strategically is a form of "leading up," which is a way of doing what needs doing in order to benefit the organization. Those who "lead up" are those who think about how they can help their boss think and act strategically. It is providing answers as well as options; it is doing what needs doing and asking for forgiveness later. Leading up begins with strategic thinking—that is, considering how you can help your team and your department add value to the enterprise. Being viewed as a strategic thinker is now considered a gateway to the top floor of management, so up-and-comers want to do whatever possible to develop those skills. Here are some questions to ask in cultivating a strategic mindset:

➤ *What are the biggest challenges facing the organization?* The easy solution is to consider market trends and the competition. These are important to know, but too often you may miss what is happening underneath. For example, Wal-Mart carved a market share that was off the consideration mark of Sears, which at the time was focused on JCPenney and Montgomery Ward. New competitors are not so easy to discern. Finding out the issues threatening your organization is essential.

➤ *What are the biggest opportunities my organization can exploit?* Adopt the mindset of a niche player. How can you turn the playing field to your advantage? Starbucks, for all its current woes, adopted a mindset of becoming the "third place" to home and office. Rather than just sell coffee, it sells an entire experience. Consider things your organization can do to increase market share or provide better service to the customer.

➤ *What can I do to help my organization overcome the challenges and exploit the opportunities?* Here is where you exert your leadership. Consider things the organization should be doing and determine how you can play a role in those action steps. It will require analytics and creativity, as well as old-fashioned gumption, to suggest things, or, better yet, carry them out.

Truth be told, those on the top rung are not always very strategic. In fact, the reason they are on top is that they were protective of their turf and their teams, and as a result made it to the top rung. Not strategic from an organizational sense at all, but strategic in terms of personal advancement.

That said, every organization needs people who can embrace the big picture and at the same time do what is necessary to move the organization forward. It is not always easy to see the forest for the trees when you are in the woods. Pulling back momentarily to assess the situation is critical. It is easier for people at the top, because they can disengage from day-to-day operations easier than a line manager can. But managers who take stock of themselves and their contributions to the company do themselves and their teams a world of good. They are not only thinking strategically, they are acting for the good of the whole. And that's very strategic.

TEACH SO OTHERS CAN FOLLOW

Now that you know where you are going, you can help others to follow. Socrates was a born teacher. In fact, it was his commitment to teaching that led to his eventual downfall; he was accused of corrupting youth chiefly because he was proposing alternate points of view. Managers who teach are those who find ways to get the most out of their people. They engage their people in work the way that teachers do. Sales managers are often excellent teachers because they not only provide information, they also show how to apply it. They accompany their salespeople on sales calls and observe them firsthand. They also role-play customer situations. All of these activities are forms of teaching.

Turn Mistakes into Lessons

In his dialogues, Socrates would lay traps for his fellow discoursers. When they fell for his gambit, he would snap shut his trap and ensnare them in their own mistakes, or hypocrisy. He would then explain what he had done and why. Managers need not lay traps, but they can go to school on the mistakes. For instance, if an employee overshoots the budget for a given project, rather than blowing a gasket, a shrewd manager can have the employee explain, line item by line item, where the costs arose. There may, or may not, be good reasons behind each expenditure. If the manager invites her employee to explain his point of view, over the course of this conversation manager and employee can arrive at a better understanding of not only the budget but also of one another. This teaching-via-conversation practice can make their continued work together more efficacious and less confrontational.

Insist on the Truth

When Socrates raised questions, he struck a raw nerve that angered those in power. They accused him of atheism and the corruption of youth. The first charge was wholly false; Socrates paid homage to the Greek gods. The second had some basis in truth, if you consider that teaching students to question those in authority could result in a "corruption" or rearrangement of the status quo. At his trial, Socrates did not back down and was sentenced to death, which he carried out by drinking hemlock. Fortunately, most managers will not have to make such choices, but every organization is faced with ethical questions.

The guidelines mandated by government regulators will help ensure that corporations are run more honestly, but these laws will not cover the day-to-day issues that managers face with their employees. For example, how vigilant must managers be with time and expense reports, invoices from suppliers, or requests for overtime? Very vigilant—not as some kind of internal affairs cop but, rather, as a manager who insists on ethical behavior. Talk about such expectations first and, like Socrates, take questions. Truth is not a "nice to have"; it's a "must-have."

To Reflect Is to Question the Status Quo

To ensure that you are connecting appropriately with your people, consider the following reflective questions:

➤ *Do people come to me with their problems?* Colin Powell has said many times that if people are not coming to you with their problems, you have a problem. When people feel comfortable enough to raise issues with you, that means you have created an atmosphere of cooperation.

➤ *Do people see me as one who deals with tough issues or one who avoids them?* A leader's job is to stay in the kitchen, particularly when it's hot. If you stand up for what needs doing and the people who do it, no matter how tough the situation, you are someone to follow. If you seek to avoid conflict, confrontation, or big problems, then leadership is not your cup of tea.

➤ *Do people see you in their workplace?* The Japanese, as well as all practitioners of lean thinking, call this *gemba,* meaning "go where the work is." By visiting people where they work, you honor them. You also expose yourself to their working conditions, the problems workers face, and the opportunities they may develop.

➤ *Do you learn from what you hear?* Listening is a commitment to others, but you must open yourself to the ideas that you hear. Listen to the problems as well as the opportunities. Leaders do not need to implement every suggestion, of course, but they need to demonstrate that they care enough to listen.

➤ *Do people view me as one who takes the blame and shares the credit?* Our proverbial kitchen can get pretty toasty sometimes, especially when things go awry. Legendary Alabama football coach Bear Bryant put it as well as I've heard: "If anything goes bad, I did it. If anything goes semi-good, then we did it. If anything goes really good, then you did it. That's all it takes to get people to win football games."

Answering yes to all questions means you are either on the right track or deluding yourself. But note the theme of these questions: they get to the heart of what you do, not so much what you are. They are designed to cast a light on how you are perceived by others rather than how you are perceived by yourself. A good trick is to ask a trusted colleague or two these same questions as they pertain to you.

EXPERIENCE IN TIME

Wisdom is not something that can be taught; it must be experienced. Therefore, managers operating in a global environment with ever-shortening product and service cycles, and ever-escalating variables creating ever more challenges, cannot always wait for wisdom to strike. That's where senior leaders can help; by making themselves available for conversations, as Socrates did for his pupils, they can help share their experience and perhaps their wisdom. The net result will be a kind of mutual wisdom, managers learning on the job and from the veterans.

It would be too much to expect people to get excited about the possibility of gaining wisdom, and that's probably beneficial, because wisdom is not something that can be obtained through outright desire. Rather, wisdom is earned by a willingness to learn. Wisdom also comes from accepting our personal limitations. Strive as we might and with the best of intentions, there are forces beyond our control, beyond our destiny. Coming to grips with such limitations is humbling, to be certain, but it can be an act of wisdom. Instead of pushing against things you cannot control—senior management, market forces, heredity—push for things you can control: your career, your relationships, and your life. In that acceptance, there is wisdom.

Leadership so often is not about you. It is about how you enable others to do their jobs and, better yet, put them into positions where they can succeed. At the same time, leadership is all about you, for it is you who make the decisions about what to do and why. That is why reflecting from time to time on your performance is an act of leadership. Sometimes you will come out on top; other times you will discover how much more you have to do and learn.

ABOUT THE AUTHOR

John Baldoni is an internationally recognized leadership consultant, coach, speaker, and author. His leadership and coaching work centers on how leaders can use their authority, communications, and presence to build trust and drive results. John is the author of eight books on leadership, including *Lead Your Boss: The Subtle Art of Managing Up* and *Lead by Example: 50 Ways Great Leaders Inspire Results.* He speaks widely to corporate, military, professional, and university groups throughout North America. Readers are welcome to visit his Web site at www.johnbaldoni.com or e-mail him at john@johnbadoni.com.

NOTES

1. Joseph L. Badaracco, Jr., *Defining Moments: When Leaders Must Choose Between Right and Right* (Boston: Harvard Business School Press, 1997); Joseph L. Badaracco, Jr., *Leading Quietly* (Boston: Harvard Business School Press, 2002).

2. Thomas Cahill, *Sailing the Wine-Dark Sea: Why the Greeks Matter* (New York: Nan A. Talese/Doubleday, 2003), especially chap. V, "The Philosopher: How to Think."

PART FIVE

Taking the Lead

➤ The X Factors

CHAPTER 20

Situational Intelligence

> **Laurence S. Lyons**

In the 1980s, when videocassette recorders (VCRs) were all the rage, a prominent Japanese company launched the "killer" application, then hastily withdrew it. The event passed by largely unnoticed and life moved on.

At the time, the business plan supporting this innovation was hailed as a once-in-a-lifetime opportunity, exceeding all known criteria for a whirlwind success. The market would beat a path to its door while the company couldn't fail to get embarrassingly rich. Early sales forecasts indicated latent demand for the new product on a planetary scale. Engineering investment turned out to be modest. Implementation involved only minor modifications to a standard VCR to deliver the special functionality. In the lab, the design was found to be extremely reliable. The smart ideas working its magic were lined up for worldwide patents. In short, concept, design, and production were a cinch.

It got better. The manufacturing cost came out close to that of a standard unit, although the new product could be sold at a respectable premium. That was because this box could do something that no other VCR on earth was able to achieve: it removed all the advertisements from recorded TV programs and movies. Seamlessly.

The unit could be set up to record for hours on end and its footage played back—totally uninterrupted by on-air commercials. Focus groups that were shown early prototypes hailed the new features as "revolutionary." All the hassle of repeatedly stopping, guessing, and restarting the videotape at just the right point in order to sift out the ads had been eliminated. For those lazy TV addicts who would regularly sit through an entire replay and take in all the commercials, this device removed hours of dead time. The ability to watch a full movie recorded off commercial TV—advertisement-free from start to finish at the touch of a button—elevated the viewing experience to the level of pure enjoyment.

Everyone in the company was hugely excited. Product management nevertheless went for a cautious market introduction and decided to debut only a few thousand units on the first production run. During this test-market phase, these seed devices were released to only a handful of friendly retailers in Tokyo, where customer reaction could be carefully captured and quickly fed back. The plan was to monitor the uptake over the first three months prior to rolling out a global launch. No fancy literature was available during this initial period, so knowledge of the product's existence spread only by word of mouth. Even so, the entire stock sold out in a matter of days.

The members of the product team held a party to celebrate their resounding success. They had clearly met the marketing textbook's definition of anticipating and satisfying customer's expectations profitably. From a financial perspective, the return on investment was exceptional and the accounting margin high. Distribution channels and customer service could easily be grafted onto the company's existing infrastructure using standard systems. Everyone involved, from inception to delivery to after-sales service, bonded together as an effective and motivated team. This perfect product checked every box on every dashboard, suggesting that the company was onto a massive winner.

At that point, the product quickly and quietly slid into oblivion. Word had gotten around. A friendly tip-off to one of the company's senior executives brought the project to an abrupt halt. In a dramatic turnaround, production lines were shut down, all work-in-progress frozen, and staff quietly reallocated to other tasks. From that moment, not a single unit was ever again offered for sale. No explanation was offered.

What did that senior executive come to realize? The issue was this: domestic users would have no need to buy the new device in a world that offered only public broadcasting. But what network could sell airtime to advertisers if it couldn't deliver its commercial content to its audience? The VCR manufacturer realized in the nick of time that large-scale uptake of the new product would eventually bring about the demise of its own market. That's because it would destroy the whole commercial broadcasting industry on which its sales depended.

As soon as it became clear that a successful product launch meant corporate suicide, the company did everything in its power to prevent the new gadget from ever again seeing the light of day.

FROM MANAGEMENT TO CITIZENSHIP

The VCR case study demonstrates what happens when a flawed theory of change gains company-wide support. Here, an apparently sound business ambition bit the dust because its formula for success was unsustainable.

The story highlights a management danger zone that is growing in scale and significance. It is exemplified in recent times by the actions of those individuals and organizations, both private and public, who brought about the credit crunch. We set out on a course of failure even though, from our unique vantage point, we apparently have the best of everything: excellent planning, effective teamwork, and inspirational leaders. Trouble surprises us from beyond the horizon, yet we fail to avoid it, primarily because of the choices we make when fixing the boundaries around our own perception. We are limited or liberated simply through the way we choose to think.

This conceptual threat becomes amplified as our business world gets more complex, global, and interdependent. Today's managers already recognize the need to hone sharper foresight in the areas of environmental impact and triple-line social accounting. The hidden danger is in failing to identify the more elusive yet vitally important extended stakeholders.

The need to bridge the gap between traditional management thinking and a more rounded definition of success extends the realm of management from the province of internal leadership into the wider arena of corporate citizenship. Corporate citizens have the ability to look outside their own organizations, understand the impact of their actions, and plan accordingly. These leaders, of course, recognize that corporations are legal entities obligated to return a profit to their shareholders. But beyond that, they also recognize the responsibility that is shared by all corporations in working toward a common good.

Figure 20.1 Some Tools of Situational Intelligence

Stakeholder-Value Wheel

Motivation-Value Constellation

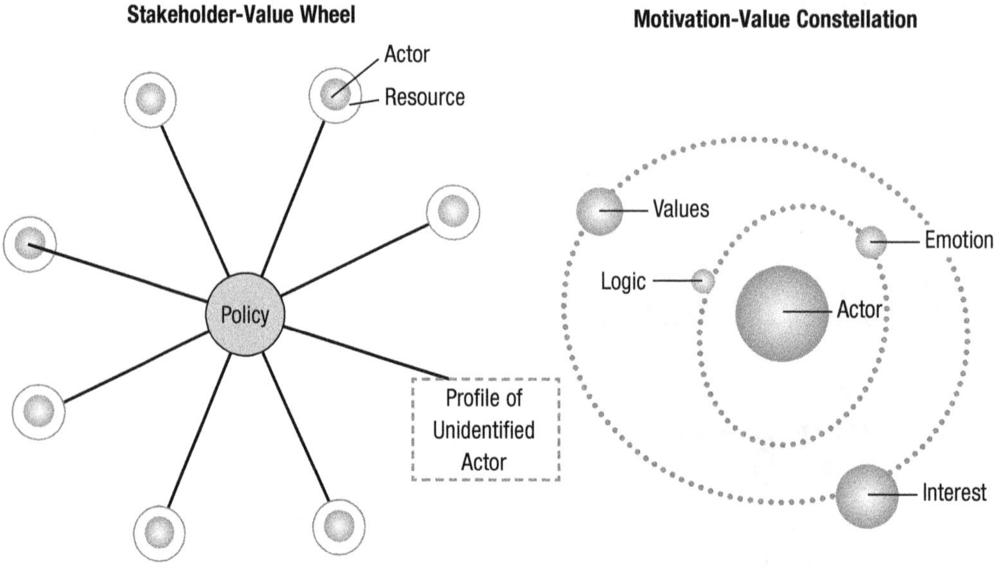

LOOKING BEYOND THE IMMEDIATE

Situational Intelligence is the ability to appreciate a situation in its wider context so that this learning can be used to inform policy. Some tools of this metatheory are shown on the left in Figure 20.1.

In the figure, the Stakeholder-Value Wheel shows the organization as a distributor of value to its various stakeholders through its policy decisions. Perhaps the most familiar stakeholder values are customer satisfaction and the monetary distributions to shareholders. There are myriad others—such as the frustration of competitors—that remind us that "value" is not always positive. The specific distribution of value is the situation in which the organization finds itself. One important use of this model is in the profiling through policy of important actors who have not yet been identified; in the case of the VCR company, this was the commercial network industry.

Of course, the value experienced by each stakeholder actor is knowable only by them. Since the actions of actors can often be complex and difficult to understand (especially where they are being deliberately deceitful), a motivational framework surrounds each actor in the Situational Intelligence model. It recognizes four interrelated motivational elements, shown on the right in

Figure 20.1: *logic,* or the actor's particular theory linking cause and effect; *interest,* or his or her ranking of beneficiaries; *values,* or his or her ranking of ethics; and *emotion,* or the feeling each actor associates with his or her situation.

Situational Intelligence does not set out to dictate the precise content of a richer policy; instead, it encourages the generation of relevant questions by offering models and frameworks on which theories may be tried out. Its practical application often leads to research activities designed to identify actors, motivations, or stakeholders currently unknown. As part of the planning process, further research typically follows in order to establish the motivation of these new actors, so that their values can be factored into emerging policy. As it deals with the alignment and misalignment of the motivations of all relevant actors, the system can be extremely powerful when working in situations involving the management of change. Tomorrow's successful manager will be a corporate citizen with a forensic mind (see case study).

CASE STUDY
FORENSICS

On a sweltering night in the city, another homicide goes down. The autopsy sheds no light—an inexplicable dead body. There are no clues at the scene of the crime, no fingerprints, no weapon. Inspector Mulligan grabs her phone.

"Joe," she says to her officer, "the lab's turned up zilch. Go see the victim's attorney and check if he's got a safe-deposit box down at the bank."

"Sure," says Joe, "but what should I be looking for?"

"Just use your intelligence, Joe," says Mulligan. "I want to know if the deceased left a will."

ABOUT THE AUTHOR

Laurence S. Lyons is an accomplished business consultant, coach, author, and public speaker who is engaged by the boards and management teams of the world's top companies to develop teamwork, strategy, and leadership. Larry spent the early part of his career as an accomplished leader in the IT and telecommunications industries, in both line and staff appointments.

An acclaimed expert in organizational transformation, Larry holds a PhD and a master's degree in management from Brunel University in London and is a visiting academic fellow at Henley Business School, England. Larry is honored to be a member of the International Advisory Committee of the Worldwide Association of Business Coaches (WABC), Vancouver, for which he writes a regular column "Ask the Expert" for its tri-yearly publication, *Business Coaching Worldwide*. A library of Larry's work can be found at www.lslyons.com, and he can be contacted at lslyons@lslyons.com.

CHAPTER 21

The Arts and Leadership

> Nancy J. Adler

"The MFA is the new MBA.... An arts degree is now perhaps the hottest credential in the world of business."
—DANIEL PINK, *Harvard Business Review*

Twenty-first-century society yearns for a leadership of *possibility,* a leadership based more on hope, aspiration, and innovation than on the replication of historical patterns of constrained pragmatism. Luckily, such a leadership is possible today. For the first time in history, companies can work backward from their aspirations and imagination rather than forward from their past. According to Gary Hamel, author of *Leading the Revolution,* "The gap between what can be imagined and what can be accomplished has never been smaller."[1] The defining question—and opportunity—for this century is, "Now that we can do anything, what do we want to do?"[2]

Responding to that question demands anticipatory creativity. Designing options worthy of implementation calls for levels of inspiration and passionate creativity that have been more the domain of artists and artistic processes than of most managers. As Harvard business professor Rob Austin well understands, "The economy of the future will be about creating value and appropriate forms, and no one knows more about the processes for doing that than artists."[3]

Adapted from Nancy Adler, "The Arts & Leadership: Now That We Can Do Anything, What Will We Do?" *Academy of Management Learning and Education Journal* 5, no. 4 (2006): 486–499.

ENTERING THE 21ST CENTURY: THE TIME IS RIGHT FOR THE CROSS-FERTILIZATION OF ARTS AND LEADERSHIP

According to poet David Whyte, who worked with the senior executives at McDonnell Douglas for more than a year, "The time seems right for this cross-fertilization [of the arts and leadership]. It seems that all the overripe hierarchies of the world, from corporations to nation-states, are in trouble and are calling, however reluctantly, on their people for more creativity, commitment, and innovation."[4] Indeed, why else, as we enter the 21st century, would we be seeing increasing numbers of corporate leaders bringing artists and their artistic processes into their companies? According to management consultant and opera singer David Pearl, "Business and the arts [are] not . . . different fields, but . . . different aspects of the creative process." As he explains, "Shakespeare, remember, was a manager and an artist. He ran a company and wrote the plays. If the two fields weren't separate for someone like [Shakespeare] . . . why then for us normal mortals?"[5]

Our contemporary world is already anything but business as usual, and most business leaders know it. Options and approaches that worked well in the 20th century no longer work as well, if at all, today. New strategies unimaginable a mere decade ago are being realized daily, if not by one's own company then by competitors half a world away. So, the challenge facing business leaders now is to design strategies worthy of implementation, not simply to select from among approaches that have succeeded for them in the past.[6]

OLD APPROACHES NO LONGER WORK: BUSINESS TURNS TO THE ARTS

What has changed so dramatically in the last decade that increasingly has leading business executives turning to artists and to artistic processes to guide their thinking and action? Five defining trends are outlined next.

Rapidly Increasing Global Interconnectedness

The world today is dynamically interconnected in ways we could not have imagined even a decade, let alone a century, ago. Few organizations have experience in successfully managing in the midst of such an environment.

Indeed, in a world in which everything is interconnected, everything matters; nothing is inconsequential.[7] Leaders search for successful strategies only to discover that the most viable options need to be invented; they cannot simply be replicated. Designing innovative options requires more than the traditional analytical and decision-making skills; it requires the skills that creative people have used for years.

Increasing Domination of Market Forces

Within our global society, power has increasingly been shifting to the private sector. In fact, 49 of the 100 largest economies in the world are now multinational companies, not countries.[8] In recognition of this development, former U.N. Secretary-General Kofi Annan invited business to become a cocreator of society's success: "Let us choose to unite the power of markets with the strengths of universal ideals . . . let us choose to reconcile the creative forces of private entrepreneurship with the needs of the disadvantaged and the requirements of future generations."[9] Such pleas for global corporate citizenship recognize that, without the private sector, no attempt to create and maintain a vibrant, equitable, and sustainable society can succeed. Leaders from all sectors are searching for new partnership options that include business as a cocreator of a society we can be proud of. In this, business leaders have been among the first to realize that they must create new ways that will work.

An Increasingly Turbulent, Complex, and Chaotic Environment

Extremely high rates of change, greater business ambiguity and unpredictability, and economic turbulence define the environment faced by business today. In contrast, the greater levels of stability, continuity, and certainty that characterized most of the 19th and 20th centuries allowed leaders to rely on hierarchical, military, industrial, and machine-based models to guide their actions. Those models no longer work well in the midst of present-day chaos and complexity, and contemporary leaders are shifting to more human and organic metaphors to guide their strategies. Among the most powerful human metaphors are those found in the arts.

Within this trend, three distinct dimensions help explain the appropriation by business of arts-based approaches to change.

1. *Discontinuous Change.* Continuous improvement is no longer good enough. Inventing the next-great-thing defines a business's success, or if it is invented by its competitors, its demise. It is not that enhancements and increased efficiency—including at the level of Six Sigma—are not important; it is just that they are no longer sufficient for economic survival, let alone business success. Instead, creating the next-great-thing demands continual innovation. It's a design task, not an analytical or administrative function. Historically, design creativity has been the primary competence of artists, not managers.

2. *Networked Teams.* Prior structures—hierarchies and individuals— no longer work the way they used to. Organizations have increasingly shifted from single-company hierarchies to flatter, more networked, multiorganizational structures, or teams, including global strategic alliances; international joint ventures; and cross-border mergers, acquisitions, and partnerships. Within such networked partnerships, people are asked to collaborate in colocated and geographically distanced arrangements.

   Unfortunately, the success rate of such globally networked organizations and their teams has not been impressive yet. Historically, three-quarters of all international joint ventures and strategic alliances fail.[10] But actors, dancers, and musicians— performing as ensembles—have always demonstrated team-based, collaborative skills. Harvard business professor Rob Austin and his colleague, theater director Lee Devin, advise managers to "look to collaborative artists rather than to more traditional management models if they want to create economic value in this new century."[11]

3. *Simultaneity.* Planning no longer works the way it used to— time has collapsed. The manager's ability to improvise increasingly determines the organization's success. Strict reliance on traditional planning models no longer works. Without the luxury of the lead time necessary for planning, managers must now use their professional expertise and experience to respond spontaneously— in other words, to improvise. Not surprisingly, managers are increasingly turning to improvisational actors, dancers, and musicians for guidance as they attempt to shift from sequential planning to approaches incorporating spontaneity.[12]

Advances in Technology Decrease the Cost of Experimentation; Organizations' Scarcest Resource Becomes Their Dreamers, Not Their Testers

With the advances in technology we've experienced over the past decade, the cost of continuous experimentation to test new ideas is at an all-time low, and it continues to decrease. Advanced computer technologies, and rapid and cheap iteration, allow managers to substitute experimentation for planning.[13]

The challenge now, according to Harvard's Rob Austin, is not to test new ideas but, rather, to dream up novel ideas worthy of testing. Inventing new "things to test . . . is fundamentally a creative act." Organizations' scarcest resource has become their dreamers, not their testers. Austin cautions, however, that "managers and management students don't understand how to create on cue, how to innovate reliably on a deadline. . . . Artists are much better at this. . . . [It's] something theatre companies [for example] do all the time."[14]

Yearning for Significance—Success Is No Longer Enough

After a century focused on the efficiencies gained through mechanistic and reductionist techniques, both individuals and society yearn for wholeness and meaning in this modern world. As business strategist Gary Hamel recognizes, "What we need is not an economy of hands or heads, but an economy of hearts. Every employee should feel that he or she is contributing to something that will actually make a genuine and positive difference in the lives of customers and colleagues. For too many employees, the return on emotional equity is close to zero. . . . To succeed in the [21st century] . . . a company must give its members a reason to bring all of their humanity to work."[15]

Similarly, poet David Whyte recognizes the greater humanity that each of us yearns to bring to work: "The artist's sensibility . . . understands that our place in this world can never be measured by the Dow Jones, that our ultimate arrival on our deathbed entitles us to other perspectives than mere fiscal success or the size of our retirement account."[16]

It is no coincidence that the beginning of the new century (and millennium) produced a confluence of people yearning for societal significance and the invitation from business leaders for artists to partner with them. Indeed, examples of business leaders incorporating arts-based approaches are gaining prominence. Industrialist and founder of ISCAR Stef Wertheimer, whose aspiration is no less than the simultaneous achievement of outstanding financial success and the creation of peace in the Middle East, has built a series of industrial parks that bring together Arab, Druze, and Jewish Israelis. Are they profitable? Yes, his industrial parks already account for more than $2 billion in annual revenue and produce 10 percent of Israel's industrial exports. Do they rely on the arts? Absolutely, as Wertheimer describes: "Tefen [Industrial Park] is a collaborative creation by both industry and art, to the point that we cannot separate . . . them."[17]

FROM PREDICTION TO ASPIRATION: A LEADERSHIP OF HOPE

Leaders now recognize that we cannot create financially successful companies, as well as an equitable, peaceful, sustainable world, simply by applying yesterday's approaches to business. Global society's hoped-for future can never be achieved through mere projections—linear or otherwise—extrapolated from past trends. Not even the best set of marketing, accounting, finance, and IT techniques, no matter how rigorously applied, will get us from here to where we want to go.

Similar to great artists, whose passion moves them beyond mastered techniques to meaningful new statements, today's business leaders require passion and courage to achieve these ends. This kind of leadership relies on three different types of courage: the courage to see the world as it actually is and not as others would have you see it, the courage to aspire to previously unimagined possibilities, and the courage to inspire others to bring possibility back to reality.

The Courage to See Reality, Not Illusion

Escaping societal conformity has long been the hallmark of most artistic traditions, but considerably less a part of managerial practice. Managers have stressed conformity, not unique perception or vision. Now they must have the courage to see reality as it is, even when no one else appreciates that reality.

Strategy professors C. K. Prahalad and Stuart L. Hart, in their bottom-of-the-pyramid approach, counsel major multinationals to "see" markets that previously were invisible to them—and remain invisible to most of their competitors.[18] They dispel the illusion that the world's poorest people do not constitute a market, that they do not posses buying power, and that there aren't significant profits to be earned by the companies serving them. Bottom-of-the-pyramid strategies dramatically use their concept of "collusion against illusion" for the mutual benefit of business and society. As the *Journal of Financial Planning* summarizes, "One of the first jobs of a leader is defining reality—and that requires a new discipline of seeing."[19]

Hope Made Real: The Courage to Envision Possibility

In addition to accurately seeing reality, today's leadership requires the courage to envision possibility—to dream the big dream. Envisioning possibility means maintaining hope and not descending into cynicism, even when colleagues and friends misinterpret one's aspirations and disparagingly label them as naïve.

More than 150 years ago, the poet Emily Dickinson wrote, "I dwell in Possibility." Echoing this optimism in 2000, Harvard Business School Press published *The Art of Possibility,* by Rosamund and Benjamin Zander. Benjamin Zander has been the conductor of the Boston Philharmonic Orchestra for 30 years—not your expected authority for a business publication. But perhaps Harvard Business School Press recognized that artistic traditions offer a better means for creating possibility—for supporting human aspirations and generating greater business expectations—than have our traditional managerial models. Perhaps "executive thought" leaders finally understand that Albert Einstein's warning applies to them: "We cannot solve our problems with the same thinking we used when we created them."

Business strategist Gary Hamel advises, "Companies fail to create the future not because they fail to predict it but because they fail to *imagine* it."[20] That is, success is driven by imagination and design, not by the commonly taught managerial problem-solving and decision-making techniques.

Inspiration: The Courage to Bring Possibility Back to Reality

Leaders must be able to inspire people to move from their current reality toward more desirable possibilities. Whereas traditional managerial frameworks have focused primarily on motivation, the 21st-century challenge is to *inspire* people, not simply to motivate them.

What inspires people to give their best to an organization? Most motivation systems focus on extrinsic rewards; in contrast, most artists are motivated intrinsically—that is, they have the inner drive to create something unique. It is therefore not surprising that British theater director Richard Olivier uses Shakespeare's *Henry V*—and not some set of standard motivation theories— to teach executives about inspirational leadership. Olivier sees this dramatic portrayal of England's King Henry V as "Shakespeare's greatest leader— inspired and inspiring, visionary yet pragmatic, powerful yet responsible."[21]

Gary Hamel, the business strategist mentioned previously, coaches executives that they need "a cause, not a business." He explains that "without a transcendent purpose, individuals will lack the courage" they need to innovate beyond the ordinary. "Courage . . . comes not from some banal assurance that 'change is good' but from devotion to a wholly worthwhile cause."[22]

THE ART OF LEADERSHIP: HOPE MADE REAL

Calling business leadership an "art" is no accident here. Who are we as "artists"? Perhaps more important, who are we as human beings? How does business hope to influence life on the planet? What skills does business bring to the art of creation? According to Ivan G. Seidenberg, Chairman and CEO of Verizon, "creativity is the one irreplaceable human skill in an increasingly automated world . . . the only sustainable source of competitive advantage."[23]

At this seemingly unique moment in history, we are beginning to see a confluence of business and artistic skills in the service of humanity. The multiple crises in the world today remind us daily that mere prediction, whether for business aims or society's good, will not bring us anywhere near our hoped-for outcomes. If the world is to have peace and the economy is to foster widespread prosperity, only the entrepreneurial skills of business, combined with the creativity and adaptability of the artistic community, can give us the hope that we will reach our highest levels of aspiration, that we will create the world we all wish for and that our children deserve.

ABOUT THE AUTHOR

Nancy J. Adler holds the S. Bronfman Chair in Management at McGill University. She received her doctorate from UCLA. Dr. Adler conducts research and consults on global leadership, cross-cultural management, and women as global leaders. She has authored over 100 articles, produced a film, and published four books. She is a Fellow of the Academy of Management, the Academy of International Business, and the Royal Society of Canada. She was named a 3M Fellow, recognizing her as one of the top university teachers, among all disciplines, in Canada. Nancy is also an artist working primarily in watercolor and ink. Her last exhibition was "Reality in Translation" at The Banff Centre.

NOTES

1. Gary Hamel, *Leading the Revolution* (Boston: Harvard Business School Press, 2000), 10.

2. Bruce Mau and the Institute without Boundaries, from the "Massive Change" Exhibition at Toronto's Art Gallery of Ontario, March–May, 2005.

3. Rob Austin, professor of technology and management at Harvard Business School, in e-mail to the author, as a part of the AACORN Network, April 2005.

4. David Whyte, *The Heart Aroused* (New York: Currency Doubleday, 1994), 21.

5. As cited in Lotte Darsø, *Artful Creation: Learning-Tales of Arts-in-Business* (Frederiksberg, Denmark: Samfundslitteratur, 2004), 182.

6. Richard Boland and Fred Collopy, eds., *Managing as Designing* (Palo Alto, Calif.: Stanford University Press, 2004).

7. Paraphrased from Bruce Mau's observation "When everything is connected, everything matters," Bruce Mau (2004).

8. As cited in report of the Aspen Institute and the World Resource Institute, October 8, 2003, ranking business schools on their social impact.

9. Speech given by U.N. Secretary-General Kofi Annan, 1999 World Economic Forum, Davos, Switzerland.

10. See A. T. Kearney's study reported in Haebeck et al. (2000) and in Schuler and Jackson (2001).

11. Rob Austin and Lee Devin, *Artful Making: What Managers Need to Know About How Artists Work* (Upper Saddle River, N.J.: Financial Times/Prentice Hall, 2003), xxii.

12. For example, see the improvisation work of Rob Nickerson with corporate clients; http://www.robnickersonimprov.com.

13. Austin and Devin, *Artful Making,* xxv, xxvii.

14. Ibid., xxvii.

15. Hamel, *Leading the Revolution,* 249.

16. Whyte, *The Heart Aroused,* 242.

17. See http://www.gemsinisrael.com/e-_article000047913.htm, for a description of the Open Museum at Tefen, Israel.

18. For a good introduction to bottom-of-the-pyramid strategies, see Prahalad and Hart (2002).

19. Fred Mandell, founding principle of Lennick Aberman Leadership Group, as cited in the *Journal of Financial Planning* 17, no. 4 (April 2004): 12. See also www.lennickaberman.com.

20. Hamel, *Leading the Revolution,* 120.

21. As expressed in a description of Olivier's 2003 book; see http://www.sfb.co.uk/cgi-bin/profile.cgi?s=55andt=4.

22. Hamel, *Leading the Revolution,* 248–49.

23. Gary P. Steuer and Julie Peeler, "The Benefits to Business of Participating in the Arts," *Arts & Business Quarterly* (Spring 2001): 3; http://www.artsandbusinessphila.org/documents/BenefitstoBusinessofParticipatingintheArts.pdf, accessed July 19, 2009.

REFERENCES

Adler, Nancy J. "The Arts and Leadership: Now That We Can Do Anything, What Will We Do?" *Academy of Management Learning and Education* 5, no. 4 (2006): 466–99.

Austin, Rob, and Lee Devin. *Artful Making: What Managers Need to Know About How Artists Work.* Upper Saddle River, N.J.: FT Prentice Hall, 2003.

Boland, Richard, and Fred Collopy, eds. *Managing as Designing.* Palo Alto, Calif.: Stanford University Press, 2004.

Darsø, Lotte. *Artful Creation: Learning-Tales of Arts-in-Business.* Frederiksberg, Denmark: Samfundslitteratur, 2004.

Haebeck, M. H., F. Kroger, and M. R. Trum. *After the Mergers: Seven Rules for Successful Post-Merger Integration.* New York: FT Prentice Hall, 2000.

Hamel, Gary. *Leading the Revolution.* Boston: Harvard Business School Press, 2000.

Mandell, Fred. Founding principle of Lennick Aberman Leadership Group as cited in the *Journal of Financial Planning* 17, no. 4 (April 2004).

Mau, Bruce, and the Institute without Boundaries. *Massive Change.* London: Phaidon Press, 2004.

Olivier, Richard. *Inspirational Leadership: Henry V and the Muse of Fire.* London: Spiro Press, 2003.

Palmer, Parker J. *The Active Life: A Spirituality of Work, Creativity, and Caring.* New York: Harper & Row, 1990.

Pink, Daniel H. "Breakthrough Ideas for 2004." *Harvard Business Review* 82, no. 2 (February 2004): 21–22.

Prahalad, C. K., and Stuart L. Hart. "The Fortune at the Bottom of the Pyramid." *Strategy + Business* 26 (First Quarter, 2002): 2–14.

Schuler, Randall S., and Susan E. Jackson. "Seeking an Edge in Mergers and Acquisitions." *Financial Times,* Special Section, Part Two, "People Management," October 22, 2001.

Whyte, David. *The Heart Aroused: Poetry and the Preservation of the Soul in Corporate America.* New York: Currency Doubleday, 1994.

Zander, Rosamund Stone, and Benjamin Zander. *The Art of Possibility: Transforming Professional and Personal Life.* Boston: Harvard Business School Press, 2000.

CHAPTER 22

Client Leadership: Leading in the Marketplace

➤ **Andrew Sobel**

In any service organization, leadership in the client marketplace is a fundamental competency. In a professional service firm or financial institution, or at any company that sells a service to other businesses, it is not enough to be a good internal manager. Individuals who aspire to lead must also be capable of developing and sustaining consultative client relationships.

How important is strong client leadership? I have seen data on this from a number of leading service firms, and research suggests that assigning an individual with strong client-relationship management skills to a major client can double the rate of your fee growth.

More important, an organization cannot develop a client-focused culture without leaders who set the example. I once advised a large, international consulting firm that had become internally focused and lost its edge in the marketplace. It turned out that the top eight executives, including the CEO, were spending an average of only 5 percent of their time with clients. Over a period of years, the rest of the organization had begun to emulate its leaders, and internal meetings became more important than seeing clients. Growth stagnated.

A senior executive who also is a great client leader can revitalize an organization. Diana Brightmore-Armour, the CEO of corporate banking at Lloyds Banking Group, is an excellent example of this. Brightmore-Armour heads this leading UK bank's efforts with clients that range from middle-market local companies to large multinationals. Since joining the bank several years ago, she and her team have dramatically grown their corporate business, and UK finance directors have consistently voted Lloyds "Bank of the Year." Describing this journey, Brightmore-Armour told me:

> After I joined Lloyds three years ago, the first thing we did to create a more collaborative, client-focused organization was to merge our relationship and product organizations. We created a corporate markets business centered on our clients, from product development through to relationship management. We also aligned our measurement and reward system with our goal of building broad-based relationships, and created a scorecard that includes financial measures for cross-selling as well as relationship development. I personally try to role-model our values—in 2008, for example, I have personally met with 645 of the bank's clients. When you have client focus coming from the top, it really lifts the game of your relationship managers throughout the organization.

During her first month at the bank, Brightmore-Armour found herself at Wimbledon with several major clients. As they walked through the corridor to enter the tennis stadium, she asked one of the CFOs where Lloyds Banking Group ranked among the banks he used. "Eighteenth" was his blunt answer. Shocked, she stopped dead in her tracks and nearly blockaded the entrance. But then she boldly told the CFO that within a year her bank would be in his top three. She later sat down with the client team, and they set an even higher aspiration: to be in the top three banks for the client within a year, and to be number one in two years—goals they subsequently have reached.

This example highlights the importance of what I call "inculcation"—the role-modeling and communication from senior management that shapes the organizational culture and creates a client-centered ethos.

THE ROLE OF THE CLIENT LEADER

What do great client leaders actually do, and how do they do it? As we will see, there are definite overlaps between organizational leadership and client leadership. However, the task of client leadership requires some particular capabilities. Let's first look at the six main roles that a great client leader fulfills with regard to building and managing external client relationships.

Aspiration Setting

Client leaders have to articulate aspirations for both the client's business and the relationship itself. First, they need to have a deep understanding of the client's business and personal agenda, and a vision for how to accomplish it. This is achieved by investing time in understanding the client's strategy and organization, walking the halls, and having explicit agenda-setting discussions with the client. Second, they need to set aspirations for their firm's relationship with the client. Aspirations, of course, are not just about revenues—they can include things like impact, influence, positioning, and so on.

Relationship Strategy

Client leaders have to make decisions about which issues to focus on, which opportunities to actively pursue, and which executives to build relationships with. At any large corporate client, you could flail away for years and never get anywhere if you're not discerning about where and how you invest your firm's resources. Some clients must be approached centrally, and the client leader has to exercise a great deal of control and discipline in terms of managing the senior contacts at the client. Others give wide budget latitude to multiple buying units throughout the organization.

Client Leadership

The degree of specific content expertise that client leaders have will vary; but in any case, the client must perceive them to be thought leaders. They must come across as people who have a deep knowledge of the client's business and people, a thorough understanding of its agenda, and a point of view on how it can achieve its goals. Client leaders cannot be an "empty suit" who are just there to coordinate delivery resources and sell more work; today's clients are just too sophisticated and demanding for that role to have much value for them. They don't have to be *the* content experts—indeed, their expertise can and will limit the growth of your relationships if they cannot step back from them—but they do have to exercise *thought leadership*.

Team Leadership

Effective client leaders spend a great deal of time ensuring that their teams have the right mix of skills and experiences. They actively coach and mentor team members, set goals for them, and follow up. They create client teams that are magnets for talent in the organization—exciting, fun places to work that attract other professionals.

Ambassadorship

Great client leaders are ambassadors for their organization, and they act as a window for the client into the rest of their firm's capabilities. Clients should view a client leader as someone who knows exactly where to go to get the right skill set for a given issue, but who will also say, "We're not the best at that"—and recommend someone else. Client leaders are door openers, not gatekeepers. They build strong networks within their firms, and invest time to fully understand their firm's complete capabilities and resources.

As simple as this may seem, it doesn't always happen as it should. One client commented to me, "Surprisingly, I still see e-mails shooting around with questions like, 'Does anybody know if we do X or Y?' For some of our partners, a lack of understanding of our service offerings is still a barrier to relationship growth."

Commercial Management

Client leaders, depending on their level in the organization, are often responsible for the financial aspects of a client relationship. These may include negotiating contracts, ensuring that profitability targets are met, managing overruns, and so on. They also have the overall task of ensuring quality control.

THE CAPABILITIES OF THE CLIENT LEADER

There are specific capabilities that client leaders need in order to fulfill the six roles outlined in the previous section. "Capabilities" refer to a combination of skills, talents, and behaviors. What are the differences among these three? A skill is the *how-to* for accomplishing something; a talent is a *natural ability* you are born with; a behavior is how you *react to* other people or situations.

These distinctions are important because great client leaders are successful owing to a combination of all three, and you select for and develop these in different ways. Because skills, talents, and behaviors are so closely related and at times bound up with each other, I use "capabilities," and sometimes "skills," as catchalls to describe the overall set of abilities that relationship managers need to possess and display. Certain processes—such as building trust—are clearly part talent, part skill, and part behavior. But there are six major, underlying capabilities that relationship managers need to accomplish their mission—to fulfill the roles that I just outlined:

1. *Relationship-Building Skills.* Client leaders need to master the core skills required to form meaningful interpersonal relationships. These include empathy, social skills, self-awareness, self-control, and the ability to build trust.

2. *Thought Leadership.* Client leaders must be recognized by clients and peers as thought leaders who offer keen judgment and big-picture thinking. Thought leadership is based on many different skills and talents, one of which is big-picture thinking: the ability to see patterns, prioritize the most important issues, make knowledge connections, and draw insights from data. It also requires that client leaders have a strong "point of view" and general business savvy.

3. *Network Development.* Client leaders need to be able to develop and maintain a vibrant, long-term network of relationships with key individuals in the client's organization, across their firms, and with other key constituencies. For example, client leaders must systematically build a multilevel network of many-to-many relationships with their clients. They also need strong internal relationships within their firms so that they understand and have access to a wide range of capabilities.

4. *People Leadership.* Client leaders must be able to assemble, manage, and lead successful teams whose members learn and grow from the experience. They need to form strong, trusted relationships with delivery team leaders and members; set clear goals; and coach and delegate effectively.

5. *Relationship Management.* Client leaders must be able to develop, manage, grow, and institutionalize complex relationships on behalf of their firms. A number of abilities fall under this topic, including using solution-selling strategies to win the sale, account planning,

communications, expectation setting, and forecasting and communicating value.

6. *Personal Leadership.* Client leaders must engage in continual personal development. The personal leadership task for individual delivery experts is more straightforward than for a client leader, who must possess a breadth of knowledge and a wide range of skills in order to perform what is a very complex job. Personal leadership would include such things as setting priorities, time management, personal renewal, and career management.

THE CLIENT LEADER AS TRUSTED ADVISER

In *Clients for Life,* I introduced, with my coauthor Jagdish Sheth, a framework of seven attributes that differentiate the client adviser from the expert for hire. Nearly 10 years later, this model has been thoroughly validated and reinforced by tens of thousands of professionals. The seven attributes highlighted in this model can be characterized as follows: Experts are for hire; advisers have *selfless independence*—they balance dedication with objectivity. Experts tell; advisers ask great questions and listen—they have *empathy.* Experts are narrow specialists; advisers are *deep generalists.* Experts analyze; advisers analyze and *synthesize*—they bring *big-picture thinking* to their clients. Experts make decisions based singularly on the evidence, while advisers offer *judgment* that incorporates the client's values and organizational capabilities. Experts have credibility based on their facts; advisers have *conviction* rooted in deeply held beliefs and values. Experts build professional trust; advisers also develop deep *personal trust* with their clients. Figure 22.1 summarizes the major client leader roles and capabilities that I've been discussing.

RECRUITING POTENTIAL CLIENT LEADERS

Most companies look for a wide variety of skills, talents, and experiences when they recruit young professionals; but they aren't necessarily thinking about whether or not a candidate will be able to relate to their clients' CEOs 15 years down the road. This is partly because of short-term needs; they want someone who can do the job now, not in the distant future. It's also due to

Figure 22.1 Key Roles of the Client Leader

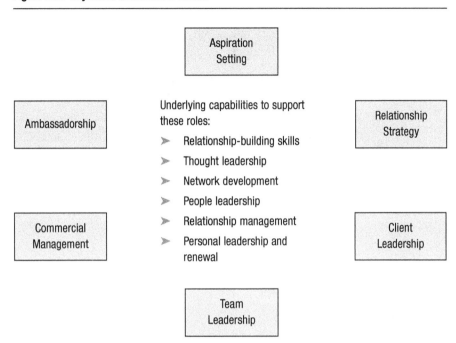

Aspiration
Setting

Ambassadorship

Underlying capabilities to support
these roles:

➤ Relationship-building skills

➤ Thought leadership

➤ Network development

➤ People leadership

➤ Relationship management

➤ Personal leadership and
renewal

Relationship
Strategy

Commercial
Management

Client
Leadership

Team
Leadership

the fact that—given the huge turnover among young professionals—it's no sure thing that this person will even be around in 5 or 10 years. Analytical and technical skills are thus highly sought after, and they have the advantage of being much easier to measure and assess than emotional intelligence. I am convinced that many organizations reject highly promising candidates who have broad intellects and strong interpersonal skills, but who are not perceived as having "good enough" analytical skills.

Creating a pipeline of client leaders, in short, starts with the hiring decision. Here are some of the qualities you ought to look for in hiring young professionals if you'd like to create a better gene pool of individuals capable of leading major client relationships:

➤ *Emotional Intelligence.* Are they self-aware? Can they control their emotions and impulses and adapt to changing circumstances? Do they possess social awareness and empathy? Can they inspire and influence others?

➤ *A Relationship Orientation.* Do they have a genuine interest in other people? Are they interested in how their decisions may affect others? Do they invest in building their own networks?

➤ *The Ability to Both Be a Team Player and Lead Teams.* Do they have a track record of successfully working in a team environment? Do they talk about "I" all the time, or "We"? What philosophies and strategies did they use as a team leader?

➤ *Curiosity and Intellectual Breadth.* Do they ask good questions? Are they motivated to learn? Do they read widely? What outside interests do they have? Are they fluent in current events and business issues? Are they able to make knowledge connections between disparate topics?

➤ *Conviction and Persuasion.* Do they communicate effectively? Are they articulate? Are they passionate and enthusiastic when they talk about their interests and experiences?

DEVELOPING CLIENT LEADERS

I am often asked if you can teach someone to become a trusted client adviser who is capable of building relationships with top executives. The short answer is that it's hard to *teach* this, but professionals can *learn* to do it. In other words, traditional training methods can instill some of these qualities, but many of them must be acquired through experience. There is no question that some individuals who have a strong natural talent for relationship building are innately better at this role than others. But at the same time, most professionals can significantly improve their game—if they are *motivated to do so.*

Another issue that affects service firms' ability to develop client leaders nowadays is their sheer size and the consequent weakening of the apprenticeship system. When I started with the MAC Group right out of business school, the firm had about 100 consultants; when I left Gemini Consulting (its later incarnation) 15 years later, we had several thousand professionals. But that's nothing: Ernst & Young now has 130,000 employees, Accenture 180,000, and an industrial behemoth like GE employs over 300,000. Even law firms, which represent a very fragmented industry, have gotten large; Clifford Chance leads the way with nearly 4,000 lawyers. Historically, most of us learned how to build client relationships by watching and doing—as one of my clients told me, by "sitting at the feet of the masters." Today, a young professional may be part of a team of 25 or 50 serving a client, and get little or no exposure to the partners or senior executives leading the account.

Because of these changes, you have to take a more institutional and systematic approach to developing the next generation of client leaders. But what's the best way to go about doing this? In the rest of this section, I describe a number of developmental activities and programs that can be effective in improving the capabilities of client leaders. These are:

➤ Career management

➤ Coaching and mentoring

➤ Formal training

➤ Experience-sharing summits

➤ Fast-track or high-potential programs

➤ E-learning programs

Let's look at each of these in turn.

Career Management

Great client leaders possess both knowledge *breadth and depth*—they are, as I say in *Clients for Life,* "deep generalists." Deep generalists are able to connect to senior executives' business issues more readily than narrow specialists, and they consistently put their expert knowledge in the context of their client's overall goals and strategy. Deep generalists tend to be naturally curious people who ask a lot of questions and read widely. You can encourage the development of this type of breadth by giving professionals a rich and varied set of career experiences during their first 5 or 10 years of work.

The career of Steve Pfeiffer—current Chair of the Executive Committee for international law firm Fulbright & Jaworski—is a terrific example of how these experiences can prepare a professional to develop and lead large-scale, trusted-partner client relationships. After graduating with a BA from Wesleyan University, Pfeiffer went to England as a Rhodes Scholar at Oxford University. He subsequently earned a master's degree in African studies at the University of London, and won a Thomas J. Watson fellowship that enabled him to travel extensively in Europe, the Middle East, and Africa. He then joined the U.S. Navy, later served as the special assistant to the Secretary of the Navy, and eventually retired as a commander in the naval reserves nearly 20 years later. After graduating from law school in the mid-

1970s, Pfeiffer went to work as a young attorney in Fulbright & Jaworski's main office in Houston, Texas. After a few years he moved to Fulbright's nascent London office, where he spent seven formative years encountering a wide variety of international corporate transactions and developing important client relationships that would endure for many years to come. Pfeiffer then transferred to Fulbright's Washington, D.C., office, and later became its Office Managing Partner.

Interestingly—and not coincidentally—each experience that Pfeiffer accumulated helped create a foundation, not only for his ability to lead major client relationships but also for his eventual chairmanship. The internal relationships that he developed during stints in Houston, London, and finally Washington gave him a deep knowledge of the firm's people and service offerings, and a base of support to both marshal resources into his client relationships and assume leadership positions in the firm. His broad knowledge of international law and cross-border business transactions gave him a leg up in a fast-growing area of legal practice that has increased in importance over the years. His nonlegal experiences have also been absolutely invaluable to his career: his time in the U.S. Navy, for example, provided him with invaluable contacts in Washington, and his extensive involvement in nonprofit organizations, such as Wesleyan University's Board of Trustees, also expanded his network in the business community. Even his degree in African studies figured into his rainmaking capabilities: while in London, Fulbright pitched a major South African company, and Pfeiffer's keen understanding of the history and culture of that region turned out to be the deciding factor in winning the business. Twenty years later, this major, publicly held company is still a client of the firm, and Pfeiffer sits on its Board of Directors.

While Pfeiffer's résumé is unusually impressive, it's not atypical—in its variety and diversity—of many of the hundreds of successful client leaders I have studied in dozens of firms. As you look at your own high-potential professionals, think about how you can systematically give them a similar diversity of experiences as they mature and grow. These might include things such as:

➤ Spending time abroad

➤ Working in different offices

➤ Being involved in a start-up (e.g., of a new service offering or office)

➤ Moving to a new practice area or subspecialty

➤ Working for a variety of senior professionals

Coaching and Mentoring

Coaching and mentoring young professionals in how to develop client relationships should obviously be an important task for every partner or senior
executive in any company that provides business-to-business services.
Changing a client leader's behaviors is often best accomplished through the
intimate, one-on-one feedback and follow-up that expert coaching affords.
Unfortunately, crushing time demands on most professionals have made it
harder for them to make room for this in their schedules. I can remember
being a young associate myself, and debriefing with the relationship partner
after a client presentation. I listened to him talk about what went well, what
we could have done better, why different client executives had reacted the
way they did to our materials, and what our next steps ought to be. Today, I
see senior relationship managers rushing off to the next meeting and catch-
ing up the next day with a cursory e-mail, or delegating these discussions to
junior managers. Learning by "sitting at the feet of masters" has become, all
too frequently, a catch-as-catch-can jumble of late-night e-mails and spo-
radic feedback.

When I lived in London and worked for the MAC Group in the 1980s, one
of our senior partners was Dean Berry, a former business school professor
who had also been one of the early heads of INSEAD, the renowned business school outside of Paris. Dean was a big bear of a man who loved ideas,
relationships, good food, and wine. He was also well connected to many
CEOs across Europe. I was a young partner struggling to master my new
role, and Dean was always available to talk to me, no matter how busy he
was. I would pull my chair over next to his leather-topped partners' desk and
ask him about a client dilemma I faced or perhaps even a personal issue I was
grappling with. Dean would listen deeply, ask thoughtful questions, and help
synthesize the critical issues for me. It was nothing for him to take an hour
out of his hectic day to just talk with me. At the end, he would usually offer
one or two incisive observations or suggestions, but always in the spirit of,
"Here's something you might just think about. . . ." Dean knew what mentorship was, and took time for it. I don't see enough of that today.

To encourage the apprenticeship model, you have to reinforce a culture of
mentorship among your senior professionals. This begins at the top and you
have to lead by example. There is no better exemplar of this than the former
chairman of Citigroup, Sir Win Bischoff. Sir Win always made time in his
demanding schedule to sit down and talk with one of Citigroup's relationship
managers about a key client relationship. He sponsored a mentoring program

at Citigroup called "Passing down the Wisdom" where he spent entire evenings sitting down with younger professionals and sharing his 40 years of experience in developing long-term clients.

Formal Training

I was approached several years ago by a large, global services company about creating a training program for its key account managers. The company had recently instituted a key account manager organization, and wanted to train these professionals to build trusted CEO relationships. However, after interviewing a number of its senior executives and reviewing its strategic plans, I concluded that a training program would be a disaster at that point in time. This company had not put into place any of the infrastructure needed to support a group of client leaders. All of the client relationships were still controlled by local office heads and practice leaders, who were resentful of the new key account management structure; the roles and responsibilities for these individuals had not been clearly defined; the measurement and reward system had not been adapted to reflect the particular goals and challenges of a client leader; and so on. Unfortunately, the client was quite fixated on a training program as the solution, and my assessment was received rather coolly. The point is that training only works if all of the other appropriate organizational structures, systems, and processes have been put into place.

If you do want to use training, what exactly do you train client leaders *in*? Relationship building is such a large topic that it can be intimidating. Can you really cover all of it in a one- or two-day training session? After working with numerous service firms on a wide variety of training initiatives, I have developed a fairly straightforward model for what needs to be taught to client leaders to help them build their capabilities. There are three broad dimensions that you need to think about: principles, skills and behaviors, and best practices.

> ➤ *Principles* are those underlying assumptions or beliefs that drive your behavior as a client leader. Examples include statements like, "Build your network before you need it," "Follow the person, not the position," and "Great relationships start with great conversations, not one person trying to show the other how brilliant he or she is." You teach and instill these principles by sharing them, encouraging people to think of some of their own, telling

stories that illustrate them, and so on. You sprinkle them through-out a training session, as opposed to creating a special module enti-tled "principles."

➤ *Skills and behaviors* refer to, among others, the core trusted adviser attributes described earlier, along with characteristics like self-awareness, interpersonal skills, and social awareness. These soft skills reside in your brain's primitive limbic system, which controls emotions and impulses, as opposed to in your neocortex, where logical thinking occurs. Because of this, soft skills are very difficult to learn from a lecture or PowerPoint slide; you won't become more empathetic by reading a series of bullet points. Rather, you need to use case studies, personal exercises, self-assessments, videos, small-group discussions, individual feedback, and role plays to help people improve these aptitudes.

➤ *Best practices* focus on effective ways of handling the different client situations and issues you encounter as you move from contact to trusted adviser. What's the best way to handle a first meeting? How do you defuse a client crisis? How do you connect with a C-level executive? How can you gain access to the econom-ic buyer? What are effective strategies to broaden a narrow relationship? How do you build relationships with clients who are probably much older than you are? Obviously, as you resolve these challenges, you will use the principles, skills, and behaviors from the other two categories.

In short, you need to emphasize all three of these capability enablers in any kind of training initiative.

Experience-Sharing Summits

It can be extremely valuable for client leaders to simply gather to share expe-riences and brainstorm common issues. A good example of this is the Client Service Officer experience-sharing summits organized by the consulting firm Booz Allen Hamilton. The summits last one day and usually involve about 20 experienced partners who are all managing major client relation-ships. The format varies, but the core of the session revolves around individ-ual partners who each take about 20 minutes to present and discuss a case study of their relationship, which is summarized on a *single* slide. The slide highlights the client's background and key issues, the consulting work Booz Allen has done, and five or six bullet points summarizing lessons learned.

Client confidentialities are carefully respected during this session—client details are disguised when appropriate, and relationships with competitive companies are not considered on the same day. Other partners get to ask questions, and there is usually some very vibrant discussion about how some of the lessons learned can be used to improve other relationships. Participants in these workshops say that they are the most valuable internal meetings that they ever attend.

Fast-Track or High-Potential Programs

Several of my clients have created fast-track or high-potential programs for up-and-coming client leaders who will soon be expected to manage major client relationships. Sometimes the participants are existing relationship managers who have the potential to raise their game and go to the next level; in other cases, they are younger professionals (in their late 20s or 30s, possibly early 40s) who are managing small relationships and need additional experience and training to be qualified to take on a major client. These programs usually last anywhere from nine months to two years, and they are invariably sponsored by senior management. They usually cover a broader array of subjects than just relationship building, and may include:

> ➤ The role of the client leader

> ➤ The firm's service offerings and intellectual capital

> ➤ Team leadership

> ➤ Client relationships

> ➤ The commercial and contractual aspects of client management

A fast-track program must be tailored to your particular needs and goals. For example, HR consulting firm Towers Perrin has a holistic fast-track program that is aimed at creating well-rounded client leaders. It puts equal emphasis on tools and techniques to perform the client-relationship management role: understanding the firm's service offerings and capabilities, teaching client leaders how to build senior-level client relationships, and developing business acumen. It lasts over a year, and incorporates many different learning approaches.

Executive search firm Heidrick & Struggles has implemented a somewhat different version of this fast-track approach. Its program is intended to help implement a strategic shift from transactional search services to a more integrated talent management model, where the firm provides both search and leadership consulting to help grow talent internally. It was rolled out regionally and comprises three workshops over a nine-month period, each of which focuses heavily on understanding the firm's complete offering of consulting services, how to identify client needs for them, and how to take a more integrated approach to talent management.

A different but also very effective approach has been implemented by another leading HR consultancy, Hewitt Associates. This program exposes Hewitt's high-potential professionals to a series of well-known academic thought leaders in different aspects of HR management and practice, and also to the top management of the firm.

E-Learning and Other Approaches

It's difficult to learn how to become a client leader from an online learning program, but e-learning and digitized resource libraries can play an important support role for other initiatives. Several firms I know have created online resource centers to which client leaders and their teams can turn for a variety of content about relationship-building strategies, including case examples, best-practices compilations, tools, articles, videos, and so on.

Other distribution channels that can work well include short teleconferences, webcasts, weekly or monthly e-mails with a short case example or lesson learned, and other similar "short bursts" of content. Ernst & Young, for example, has long used a format called the "19 Minutes," where outside guest speakers are asked to lead a 19-minute conference call with several hundred or more interested E&Y professionals who sign up for the teleconference. E&Y found that when the calls were scheduled for a full hour, there was limited participation; when the calls were compressed to 19 minutes, however, the number of participants grew enormously.

For one client, we videotaped interviews that I conducted with 20 of the most accomplished senior client leaders (with some 400 years of experience among them) about their approach to building trusted client partnerships. We then edited these conversations down to short (5 to 10 minute) compilations organized around eight important topics such as listening, building your network, developing C-suite relationships, and so on. Interviews with a few outside experts were also incorporated into the videos. These video clips were then loaded onto video iPods and distributed to every client leader in the firm, and also made available online. The client's professionals began enthusiastically using the iPods to watch this material on airplane trips and during their downtime while traveling.

SUPPORTING CLIENT LEADERS ON AN ONGOING BASIS

Client leaders need to be supported, on an ongoing basis, in several ways. First, they must have the backing of senior management. If client leaders are viewed as "third wheels" or interlopers by practice and geographic leaders, they will never be very effective. They must have the power to lead key relationships, marshal resources, and have tie-breaking votes on relationship strategy.

Second, client leaders need to be connected to each other. This can happen in person or virtually through collaboration technologies and online forums. As I mentioned earlier, Booz Allen Hamilton has implemented experience-sharing summits for its client service officers, to spread best practices and allow client leaders to discuss their toughest issues with their peers. International law firm Fulbright & Jaworski routinely gathers its relationship partners together in small-group settings, organized by office or sometimes by industry. Towers Perrin has created a very well-developed support network for its 400 client relationship managers (CRMs). The firm organizes a once-monthly 90-minute conference call (held twice to accommodate different time zones around the world) in which all CRMs participate. Written materials are circulated in electronic form two days prior to the conference call. During the call, managing partners provide an update on the state of the firm, a win-loss analysis that reviews two recent client successes and one loss, and a report on new intellectual capital that the firm is developing. The calls are taped, so even if people miss one, they have access to the full content. Towers Perrin also supports its network of client leaders with a highly sophisticated online knowledge management system called TP World, which provides a vast array of resources about the firm's service offerings, research and publishing, best practices, and client case studies.

MEASURING AND ASSESSING CLIENT LEADERS

Client leaders need to be assessed against a balanced scorecard of both quantitative and qualitative measures that reflect their fundamental goals; short-versus long-term impacts must also be evaluated. If you get the balance right, you'll be able to create a very robust snapshot of a professional's performance. Important questions might include:

➤ Has this individual helped us grow our revenues with specific clients? Has he or she successfully broadened and deepened key relationships?

➤ Does he or she role-model the client-centric, collaborative values and behaviors that are needed to build long-term client relationships on a systematic basis?

➤ Is the client leader considered a leader in the eyes of our clients? Do clients believe that he or she adds value and is a thought leader?

➤ Has the client leader built a team and been an effective team leader? Is this a client relationship that other professionals want to work on?

➤ Has the client leader been an effective ambassador for the firm, in terms of bringing the best the firm can offer to this client? Is he or she a door opener or a gatekeeper?

Striking a balance between short- and long-term measures is essential, but difficult because of the intense quarterly and yearly focus on financial results that characterizes many firms. ERM, the world's largest environmental consulting firm, uses two separate balanced scorecards for a key group of 50 senior partners. One scorecard focuses on achievement of short-term financial results, and it drives cash bonuses. A second set of measures focuses on long-term developmental goals, such as recruiting, new skill development, and building long-term client relationships, and it drives stock awards. Together, these scorecards help create a balanced focus on both the short- and long-term needs of the firm.

SUMMARY

The client leader plays a fundamental role in developing and sustaining trusted client partnerships and in promoting a client-centered culture. The skills required to accomplish these overlap with, but go beyond, what are thought of as traditional leadership capabilities. You need to create a systematic client leadership talent pipeline to ensure you will have a sufficient number of these individuals available to lead major client relationships and drive your future revenue growth.

ABOUT THE AUTHOR

Andrew Sobel is the leading authority on client relationships and the skills and strategies required to earn lifelong client loyalty. His books include *All for One: 10 Strategies for Building Trusted Client Partnerships, Clients for Life,* and *Making Rain.* He has also written more than 75 articles on building long-term relationships, and contributed chapters to four books on leadership, strategy, and marketing.

A former Senior Vice President and Country Managing Director with Gemini Consulting, Andrew lived and worked in Europe for 13 years, and speaks four languages. He graduated from Middlebury College with honors and earned his MBA from Dartmouth's Tuck School. Since 1995 he has been president of Andrew Sobel Advisors, an international consulting firm that helps organizations develop their clients for life. His Web site is www.andrewsobel.com, and he can be reached at andrew@andrewsobel.com.

CHAPTER 23

Leading for Sustainability

➤ **Fons Trompenaars and Peter Woolliams**

While organizations share similar problems during these difficult times, the approach their leaders adopt to solving them will be different and often rooted in the culture and past behaviors of the organization. The challenge today in defining appropriate and effective leadership to realize a successful and sustainable future is to include a perspective that transfers to the dynamics and competing demands of modern (global) business. Too rigid adherence to any one strategic approach—ranging from scientific management, or a Theory Y human resource dimension basis, to customer orientation, shareholder value, or corporate social responsibility—has been shown over time to be unduly restrictive. Similarly, the plethora of competing leadership models—including those derived from trait, behavioral, participative, situational, contingency, transactional, and transformational theories—does not inform leaders how they should lead their organizations and people into the new future.

Survival needs to be based on a reconciliation of the dilemmas created between the competing demands of all stakeholders, including employees, shareholders, and customers. New solutions are required that are grounded in a strategy that is aligned with the organization's values. We submit that a new paradigm of leadership is required to revitalize business from the credit crunch and beyond in an approach that is more akin to the "Servant Leader." This chapter identifies how to connect and embody the many competing values that make an organization so complex and explains how Servant Leaders enable others to consistently achieve their highest performance and innovative pathways.

THE ORGANIZATION AS A CULTURAL CONTEXT FOR LEADERS

During the last 20 years, the fact that national and organizational cultures both need to be considered in modern business management has been increasingly recognized. More and more, a leader in a local company will find that she or he is leading and managing a workforce that is multicultural. Many of the conceptual frameworks for explicating culture are based on describing how different cultures give different meanings to relationships with other people, to interactions with the environment, and to use of time. Similarly, much attention has been given to the recognition and respect for cultural differences. However, if we stop at only these first two stages, we run the risk of supporting only stereotypical views of cultures. In our extensive cross-cultural database, we have found enough variation in any one country to know that it is very risky to speak of a national, corporate, or even functional culture in terms of simple stereotypes.[1]

The starting point is to ask how leaders deal effectively in situations where there are competing demands from different stakeholders and a multicultural workforce. Take these alternate descriptions as examples. Which would you choose?

➤ Today's effective leaders are people who continually help their subordinates to solve the variety of problems that they face. They are like parents, not teachers.

➤ Today's effective leaders occupy a position between that of a private coach and a teacher. Their effectiveness depends on how they balance both roles.

➤ Today's effective leaders get things done. They set goals, give information, measure results, and let people do their own work in that context.

➤ Today's effective leaders give a lot of attention to work streams so that goals, tasks, and achievements are aimed at improving those processes.

➤ Today's effective leaders get things done. They set goals, give information, and measure results so that everyone is embedded in continuous work streams.

We posed these types of questions to many top leaders during our research into organization sustainability through innovation and leadership.[2] Their answers are consistent with our finding that leaders such as Richard Branson of Virgin, Michael Dell of Dell, Kees Storm of AEGON, and Laurent Beaudoin of

Bombardier made significantly different choices than did the more "ordinary" managers in our study. Do you know what the difference was?

The leaders described in statement no. 1 look like those from the beginning of the 20th century: listen to "father" or "mother" and everything will be okay. This style is still very popular in Latin America and Asia, compared to Europe and the United States.[3] There is nothing wrong with this approach—simply that it is limited in its applicability outside these regions and cultures.

Statement no. 2 is a typical compromise and will work anywhere—but it is certainly not the optimal approach. Statement no. 3 is very popular among Anglo-Saxons and northwest European managers. However, the ever-popular "management by objectives" is often applied recklessly. Add some vision and mission, and you're the modern leader; but the French would quickly argue, "Whose vision and mission is it?"

Statements no. 4 and 5 are two alternative ways to integrate seemingly opposing values on a higher level and would therefore have our approval. Statement no. 4 suggests that good leaders guide people who make mistakes and learn from them, while statement no. 5 integrates the dichotomy between task orientation and work streams beginning from the opposite direction. In our research, more successful leaders selected the last two statements much more frequently than did their less-successful counterparts.

REDEFINING SUSTAINABILITY

The evidence from our research and consulting practice reveals that "organizational sustainability" is not limited to the "traditional" environmental factors such as controlling emissions, using green energy, conserving scarce resources, and the like. The future strength of an organization depends on the way leadership and management deal with the tensions between the five major elements of any organization: efficiency, people, clients, shareholders, and society. The way in which these tensions are addressed and resolved determines the future strength and opportunities of an organization.

We therefore define *sustainability* as the degree to which an organization is capable of creating long-term wealth by reconciling its most important ("golden") dilemmas created between these five components. The task for today's leader is to connect and integrate these drivers in ways that are more than just compromise.

We have collected and analyzed some 8,000 of these "tensions" from our Web-based online surveys of leaders and senior managers from around the globe, representing the top Fortune 500 global companies and familiar household names, but focused primarily on more local or specialist companies. From these data we have identified frequently recurring "10 Golden Dilemmas" that exist between these five components, as shown in Figure 23.1.

Figure 23.1 10 Golden Dilemmas

Component	Sectional Interest
Business processes	Corporate effectiveness
Employees	Employee development and learning
Shareholder	Shareholder return, financial performance, and growth
Client, customers, and suppliers	Satisfaction
Society at large	Contributions to society

We can now create 10 dimensions from our five components because each component competes with the other four, as shown in Figure 23.2.

Figure 23.2 10 Dimensions of Sustainability

	Business Processes	Employees	Shareholder	Client Customer Suppliers	Society at Large
Business Processes		1	2	3	4
Employees			5	6	7
Shareholder				8	9
Client Customer Suppliers					10
Society at Large					

Table 23.1 10 Golden Dilemmas in Generic Format

Golden Dilemma	On the One Hand	On the Other Hand
1	*(B: Employees)* We need to develop our people for their future roles.	*(A: Business Processes)* We need to become more cost conscious and results oriented.
2	*(C: Shareholder)* We need to cut costs wherever we can for the sake of our shareholders' return.	*(A: Business Processes)* We need to invest for long-term sustainability.
3	*(A: Business Processes)* We need to supply standard products/services as defined from HQ.	*(D: Clients)* We need to supply products/services that respond to local tastes and needs.
4	*(A: Business Processes)* We need to focus on cash flow and working capital.	*(E: Society)* We need to serve the wider community in a sustainable and responsible way.
5	*(B: Employees)* We need to motivate and reward our people.	*(C: Shareholder)* We need to satisfy our shareholders.
6	*(B: Employees)* We need to educate clients/customers about new solutions we can offer.	*(D: Clients)* We need to keep the customer in focus ahead of our own personal preferences.
7	*(B: Employees)* We need to retain equal opportunities for all existing staff.	*(E: Society)* We need to apply some positive discrimination to increase diversity.
8	*(D: Clients)* We need to satisfy our clients'/customers' needs.	*(C: Shareholder)* We need to generate both revenue and capital growth for our shareholders.
9	*(C: Shareholder)* We need to maximize shareholder return from our existing business.	*(E: Society)* We need to adapt to the future as society evolves.
10	*(E: Society)* We need to supply products and services that enhance our reputation in the wider community.	*(D: Clients)* We need to supply products that our clients and customers are asking for.

The value conflicts between these components are precipitated by scarcity and different sectional interests; the role of the leader is to reconcile these dilemmas over time. Table 23.1 shows the 10 Golden Dilemmas in a generic format with a relatively high level of abstraction. In practice, our respondent leaders were asked to take the generic versions and restate them as to how they apply more specifically to their own organizations.

THE CHALLENGES FOR THE LEADER

Leaders frequently suffer from insomnia because they have not been able to resolve a dilemma they face. It is difficult "not to have made it," but it's even more difficult not knowing "what to make." Then, worse, the successful integration of conflicting values frequently leads to the creation of one or more new dilemmas. It is a continuous process.

Of course, you have to inspire as a leader and you also have to listen. You need to follow the orders of headquarters (HQ) to fulfill the global strategy, and you have to have local success by adapting to regional circumstances. You have to decide when to act yourself, but also when and to whom to delegate. As a professional, you need to input your own day-to-day contribution, and at the same time be passionate about the mission as a whole. And you need to simultaneously use your brilliant analytical power while enabling the contributions of others. You need to develop an excellent strategy while simultaneously having answers as to why the strategy misses its goal.

Leaders find themselves caught between conflicting demands and are subject to an endless series of paradoxes and dilemmas. There are nonstop culture clashes; by "culture" we mean not simply the cultures of different nations but also the cultures of different disciplines, functions, genders, classes, and so on.

LEADING FOR SUSTAINABILITY

Let's explore some of the Golden Dilemmas and how successful leaders might approach the tensions and resolve them.

Golden Dilemma 1

B: Employees	A: Business Processes
We need to develop our people for their future roles.	We need to become more cost conscious and results oriented.

Is the leader of the 21st century a cool analytic brain, able to chop the whole into piecemeal chunks and strive monolithically for corporate efficiency? Or a person who puts everything into a larger context and prioritizes the contribution of people? At Shell, Gijs van Lennep's concept of "helicopter quality" was introduced to focus on an important quality of the modern leader: the competence to transcend the problem by elevating to higher levels of abstraction but at the same time the ability and drive to zoom in on certain aspects of the system of problems.

Jan Carlzon, of Scandinavian Airlines (SAS), called this integration of more specific moments with the ability to go deeper when one approaches a client "moments of truth." Here also we find an important new quality of the effective leader: the competence to select where to go deep. Pure analysis leads to paralysis and an overdone synthesis leads nowhere, either.

Michael Dell of Dell, Inc., has had to grasp the dilemma of selling to a broad array or to a special group with whom deep relationships were developed. His newly developed Direct Selling Model has the advantage of being very broad and simultaneously very deep, personal, and customized. Dell broke with the conventional wisdom that you either aim for many customers *or* you aim for just a few clients with complex problems and specialized needs who need complex high-end service. The first strategy is cheap, but rather superficial. The second strategy is intimate and personal, but typically niche oriented and attracts premium prices.

The risk is obviously that if you go for the first strategy, distribution channels might clog very quickly and there is no differentiation between you and competitors. This strategy also runs the risk of swamping the intermediaries. On the other hand, Dell could have focused on creating a very narrow but deep strategy with the risk of creating severely limited opportunities in small niche markets. The reconciliation he created was as powerful as it was simple. By direct sales via face-to-face interaction, telephone, and Internet, Dell reconciled breadth with depth and complexity. The genius of direct selling via the Internet is that you reach an ever-increasing spectrum of customers *and* you can give personalized, detailed, information-rich services to those customers via premium pages for each.

Golden Dilemma 5

B: Employees	C: Shareholder
We need to motivate and reward our people.	We need to satisfy our shareholders.

Getting things done is important for manager performance. But doesn't the doing of mundane things need to be in balance with our private life? As a leader of others, you also need to be able to be yourself. However, from our research findings we conclude that our best leaders are *not* different from what they do. They seem to be one with what they do. One of the most important sources of stress is when being and doing are not integrated. An overdeveloped achievement orientation that doesn't harmonize with a person's lifestyle or who a person is creates ineffective leadership behaviors.

In *Building Cross-Cultural Competence* (Yale University Press, 2000), Fons Trompenaars and Charles Hampden-Turner suggest that successful leaders do things in harmony with whom they feel they are and vice versa. They have been able to reconcile their private lives and their work lives. This is not easy, but the Servant Leader doesn't use his or her ascribed status merely to have his or her people achieve better; it is also used to have family life and business support each other.

Golden Dilemma 3

A: Business Processes	D: Clients
We need to supply standard products/services as defined from HQ.	We need to supply products/services that respond to local tastes and needs.

It is striking, in our research, how often we found this in many forms. Should we globalize or should we localize our approach? Is it better for our organization to mass-produce or to focus on specialized products? Good leaders in transnational organizations are effective in finding resolutions whereby locally learned "best practices" are globalized. Thus, activities might be decentralized, but the information about the activities is centralized. Mass customization has become the credo of the reconciliation between standardized and universal products, and between customized and particular adaptations.

For example, McDonald's was able to transform local learning into global products. This company (especially in its performance in the United States), has swiftly turned around in the last three years after a doubtful start in this century. What values has McDonald's reconciled? And is reconciliation even possible in a company that is known (like Coca-Cola) to stand for an assertive approach—be as American as you can be? McDonald's universalism is reflected in several areas of the business—for example, in the promotion of global brands, common systems, and HR principles around the world.

Universalism fuels the search for the one best way of doing things and releases the synergy of a global corporation. Without this synergy, it is easy to lose the benefits of operating globally. At the same time, taken to extremes and not balanced with a healthy dose of particularism, universalism can lead to the "one best way" being pursued at the cost of flexibility to the particular circumstances and needs of the local situation.

This might explain the difficulties McDonald's faced in the late 1990s–early 2000s. (However, there is also a "particular" relationship at the heart of the company, since McDonald's at its most senior levels is family run.) This interesting bicultural set up has allowed McDonald's to create freedom within a framework of strong values. It enables McDonald's to reconcile the dilemma of how to exploit the common franchise frameworks of the brands (universalize) and how much to leave to local market adaptation (particularize). While in Indonesia, the Netherlands, and South Korea McDonald's offers Big Macs and Happy Meals, in Austria, and now the United States, its franchises contain "McCafes" that offer coffee blends for local tastes. Next to french fries, it offers rice in Indonesia. In Amsterdam, it offers the McKroket, a local Dutch snack. And in Seoul, the burger chain sells roast pork on a bun with a garlicky soy sauce.

However, McDonald's is going beyond the theme that "all business is local." In response to concerns of too much localization, McDonald's executives say they are actively experimenting with decentralized foreign operations, taking the best local practices and applying them in other areas of the world as well. McDonald's is a prime example of successfully globalizing local practices. The result is a transnational organization in which exceptions to the rules modify the existing principles.

Golden Dilemma 7

B: Employees	E: Society
We need to retain equal opportunities for all existing staff.	We need to apply some positive discrimination to increase diversity.

The most common approach to fairness in the workplace is the "equal opportunity model" (EOM). It is also the backbone of the compliance paradigm. If you can show the courts that minorities were evaluated fairly, then you cannot be blamed if the white European males keep showing up in the executive suite. Perhaps they are simply better! Possibly, but we do not think so. The problem with the EOM is that it assumes that the rules of the game are gender and culture neutral; in truth, they almost never are. Business is a game invented by men, played by men, and ruled by men for their own convenience.

What we have yet to discover is what happens to women contestants when we give them the power to qualify the rules by which they are judged. For instance, why should a woman who has taken time out to raise her children be "taken off" the career track? The underlying principle is that women and other minorities should help write rules to make the best of their unique talents. There is a fairly predictable sequence to the mess organizations keep getting into in this regard. The norms of some workplaces allow sexual "kidding" and the lives of some women become impossible. This problem is solvable by a critical mass of women setting up norms for themselves and insisting on respect as *they* define it. It would be interesting to see how the norms of a project team with over 50 percent female membership would differ from those of male-dominated teams, and to consider their relative performances.

Golden Dilemma 4

A: Business Processes We need to focus on cash flow and working capital.	**E: Society** We need to serve the wider community in a sustainable and responsible way.

The final core quality of today's effective leaders is the competence to integrate the feedback from the market and the technology developed in the organization, and vice versa. Again, it is not a competition between technology push and market pull. The modern leader knows that a push of technology will eventually lead to the ultimate niche market—that is, that part of the market without customers. Conversely, a monolithic focus on the market will leave the leader at the mercy of its clients.

Our thinking is that values are not "added" by leaders, since only simple values "add up." Leaders combine values: a fast and a safe car, good food that is easy to prepare. Nobody claims that combining values is easy, but it is possible. A computer that is able to make complex calculations can also be customer friendly. It is the more extended systems of values that will be the context in which international leadership will prove its excellence.

Laurent Beaudoin, president of Bombardier, skillfully reconciled his dilemma in this area of inner and outer direction. We might even argue that the reconciliation of this dilemma accounted for much of the success of Bombardier. An acquisition strategy is an advanced form of inner direction with powerful motives steered from within. Beaudoin has created a company that looks for the rare and valuable. Bombardier was always looking to find this ability coupled with its opposite—the readiness to understand, acknowledge, and respond to the value-creating capacity of another system outside itself.

Beaudoin used humility, listening, and patience to learn about the companies Bombardier acquired. He reconciled the inner-directed strategy of bold new acquisitions with the outer-directed policy of respecting the integrity of acquired companies. He had to let companies he acquired share their dreams so he could understand what was possible and of how much they were capable. The resolution of these contrasting abilities, hitting the acquisition trail and studying respectfully what you acquire, is also the way of the Servant Leader.

SUMMARY

In order to become a sustainable success as an organization, the business's leader must reconcile the dilemmas posed by competing interests of various stakeholders. It is the Servant Leader who has the capability to do this. Since, essentially, innovation can be defined as combining values that are not easily joined, this process is created by and leads to innovation. It is the innovative capability of organizations, from process to product, from research and development to human resources, that will make an organization sustainable. And it is far more than just corporate social responsibility.

ABOUT THE AUTHORS

Fons Trompenaars is CEO of Trompenaars Hampden-Turner (THT) Consulting, Amsterdam, an innovative center of excellence on intercultural management. A consultant, trainer, and motivational speaker, Dr. Trompenaars is the world's foremost authority on cross-cultural management. He has spent more than 20 years helping Fortune 500 leaders and professionals manage and solve their business and cultural dilemmas to increase global effectiveness and performance, particularly in the areas of globalization, mergers and acquisition, HR, and leadership development. He's the author of many books and articles, including the best seller *Riding the Waves of Culture: Understanding Cultural Diversity in Business* (Nicholas Brealey, 1993). His latest book is *Servant Leadership Across Cultures* (Infinite Ideas, 2008).

Peter Woolliams is a senior partner with Trompenaars Hampden-Turner (THT) Consulting, and also Professor Emeritus at Anglia Ruskin University, United Kingdom. Dr. Woolliams has worked extensively as an academic and practitioner management consultant throughout the world with many leading organizations and management gurus, and is visiting professor at several international institutions. He has worked closely with coauthor and business partner Fons Trompenaars's for nearly 20 years. Peter's contribution has been to support the development of the THT's cross-culture and knowledge management database and its reliability and consistency through extensive rigorous analysis. You can find out more about Peter at www.business acrosscultures.com.

NOTES

1. F. Trompenaars and C. Hampton-Turner, *Riding the Waves of Culture: Understanding Diversity in Global Business* (London: Nicholas Brealey, 1993).

2. F. Trompenaars and E. Voerman, *Servant Leadership Across Cultures* (London: Infinite Ideas, 2008).

3. Ibid.

INDEX

www.ingramcontent.com/pod-product-compliance
Lightning Source LLC
Jackson TN
JSHW061934140125
77111JS00005B/7